Feeding New Orleans

Feeding New Orleans

Celebrity Chefs and Reimagining Food Justice

Jeanne K. Firth

The University of North Carolina Press CHAPEL HILL

This book was published with the assistance of the Fred W. Morrison Fund of the University of North Carolina Press.

Set in Merope Basic by Westchester Publishing Services
Manufactured in the United States of America

Complete Library of Congress Cataloging-in-Publication Data for this title can be found at https://lccn.loc.gov/2023040807.
ISBN 978-1-4696-7632-6 (cloth: alk. paper)
ISBN 978-1-4696-7633-3 (pbk.: alk. paper)
ISBN 978-1-4696-7634-0 (ebook)

Cover photo of rice boiled with red beans by norikko/stock.adobe.com.

The author gratefully acknowledges permission to reprint excerpts from "Crisis Caring: Chef Foundations, Branding, and Responsibility in Foodscapes," *Food, Culture & Society*, October 2022.

For River and Ruthie, in hope

Contents

List of Illustrations

MAP

TABLES

Acknowledgments

Two beloved mentors, Mark Hunter of Cornell College and Sylvia Chant of the London School of Economics and Political Science (LSE), passed away before the publication of this book. If I'm doing things right, their lasting intellectual influence resonates throughout the text.

My heartfelt thanks are due to every chef, cook, philanthropist, and food justice worker who participated in this project. Thank you to the editorial team at UNC Press and specifically Lucas Church, a most caring and supportive editor. I have such appreciation for the thoughtful readers of this monograph. I owe gratitude to the absolutely wonderful Austin Zeiderman in the Department of Geography and Environment at LSE, LSE's Department of Gender Studies, Laura Murphy and Tulane University's Phyllis M. Taylor Center for Social Innovation and Design Thinking, Tulane's Albert and Tina Small Center for Collaborative Design, Lilie Chouliaraki of LSE, Lisa Ann Richey of the Copenhagen Business School, and the Food Justice Scholar-Activist/Activist-Scholar Community of Practice (FJSAAS) within the American Association of Geographers. Conversations with Regina Hansda, Liisa Maliki, Deborah Harris, Cocoa Williams, Karen Gardner, Mariama Eversley, Amelia Brandt, Jordana Ramalho, Sarah Howard, Andy Horowitz, Emma Spruce, Gwendolyn Beetham, Samantha Fleurinor, David Beriss, Yuki Kato, Leo Gorman, Krystin Rubin, Karen Heisler, Jesse Brown, Catarina Passidomo, Elizabeth Hoody, Lydia Pelot-Hobbs, Jesse Hardman, Tatiana Cary, Sarah Fouts, Joann Ricci, and Courtney Harvey were essential to this research.

There is no single individual I learn more from than my friend Jabari Carmichael Brown. Working with Jabari at Grow Dat Youth Farm and at VISIONS Inc. over the past dozen years has shaped and sharpened my analytical perspective. I'm honored to be a "land nerd" in the History of the Land collective alongside Jabari, Kevin Connell, and Theodore Hilton. The staff and young people, past and present, at Grow Dat have deepened my imagination for transformation.

I benefit from an incredible constellation of caring people: my Firth and Widmer families, Leigh Bird Khandro, Francey Russell, Kristy Magner, Alexis Erkert, Ben Depp, Emily and Ketch Morse, Tom and Jenny Krell, Rhonny Bowers, Addy Free, Carolyn Morales, Cayla Skillin-Brauchle,

J. J. Gregg, Martin de Porres House of Hospitality, Suze Gardner, Sam Yates, Nancy Wiens, Sonya Thompson, Peggy Thompson, Rod Nurse (RIP), Carl Truedsson, Stina Wassen, Johanna Gilligan, Laura Erceg, VISIONS family, Laura Antona, Jordan Falk, Lina Yaqubian, Jeff Guinn, Paroj Bannerjee, Carwyn Morris, Lauren Elliott, Asiya Islam, Adrien Martin, Sonal Shah, Alison Weisgal, Lillian Sizemore, Jenny Lee, Ruth Korsten, Melanie Berry, and Zarah Patriana. Will Widmer, you're true blue.

Feeding New Orleans

CHAPTER ONE

Introduction

Chef Humanitarianism in the "New" New Orleans

It's nighttime in March in New Orleans, the weather mild and truly gorgeous. It is 2017, and I am in the redeveloped Central Business District (CBD) in an 1820s venue that used to be a sugar mill, now dappled in blue and white lights for weddings and corporate parties. It's the John Besh Foundation's (JBF) Fêtes Fest, the kickoff event for the foundation's annual Fêtes des Chefs fundraising weekend. Tomorrow, eight private dinners with chefs Marcus Samuelsson, Emeril Lagasse, and Aarón Sánchez will be held in local homes for upwards of $1,000 a ticket. Admission to tonight's event started at the lower price point of $99 for unlimited food, drink, and music by the Brass-a-Holics, described as New Orleans's "GoGoBrassFunk Band." It has been a dozen years since the city flooded in 2005, and while attending the event that night, Katrina was completely out of my awareness. Looking back now, I understand that I was moving through a social and physical landscape shaped by the flooding.

Long lines form around dozens of chef stations throughout the enormous hall, offering cocktails and small plates from restaurants across the city. The attendees are almost exclusively white, like me, as are the chefs announced on placards in front of their cooking areas. The service crew cleaning up empty glasses and paper plates comprise the few people of color in the space. In the coming months, Besh and his company of bars and restaurants will be accused by dozens of women of rampant sexual harassment. But that reckoning is still to come, and for now, Besh is the idol of the hour. In his typical gregarious fashion, he cracks jokes onstage and poses for photographs with fans. Around midnight, I see him running in the street outside the venue, pretending to jump through the window of a Chevy Tahoe filled with laughing women as it rolls by. I imagine this is the after-hours "laissez les bons temps rouler" version of Besh's *Family Table* TV show on PBS, where the kids go to bed and the adults let the good times roll—as the popular Cajun French expression says.

A young Black man named Gaines is circulating through the crowds in a STAY WOKE T-shirt, highly visible under his blue sport coat.[1] Gaines was one of the early winners of the foundation's Chefs Move! scholarship, and he has stayed involved with the JBF's alumni program. Chefs Move! was

FIGURE 1.1 @Fêtes Fest and ready for Instagram: a step-and-repeat photo backdrop, where the John Besh Foundation's hired photographer took portraits of donors as they arrived at Fêtes Fest. The backdrop reads "Fêtes Fest" in bold, alongside the names of event sponsors Omni Hotels & Resorts and *Garden & Gun*. Photo by the author.

cofounded by Besh and philanthropist Jessica Bride, who reportedly approached Besh with the idea of increasing the racial diversity of kitchen leadership by providing aspiring "minority" chefs with the means to attend professional culinary programs.[2] Since its founding in 2011, the JBF has sent more than a dozen young people—primarily older teenagers—to culinary schools including the International Culinary Center (ICC) in New York. As the evening crescendos, Gaines is onstage in front of a packed audience, standing between chef Besh and the JBF director, Melanie, and alongside several other young people of color. STAY WOKE seems to radiate under the bright lights.

Aeriel Ashlee, Bianca Zamora, and Shamika Karikari (2017, 90) define "wokeness" as "critical consciousness to intersecting systems of oppression. Specifically, to be a woke person is to hold an unretractable embodied consciousness and political identity acknowledging the oppression that exists in individual and collective experiences." "Stay woke" has thus been mobilized as a call to be attentive to power and continued oppressions on the basis of race. I asked Gaines why he chose to proclaim this directive onstage, standing next to Besh in front of hundreds of mostly white guests:

> I wasn't scared at all, and I really wanted to send a message, it was really to my people who won it. And really to every Black person that was working alongside another white chef that the chef just decided to pick and choose and bring to the Fête des Chefs program. "Look: enjoy the moment, but think of the big picture." These people—they will use you. They will definitely use you. I've been used. . . . And you have to know what it is you're actually doing and what you're going to get out of it for yourself. And it's just the world we live in. And so the Stay Woke shirt was to Cleshey, Tajee, Marcus [recent scholarship winners]. Like "Yo, like, think. Really think about what we're doing. Think about the space we're in. Think about who is actually giving us this money to do this school scholarship. Think of who's here. Think of all of it."

Gaines was using "stay woke" in the way Ashlee, Zamora, and Shamika describe, demanding awareness of power and privilege, while also signaling his own complicated relationship with the foundation. It was important to Gaines to stand in solidarity with the new scholarship winners, as well as with the Black service workers working the event, whom he saw as tokenized. In the evening's saccharine-sweet atmosphere of affluence and elite culinary culture, Gaines's shirt ruptured any simple story of celebration and generosity.

I bump into a teenager I know from Grow Dat Youth Farm, a food justice organization for young people I helped start several years ago in City Park.[3] He's there with his grandmother, a white woman named Rhonda, who tells me her daughter became a member of one of the JBF's philanthropic clubs and has now gotten their entire family involved with the foundation. In my later interview with Rhonda, she said it was moving for her to see Gaines and the other winners up onstage that night: "So even if you didn't realize that you were there to support the Besh Foundation—you thought you were just at a food event—it became apparent, and I think you probably felt better about being there that evening."

I lead with this vignette to illustrate the themes that echo throughout this ethnography. First, I contend that the nature of humanitarianism is changing, particularly in how "helping" and "caring" show up through consumption, celebrity, disaster capitalist accumulation, and mediations of the self.

In studying the growing presence of chef philanthropists, I examine how giving and receiving are embedded within restaurant culture and create and re-create unequal interpersonal and systemic relationships that are raced, classed, and gendered. I focus on the experiences of "receivers" like Gaines—often given less attention in humanitarian scholarship—as well as "givers" like Rhonda, and question if those labels are even useful in many practices of the gift today. I study fundraising events as sites of ceremonial humanitarianism (Chouliaraki 2013), and work to unpack the increase in commodified causumer experiences, like the Fêtes Fest, as a form of giving.[4] Second, I argue that philanthropy in the present cannot be separated from the history of the land (Brown et al 2020). Gaines framed that history this way: "Think about the space we're in." In a part of town heavily targeted for investment post-Katrina, a former sugar mill had been redeveloped and become a site where white donors gathered to celebrate a celebrity chef "for a good cause"—a chef who had skyrocketed to stardom because he drastically expanded his corporation through post-disaster speculation in the same neighborhood.

THE YEAR 2025 MARKS the twentieth anniversary of when New Orleans and other areas along the Gulf Coast experienced catastrophic flooding due to the failure of the federal levee system after Hurricane Katrina. Since then, projects led by celebrities—and celebrity chefs such as John Besh—have proliferated, mirroring global trends in which corporations, celebrities, and philanthropists have become prominent development and humanitarian leaders of the "new" New Orleans.

The examples of "gifts" offered by celebrities to the city are seemingly endless. On her television show, Ellen DeGeneres gave a food truck to an aspiring entrepreneur, a Black woman who had been gravely affected by Katrina. The recipient of the mobile restaurant now serves customers (delicious) vegan cuisine over the lunch hour in the CBD (figure 1.2). Actor Sean Penn navigated the flooded city in a rescue boat, while actors John Travolta and Kelly Preston flew food and tetanus vaccines into the area in Travolta's personal plane. Actor Brad Pitt's Make It Right Foundation and President Mikhail Gorbachev's Global Green organization built green homes in the Lower Ninth Ward. Actor Wendell Pierce attempted to create a neighborhood of eco-homes in Pontchartrain Park and open a series of healthy grocery stores called Sterling Farms. Randy Fertel, heir to the restaurant chain Ruth's Chris Steak House, worked with chef Alice Waters to open a chapter of Waters's garden education program Edible Schoolyard.

FIGURE 1.2 Serving lunch in New Orleans's Central Business District from a food truck donated by Ellen DeGeneres live on *The Ellen Show*. The show's logo is on the front door of the truck. Photo by the author.

Beyond the Crescent City, Oprah Winfrey opened Angel Lane housing in Houston, while billionaire auto-parts manufacturer Frank Stronach evacuated four hundred New Orleanians and built a rural farming experiment called Magnaville/Canadaville almost overnight. And the list continues.

In the immediate aftermath of the flooding in 2005, arguments for rebuilding New Orleans often hinged on the cultural importance of the city, referencing its food, music, and way of life, which are unique in the United States and much celebrated (Beriss 2012). Simultaneously, New Orleans is marked by high rates of hunger, food apartheid, and diet-related diseases.[5] Both the celebration of New Orleans's cuisine and a concern for residents struggling to put food on their tables became justifications variously deployed by charitable interventions. In the aftermath of the COVID-19 pandemic and Hurricane Ida, chefs have continued to emerge as leaders in disaster response and rebuilding efforts (Firth 2022).

While chefs and restaurants have a long history of "caring" for New Orleans through small-scale efforts, formal philanthropic foundations led by chefs emerged post-disaster(s). This reflects the sudden proliferation of new nongovernmental organizations (NGOs) operating in the city; before Katrina, there were few nonprofit organizations and limited philanthropic activity overall (V. Adams 2013; Woods 2017b). Post-Katrina rebuilding ushered in an unprecedented surge of NGOs in the city and their attendant volunteers—what Adams (2013) documents as the "affect economy"—which mobilized the United States' largest domestic volunteer effort. More than 900 local nonprofits participated in GiveNOLA Day in 2021, an annual event started in 2014 by the Greater New Orleans Foundation to encourage people to donate to organizations working to strengthen the region. One of the consistent facets of ongoing crises in New Orleans is NGO involvement and a reliance on volunteer labor, a trend facilitated by "starve the beast" politics, which have eroded governmental systems and social supports over time (Woods 2017b, 261–71).

The Link Stryjewski Foundation (2015), the Edgar "Dooky" Jr. and Leah Chase Family Foundation (2013), and the John Besh Foundation (2011) were all launched by chefs or their companies post-Katrina. By the end of 2018, three additional chef foundations affiliated with the Besh Restaurant Group had launched: the Aarón Sánchez Scholarship Fund, Kelly Fields's Yes Ma'am Foundation, and Alon Shaya's Shaya Barnett Foundation.[6] While restaurants and chefs have been celebrated as a source of pride and resilience for the city, oppressive practices and inequities within the restaurant industry—such as sexual harassment and labor exploitation—have been largely overlooked. Charting the rapid proliferation of foundations launched by primarily white male chefs, this ethnography tells a complex story about the "new" New Orleans and the future being imagined by businesses and corporate philanthropists in the city.

In what has been called a restaurant "renaissance" and "boom" in the decade after Katrina (Firth and Passidomo 2022), New Orleans is said to have more restaurants than any other US city of its size today. I position this growth as part of government and private sector investments in the city's "cultural economy" for tourism. The city now relies on tourist spending, and the COVID-19 pandemic revealed some of the precariousness of this economy. The $1 billion dollar Louis Armstrong New Orleans International Airport opened in November 2019, just a few short months before lockdowns for the pandemic began. In April 2020, passenger traffic was down 97 percent compared to the same month the year before; by June, it was still

85 percent lower (J. Williams 2020). With few tourists visiting the city, dire forecasts predicted that half of New Orleans's 1,500 restaurants were at risk of closing. A local TV news channel implored, "The future of New Orleans restaurants is in the hands of locals" (Truong 2020). In the absence of visitors, New Orleanians were urged to care for their city by patronizing its restaurants, the city's culture and economy now fully dependent on their spending.[7]

Following calls by scholars such as Rachel Slocum (2013), I explicitly consider race and racism in the study of food geographies, attempting to highlight the deep linkages between food, regional identity, and race to stress why the study of foodscapes in New Orleans yields particularly salient information about the power dynamics present in the reconstruction of the city post-disaster.[8] Kaitland Byrd (2015, 104) argues that being committed to the histories and cultures of food means engaging with the fact that "what constitutes authentic Southern food is rooted in the history of racial oppression and the appropriation of foodways that began with African American women working in the kitchens of white plantation owners." I agree with Catarina Passidomo (2017, 432) that Southern food must be understood as "a product of the violences of colonialism, Indian Removal, enslavement, and cultural and resource exploitation by the white elite."

Chef interventions are focused on foodscapes, and most do not explicitly consider gender, race, or class. The JBF's project, Chefs Move!, is an exception, as it is explicitly about race. However, the term "racism" was rarely heard in my fieldwork with the foundation, and the initiative does not consider gender, class, other historically excluded identities, or intersectional axes of difference and oppression (see more in chapter 5). Still, Sarah Bradshaw (2013, 47) reminds us that even when there is a lack of attention to gender, "all policies have a gendered aspect." When a particular policy affects women's time or health, which is indirect or hidden, the "differential gendered impact is often not recognized." Food and food provisioning is especially relevant in this regard, as not only are women disproportionately affected by hunger, but the unpaid reproductive labor of "feeding the family" is constructed as feminine and women's work (Cairns and Johnston 2015; DeVault 1991). Sylvia Chant (2016, 59) argues that using a gendered perspective to examine food systems and poverty "requires acknowledging not only the hiatuses between women's production of food and its consumption, but also the manifold burdens associated with access, provision and preparation which devolve upon women and girls, and can add to their monetary privations in numerous ways, including physiologically, psychologically and socially." Thus, I consider how foodscape interventions are inherently gendered, raced, and classed.

While this research is rooted in New Orleans, my broader interest is in the increasing global presence of philanthropists, corporations, and public-private partnerships (PPPs) in consumer-based solutions in development and humanitarian aid. Anthropologist Erica Bornstein (2012, 16) proposes that "perhaps humanitarianism and philanthropy—the gift of an individual to a cause—have become the new development." The era of the New Poverty Agenda or New Policy Agenda has seen the growth of market-based and consumer-driven approaches to development, along with the rise of PPPs and nontraditional development actors, including philanthropists, corporations, celebrities, the public, and the poor.[9] Worldwide philanthropic contributions to development have increased more than tenfold in the last decade (OECD 2015, 1). Calls to increase private-sector involvement in development appear throughout the United Nation's Agenda 2030, which encapsulates its sustainable development goals (SDGs, or global goals). The SDGs culminate in goal seventeen, which emphasizes mainstreaming multi-stakeholder partnerships to "encourage and promote effective public, public-private and civil society partnerships" (United Nations, 2015, 32, Target 17.1). The media campaigns announcing the SDGs were indicative of the continued and developing interrelations between the development agenda and celebrity engagement. Interested members of the press have referred to the SDGs as a "star-studded, celebrity-backed campaign" featuring Beyoncé, Meryl Streep, and Stephen Hawking (Ziv 2015, 1). There is widespread consensus that philanthropy and development have not collaborated enough previously, and that "including foundations more strategically in policy discussions at the global and the local levels will help optimize development results" (OECD 2015, 1).

Bornstein (2012, 12) argues that development, charity, and humanitarianism, although "often academically considered to be in separate realms . . . are part of a larger universe of giving." In agreement with Bornstein on both points, I contend that philanthropy, as part of private sector engagement more broadly, is playing an increasingly important role in development. Geography as a discipline has been a particularly fruitful venue for seeking to understand Bornstein's "universes of giving" beyond the limitations of standard disciplinary boundaries.

I aim to establish an analytical framework for better understanding the geographies of corporate giving. In developing geographies of the gift and of giving, I propose that gift geographies must attend to giving's uneven spatiality and historicity. Geographic engagement with giving has been limited, and literature concerned with philanthropy across disciplines— both more critical and constructive or applied—has sought to identify broad patterns in the United States but has generally neglected the matter of how giving is situated spatially and constructed historically. Foodscape philanthropy by celebrity chefs stems from and contributes to the uneven redevelopment of New Orleans post-Katrina. Practices of giving are cultivated within a long arc of social inequality and social relations in New Orleans, which shapes what it means to be generous or philanthropic. Geographies of giving are shaped by the history of the land, and giving is specific to particular articulations of temporal and spatial social relations. My education about and interest in land histories comes from a workshop developed by Jabari Brown and Leo Gorman at Grow Dat (Brown et al. 2020), and I discuss the workshop in more detail in chapter 5.

I also develop a framework that builds on foundational work by Lisa Ann Richey and Stefano Ponte (2011) to analyze the geographies of corporate giving at various scales in relation to the restaurant industry and foodscape interventions. In analyzing the spatial dimensions of corporate charitable engagement, this framework reveals the nuanced formulations and implications of the politics, potentials, and limitations of business-based involvement in transformation and social change. In embedded corporate social responsibility (CSR), the ethical dimensions of the business are considered, and reforms target workplace conditions and environmental impacts. In disembedded CSR, philanthropic interventions are made outside industry locations and concern social issues that are unrelated to the corporation's practices or production. Disembedded CSR follows more traditional formulations of philanthropy (giving to others), while embedded CSR targets internal business reforms. This analysis, combined with attention to the geographies of giving, creates a more thorough understanding of the implications of elite and corporate philanthropy.

While I develop these contributions in the context of New Orleans and foodscapes, there is potential for the use of these lenses or tools in other research on giving across disciplines. More broadly, this research assists in addressing gaps in feminist scholarship in the fields of geography, development studies, gender studies, and food studies by bringing my research into conversations concerning philanthropy in foodscapes, long-term engagement in disaster and humanitarian work in wealthy countries with colonial histories, and elite projects that are privately funded and led by celebrity humanitarians and philanthropic business leaders, specifically chefs.

My research further illuminates the changing nature of humanitarianism by bringing feminist consideration of "the gift" into literatures on celebrity humanitarianism.

Entrenched Inequalities: Chef Humanitarianism in Foodscapes

In utilizing a feminist lens to study the emergent philanthropic worlds of chefs, I seek to understand how their charitable institutions are created, practiced, and contested, and how their efforts are shaped by interwoven politics of race, class, and gender in the context of racial capitalism, plantation logics and legacies, and unfinished freedom movements (Camp and Pulido 2017a; Woods 2017a). While domestic cooking and food preparation labor are overwhelmingly assigned to women, professionalized cooking, restaurant ownership, and philanthropy are now the domains of white men, who hold the majority of leadership positions—and prestige—within the culinary world (Yen Liu and Apollon 2011).

Rosalyn Diprose (2002, 10) observes that "the generosity and the gifts of some (property owners, men, wage earners, whites) tend to be recognized and remembered more often than the generosity and gifts of others (the landless, women, the unemployed, indigenous peoples, and immigrants)," and that injustices arise when the gifts of certain people are forgotten while the gifts of others are memorialized. Nonprofessionalized and low-wage cooking and restaurant work have been devalued historically, associated with people of color, enslaved persons, domestic workers, and lower-class service workers, and my research reveals how elite foodscape philanthropy not only stems from a long legacy of such inequities but also reproduces them. White male chefs with profitable businesses owe their success at least in part to privileged access to capital and resources. Bolstered by the privileges offered to white men in the restaurant industry, successful chefs are able to expand their work beyond the restaurant, positioning themselves as humanitarian leaders.

Alternative food initiatives (AFIs) in the United States have struggled with how to fund their activities. Consumer spending has been emphasized in a range of initiatives, from fair trade to organic agriculture, mobilizing a widespread belief that food systems can be reformed by "voting with your fork." Simultaneously, AFIs and food movements have largely embraced the restaurant industry and gourmet culinary culture, with chefs becoming public intellectuals (Eckstein and Young 2015) and leaders of their own AFIs and charitable foundations. To what extent chefs are leaders of food movements more generally is debatable, but I argue that chefs increasingly have a seat at the table in setting such agendas. My research studies the merging of these trends, and I attend to the troubled relationships between consumerism, the restaurant industry, and food movements.

Eric Holt-Giménez and Annie Shattuck (2011) evaluate the potential of food movements to create substantive change in the global food system and argue that the current food regime qualifies as corporate (McMichael 2009).[10] Within the corporate food regime, interventions are either neoliberal or reformist in their orientation, and food movements are either progressive or radical (Holt-Giménez 2010; Holt-Giménez and Shattuck 2011). The food sovereignty movement is one radical movement that has been a source of personal inspiration for my own work. Food sovereignty is attributed to the peasant farmers of La Via Campesina and has a distinct sociopolitical orientation that "takes a rights based approach, encompassing the right of self-determination, and the right to food and decent work" (Sayeed and Maldonado 2013, 21).[11] Calls for food sovereignty make direct connections to the history of land and inequalities in land tenure.

In response to criticisms that AFIs have been co-opted or are complicit in oppression, Charles Levkoe (2011) proposes a three-part rubric for evaluating AFIs and their potential for a "transformative food politics": (1) the transition to collective subjectivities; (2) a whole-food system approach, and (3) a politics of reflexive localization. It is not my intention to evaluate the efficacy of individual projects, but my findings suggest that philanthropic efforts in post-Katrina New Orleans are unlikely to qualify as part of the food movement in Holt-Giménez and Shattuck's framework or to meet Levkoe's criteria for a "transformative food politics." Holt-Giménez, Shattuck, and Levkoe draw distinctions between issue-based and system-based initiatives, and the New Orleans foodscape initiatives are primarily issue based and limited in their scope.

Rachel Slocum and Arun Saldanha (2013, 11) argue that food justice mobilizes food as a tool or venue for social justice, and in order for it to be effective, it must "directly build on anti-racist politics." Joshua Sbicca's (2018) work shows how food justice can do this, and Bobby J. Smith's (2019) development of the concept of "food power" can further antiracist scholarship. Food power considers both oppressive food power and emancipatory food power, the latter of which is often neglected in academic scholarship. Smith's acknowledgment of the dual processes of oppression and emancipation in food justice struggles resonates with my focus on freedom movements in telling histories of the land.

The multisite fieldwork that informs this book included extensive observation and semi-structured interviews with more than one hundred participants. Participants included celebrity chefs and representatives from their foundations; elite chefs who have decided not to start formal organizations; community cooks and food organizations (including the organization that I helped start, Grow Dat Youth Farm); philanthropic advisors; members of the newly developing industry that supports or champions chef activism; and other post-Katrina philanthropic projects.[12] Of the six chef foundations I've studied most extensively, three were started by white male chefs, one by a Latino chef, one by a white chef and his mentor (a woman), and the newest, nascent foundation is being launched by a white woman. As public figures, celebrity chefs and corporate executives are named and otherwise identified. Participants who are not public figures have been assigned pseudonyms (in text, they are referred to by first names) and are not featured close-up in photographs. Beneficiaries of charitable causes have rarely been asked to contribute to this line of research, and their perspective proved invaluable for providing insight into my research questions. Community cooks and food organizations are defined as those who use cooking and food as an axis for social engagement or change. Some of the cooks I interviewed are affiliated with formal NGOs, while others are not. Several cooks spend the majority of their time cooking and selling their food, but they do not use the title chef (see chapter 5).

I am as specific as possible when describing how people self-identify regarding race, gender, and gender expression, and I prioritize using participants' own language and descriptions. I capitalize "Black" and racial categories other than white, and I write "white" with a lowercase "w." This approach is contested, and my present rationale for doing so follows the practice long established by the Black press in the context of historical calls for capitalization (Okun 2010, xi), such as the one advocated by W. E. B. DuBois (1899, 1). Capitalizing "Black" explicitly references history, power, and enslavement because it "speaks to an unknown familial/national past" (Touré 2011, ix), whereas white familial lineages and ethnicities are more commonly known or knowable. As a white writer concerned with knowledge production and power, using lowercase for "white" denotes my ongoing intention to "decenter whiteness" (Davis and Craven 2016, 4) as the principal source of knowledge.

Donna Haraway (1998, 56) has said she wishes she had used her rhetorical apparatus more intentionally in *Primate Visions* (1989) to reassure primatologists that she "know[s] and care[s] about the way they think." I similarly feel a sense of care for the staff working at the chef foundations I studied, some of whom I knew personally before this research began. Most of them were passionate about their work, were keen to push their own growth, and shared concerns about their engagement in ways that felt open and honest. Some staff members readily and willingly identified areas in which they lacked knowledge or expertise. Foundations requested information about best practices in chef philanthropy and asked me to advise them on how to do their work better. Occasionally I was able to point them toward previous research that might be relevant (for example, scholarship on Jamie Oliver's projects), but there had not yet been critical literature designed for practitioners to use. Thus, I hope the findings of this book and the specific recommendations for chef philanthropists outlined in the conclusion are useful. At the John Besh Foundation specifically, it feels important to note that there is a spectrum of culpability regarding individual participation in the Besh institutions where sexual harassment was endemic. As I discuss more throughout the book, some staff I engaged with in this research were active enablers of harassment and harmful practices, while others seemed to brush off, ignore, or play ignorant about what was happening. Others—including youth winners of the Chefs Move! scholarship—experienced racism and sexism firsthand, and a former executive director of the foundation quit her job in protest over what was happening to her and the youth in the program.

My findings reveal how chef-led foodscape philanthropy stems from entrenched inequalities within the restaurant industry, and that charitable gifts from chefs are part of—rather than separate from—this world. Projects, regardless of intention, operate within a field in which donors, beneficiaries, and staff negotiate troubled legacies that reemerge and can be reproduced. Given the backdrop of deeply entrenched inequalities regarding race, gender, and class, is chef philanthropy addressing and redressing inequalities within its own operations? I find that chefs with foundations engage in business-aligned and business-informed philanthropy, and I explore how this can result in the sexism and racism common in the culinary world, infusing a chef's charitable work as well.

Positionality, Land Histories, and Diffraction

I am forever being crept up on and newly startled by the realization
that my people established themselves here by killing or driving out the
original possessors, by the awareness that people were once bought and
sold here by my people, by the sense of the violence they have done to

their own kind and to each other and to the earth. . . . And so here, in the place I love more than any other and where I have chosen among all other places to live my life, I am more painfully divided within myself than I could be in any other.

—WENDELL BERRY, "A Native Hill"

In this section, I begin to locate myself within this research by rooting my own engagement in a collective project I am a part of. Based on an initial workshop at Grow Dat Youth Farm discussed in chapter 5, History of the Land is both "a curriculum and pedagogical lens [that] theorizes oppressive structure within foodscapes and then imagines how such structures may be transformed" (Brown et al. 2020, 243). Here I share about my ancestral relationships to land with the goal of showing how being a white woman from the North (of the United States and in a global context) shaped much of my experience of fieldwork and forms the backdrop of my own lens to understanding what I observed in my research.

My grandparents had a light box in their living room, a backlit photograph of the town of Garrison, Kansas, taken from a neighboring hillside in the early 1950s. My grandmother would grasp a pencil and tap on locations nestled between swaths of faded green fields and the dusty brown roads of the Flint Hills tallgrass prairie. She pointed to the home where her Swedish immigrant parents settled along the Little Blue River; the Walsburg Lutheran Church off in the distance, where she was married, and its attendant cemetery, where all my family is buried; the farm with four hundred acres of "broke ground," which my grandparents sharecropped at the time my mother was born.

With dementia altering her timelines, my mimi insisted that this tiny town had not changed over seventy years—she had lost the memory of her community's fight to stop the construction of the Tuttle Creek Dam. I used to peek at a button in my mother's jewelry box that read "Stop the Dam Foolishness," a remnant from the failed resistance campaign my grandparents took part in. The dam was built in 1953 through eminent domain by the Army Corps of Engineers, and a giant reservoir quickly engulfed the land, displacing my grandparents' immigrant (settler, it feels important to also name) community. As a child visiting the Tuttle Creek State Park for Fourth of July celebrations, I watched fireworks break over the deep, glassy water. I swore to my cousins that I could see the church steeple poking out just above the shimmering waterline.

I grew up learning the history of my family through stories about the land. When the farm was flooded, my grandfather went to night school and fo-

FIGURE 1.3 My mimi, Phyllis K. (Peterson) Dettmer, narrating a history of the land of Garrison, Kansas, now under the waters of the Tuttle Creek Dam. Photo by the author.

cused on agricultural engineering. If he couldn't be a farmer, his dream was to help farmers, and the family moved frequently, following his short-term contracts across the country, moving between Dow and Monsanto petro-chemical plants. My own work in sustainable agriculture and food justice today is tied to this legacy, an attempt to account for my family's participation in extractive, petrochemical-intensive agriculture. My grandparents' siblings remained in Kansas and set up farmsteads in other rural towns, which, to my delight, we returned to again and again for vacations and holidays. Somehow, despite my own perpetual movement, I developed a sense of being a steward of the land, deeply rooted in the prairie heartland of Kansas.

I continue to learn how my own positionality—as a white person, as working class, as a holder of a US passport, as a Northerner, and more—not only shapes how I understand the world but also influences the knowledge I produce as a scholar. Working with elder Black activists in New Orleans has brought these lessons home further as I continue to learn the importance of not only knowing my own history but learning the histories of others. When I first moved to New Orleans in 2010, I participated in a series of Story Circles convened by Junebug Productions. My group was led by John O'Neal (1940–2019), a former field director of the Student Nonviolent Coordinating Committee and one of the founders of the Free Southern Theater. In our workshops, O'Neal, a legendary teacher of radical pedagogy, insisted that we must listen to others' stories. The act of hearing, of deeply listening, influences or informs our own stories in turn. Thus, it is a move from the individual to the collective.

Knowing the history of the land is not merely about providing a timeline of events but about understanding material impacts, as the history of who has control of the land is a history of power (Brown et al. 2020). Fannie Lou Hamer, the visionary founder of the Freedom Farm Cooperative in Mississippi in 1967, knew this truth about land: "In order for any people or nation to survive, land is necessary" (quoted in M. M. White 2018, 65). The histories of the land that I heard were, after all, narrated by my settler colonial ancestors. I learned that towns in Pottawatomie County were flooded when the dam was built; I knew nothing of the Bodéwadmi/Pottawatomie/Potawatomi people who were forced into the area by the US government, or that the Prairie Band Potawatomi Nation now holds an annual powwow nearby. I went to high school at Shawnee Mission East, knowing nothing of my school's namesake, the Shawnee Indian Mission. The Shawnee Mission, a forced labor school, was presented in a sunny, positive light as a popular elementary school field trip destination. Much of the suburban white-flight sprawl of the Kansas City metro area is named after it. I was unaware that the landscape I navigated daily throughout my childhood also mapped the racist legacies of both boarding schools and redlining practices. As John O'Neal might ask: How do these stories influence my own?

I moved to New Orleans the summer that BP's *Deepwater Horizon* offshore rig exploded and dumped millions of barrels of oil into the Gulf of Mexico. My spouse, photojournalist William Widmer, covered human ecology and environmental issues across the Gulf South, and I was fortunate to be hired onto the team to launch Grow Dat Youth Farm, a youth food justice program that is now the largest urban farm in the city. I spent the next five years in New Orleans at Grow Dat while serving as co-chair of the New Orleans Food Policy Advisory Committee, teaching in International Development at Tulane University, and being involved in local justice movements. I left my role as Grow Dat's first assistant director in 2015, knowing that I wanted to critically reflect on the work that I had been immersed in through this research.

Among elites within my professional networks, I follow Ananya Roy's commitment to "intimate ethnography" that "studies up": "In my work, I have charted the shift from 'studying down' to 'studying up' as a shift from a 'conscientious ethnography' of subaltern subjects and spaces to an intimate ethnography that has brought me face to face with the professionals who research and manage poverty—people like myself. Instead of rendering the strange 'familiar'—which middle-class researchers tend to do when they study the poor—this type of awkward ethnography renders the familiar 'strange,' revealing the forms of power and knowledge through which the ethnographer as subject is also constituted" (Roy 2012, 37). The spaces of formal philanthropy and fundraising events in this fieldwork were almost exclusively white and upper middle to upper class. Anthropologist Laura Nader argues that "if we look at the literature based on fieldwork in the United States, we find a relatively abundant literature on the poor, the ethnic groups, the disadvantaged; there is comparatively little field research on the middle class, and very little first hand work on the upper classes." Such research is necessary to understand power more fully and complexly, "to get behind the facelessness of a bureaucratic society, to get at the mechanisms whereby far away corporations and large scale industries are directing the everyday aspects of our lives" (1972, 5).

My professional experiences working in post-Katrina food justice movements raised questions regarding the nature of social transformation in the context of ongoing disasters. Were nonprofit organizations, such as our own, the best approach for bringing about change and heading into the future? Calls to transform the food system by "voting with your fork" had become endemic in much of the food movement in the United States.[13] What were the promises and pitfalls of such market- and consumer-based approaches in funding food movements? How does money circulate (or not) in social movements and social change? I bring these questions to the new configurations of development and humanitarianism, in which corporations, philanthropists, and celebrities are increasingly important.

FIGURE 1.4 Conducting observation at Dinner on the Farm. The intimate and awkward ethnographer (front right) at a fundraising dinner for Grow Dat Youth Farm. Here I chat with other guests (donors?) in a photograph Grow Dat featured on its Facebook page. Photo by Grow Dat Youth Farm.

Witnessing the role that private funding and philanthropists had played in rebuilding New Orleans brought these research interests close to home. Developed as a social entrepreneurship project, Grow Dat recognized that some market-based fundraising might help break our reliance on foundation funding, responding to the worry that such funding would soon be scarce as the influx of Katrina-related philanthropy waned with each passing year. As I began this research, the organization had just started hosting Dinners on the Farm, which featured guest chefs (and their foundations) serving gourmet meals to wealthy diners on our land. Grow Dat is located on seven acres in New Orleans City Park, a land that holds hundreds of years of complex stories (see chapter 5). What could celebrity chefs cooking Dinners on the Farm in post-Katrina New Orleans tell us about food movements and the changing nature of humanitarianism?

As the poet and agricultural thinker Wendell Berry expresses in the quotation that opens this section, white people's relationship to beloved ancestral land divides our sense of self, ruptures any one way to be or to feel about that relationship and our belonging to it. An early methodological inspiration for this research approach was the concept of diffraction, as developed by feminist historian of science Donna Haraway. Diffraction engages an optical metaphor, which Haraway (1998, 103) describes as such: "When light passes through slits, the light rays that pass through are broken up. And if you have a screen at one end to register what happens, what you get is a record of the passage of the light rays on the screen. This 'record' shows the history of their passage through the slits." Diffraction offers a methodology that both records histories of "how something came to 'be' as well as what it is simultaneously" (Haraway 1998, 104). Methodological practice using diffraction registers the "interference" between how an object of study is currently contextualized and shows "that it has many more meanings and contexts to it and that once you've noted them you can't just drop them . . . to make visible all those things that have been lost in an object; not in order to make the other meanings disappear, but rather to make it impossible for the bottom line to be one single statement" (Haraway 1998, 105). Diffraction records history: it documents the school established by the Shawnee Methodist Mission and my own graduation from a school named after it 140 years after the original school closed. Since diffraction asserts that it is impossible for there to be a single statement about an object—and I extend this to places—the geography of my youth (or the land where Grow Dat is located today) comprises places of comfort *and* of violence. This ethnography is based on careful attention to the specific historical contexts and places in which the philanthropic projects I study are being enacted. I have attempted to record history over time and register "interferences" that arise.

Robin Wall Kimmerer (2013, 9) writes that "our relationship with land cannot heal until we hear its stories." Land is essential to agriculture and foodscapes, and in weaving the history of the land throughout this book, I aim to contribute to the collective endeavor to move toward healing and liberation. Land, agriculture, community, resistance, and narration—these themes have not only underpinned my personal biography but also shaped my scholarship.

Conceptualizing (and Living with) Disasters

Rather than isolate "the disaster" of Katrina, I argue that we need to conceptualize *disasters* in New Orleans; in other words, disasters must be understood as historical, ongoing, interconnected, and *not* limited to Katrina, the COVID-19 pandemic, Hurricane Ida, and so on. By the time the COVID-19 pandemic swept through the city in 2020, chef foundations that had originally formed post-Katrina had become normalized—and perhaps even essential—components of the city's disaster infrastructure (Firth 2022). In my framing, I follow Woods's (2017b) analysis that "disaster capitalism," while useful, focuses too much on disasters as distinct and isolated phenomena rather than ongoing and multifaceted, more akin to Gotham and Greenberg's (2014) conceptualization.[14] Disaster capitalism thereby fails to grasp the significance and lasting legacies of enslavement and racial capitalism.

In my experience, flooding shaped the contours of daily life in New Orleans. Weather events are both extreme and ordinary in the city, from Hurricane Isaac, which left us without electricity for almost a week in August 2012, to heavy rains that flooded my new apartment in the Broadmoor neighborhood five times in four months in 2019. The first flooding incident occurred while we were still unpacking moving boxes, the second brought two feet of water into our downstairs and forced us to evacuate to Mississippi in advance of Tropical Storm Barry in July 2019, and it continues.

In August 2016, heavy rains in Baton Rouge, just north of New Orleans, flooded a large area surrounding the city. I helped with grassroots relief efforts to gut two flooded homes, removing rotting carpets and drywall and painstakingly helping families search through mounds of personal effects for mementos that could be salvaged. I worked with my spouse, Will, on a story about the impacts of the flood on elderly residents (Widmer 2016). A couple in St. Amant had raised their home forty-seven inches off the ground, but it still took on nine inches of water. We visited emergency shelters swelling above capacity and watched Red Cross trucks deliver canned water to residents as they returned to their ransacked homes. Celebrity chefs fed hungry evacuees (which I discuss in chapter 5).

We finished the photography for the story, and the next day I visited a celebrity philanthropic project, a farm and residential community designed and funded by Frank Stronach. The project was officially named Magnaville, after Stronach's company, but it was called Canadaville by residents. Located in rural Simmesport, Louisiana, hundreds of evacuees from New Orleans were relocated to Canadaville after Katrina. In my field notes I wrote about how eerie and unsettled I felt, sensing the parallels between the devastating flooding that I had just witnessed and the flooding in New Orleans that had occurred almost exactly eleven years ago to the day. The heat of the August summer, the rushing water and closed roads, the dank smell that lingered on our clothes—a mix of rotting wood and the cleaning products used in trying to stop mold from taking hold in the innards of the houses we had visited. As someone who had not experienced Katrina firsthand, the visceral realities of flooding and the relief response were shocking and seemed to create a link across time and space: Was it just as brutally hot when residents left their homes in New Orleans and moved here, to Canadaville? Did it smell the same? Many friends who had survived Katrina went to Baton Rouge to assist in solidarity; others shared that PTSD prevented them from offering the support they wanted to. Social and environmental disasters shape the landscape of my (and our collective) daily life and research.

Chapter Overview

Chapter 2 begins with an expansive consideration of scholarship that has theorized the gift and giving. I examine the gift's analytical use in understanding power, such as in donor-recipient (or beneficiary) relationships and hierarchies. Does a gift require inequality or unequal power relations? I position this examination within the broad changes surrounding what development is and how it is funded and financed. I discuss how I position celebrity humanitarianism—and my ethnography of celebrity chefs— within these evolutions and trends. I outline feminist scholarship that examines CSR in development agendas, and tie this to research on ethical consumption and causumerism—"voting with your fork."

Chapter 3 establishes why a particular formulation of aid—that of chefs as humanitarian leaders—has emerged in New Orleans. I outline national trends that increased the prominence of celebrity chefs in New Orleans and across the country, and I argue that government and private investments in the cultural economy for tourism, combined with the sociohistorical importance of culinary culture, imbued chefs with economic power and compelling forms of culinary capital, which positioned them to become humanitarian leaders in the "new" New Orleans. With this background in place, I document the chef-led interventions that have emerged in the city and establish how the post-Katrina disasters and processes of rebuilding provided the context for celebrity humanitarian interventions.

Chapter 4 considers a prominent spatiotemporal configuration of chef philanthropy that I regularly observed: the fundraiser. I argue that fundraisers are not simply a means to an end but worthy of study and theorization as essential to the practices and operations of elite chef philanthropy. Chef foundations fundraise extensively through events that are key to both their income-generating and operational activities. I discuss how, despite their use of the term "foundation," chef organizations do not function as private foundations, public foundations, or community foundations—structures in which financing would primarily come from a chef's wealth or profits from the chef's restaurants. Instead, most chef foundations function as charities that fundraise and run their own programming, as would any standard 501(c)(3) charity or nonprofit organization. Marketing for fundraising events often hinges on the exceptional and ephemeral nature of these events, creating a sense of urgency and exclusiveness. However, I argue that these events need to be conceptualized in a way that is equally attentive to their consistencies and repetitions as sites of ceremonial humanitarianism (Chouliaraki 2013).

Throughout chapter 4 I draw on an extended ethnographic vignette from a JBF fundraising event to illustrate my findings. Centering the perspectives of staff, attendees/donors, and beneficiaries, I analyze how fundraising events are racialized, classed, and gendered. I show the polyvalent nature of fundraisers: as sites of financial gain for foundations; sites of branding and meaningful charitable work for chefs; sites of pleasure and ethical consumption for attendees/donors; and sites of opportunity, intense racialized histories, and contested representations for beneficiaries. I highlight how beneficiaries experience public fundraising events, an area that is currently understudied in academic research, and I explore how beneficiaries view and understand the gift.

Chapter 5 considers raising money and doing "good work" in foodscapes more broadly. I discuss Grow Dat Youth Farm's partnership with celebrity chefs and their foundations to raise money through Dinners on the Farm. Grow Dat's Dinners on the Farm are illustrative of attempts by NGOs to develop partnerships and associate with celebrity humanitarians. The dinners aimed to utilize the culinary capital held by celebrity chefs to generate market-based revenue. I discuss Grow Dat's History of the Land workshop— both a workshop and a way of seeing—in relation to the dinners. As a way of understanding the present by honoring and learning from what came before, consideration of the history of the land has influenced my analytical lens for this research overall. In her study of Black agricultural cooperatives and freedom movements in the US South, Monica White documents how Black farmers have used—and continue to use—the land as "a strategy to move toward freedom" (M. M. White 2018). The land where Grow Dat currently has tenure holds histories of both oppression and freedom. As I found at the Besh Foundation's crawfish boil fundraiser analyzed in chapter 4, raising money cannot be separated from the history of the land. I continue to develop the argument that we must carefully consider place, history, and power in order to understand the gift and its manifestations in foodscapes.

In the second half of chapter 5, I broaden my scope to study chefs who do not have foundations. I work to understand how other chefs (some of whom self-identify as cooks) attempt to "do good" in foodscapes. I discuss findings from interviews with elite chefs who have decided not to start foundations and with women who left careers as professional chefs to work for community organizations instead. I end with a discussion about the pressure chefs feel to engage in charitable causes, and I tie this demand to national trends of professionalization and formalization in which chefs are starting their own foundations and NGOs.

Chapter 6 considers the restaurant industry and looks closely at the relationships between chef humanitarianism and business. I build on Richey and Ponte's (2011) work to establish embedded and disembedded CSR, which emphasizes the spatial dimensions of both the physical location of interventions or reforms and the social problem being addressed. In embedded CSR in restaurants, workplace conditions and politics, environmental impacts, and the purpose of the space (beyond food service) are the focus of reforms. In disembedded CSR, interventions are made outside the restaurant and concern social issues unrelated to food and foodscapes. I outline how evaluating embedded and disembedded CSR is a useful analytical tool.

Chapter 6 also highlights how the lack of focus on power and oppression in charitable work can have consequences for beneficiaries. Here I center narratives from beneficiaries and employees that experienced sexual harassment connected with chef philanthropy. Their stories are evidence of the importance of considering questions of embeddedness in CSR. Evaluating the effectiveness of chefs' programs is not one of my research goals, but I can assert that ignoring gender, class, and other axes of difference affects beneficiaries and can inhibit a foundation's ability to meet its social mission. Following theorizing by Richey and Ponte (2011) regarding "brand aid," I explore how chef philanthropy provides a form of aid to the restaurant industry, working to brand and rebrand the gourmet culinary world as ethical. The chapter concludes with a discussion about causumerism and the role that ethical consumption plays in funding chef projects.

In the final chapter, I review my core arguments and findings, highlight limitations of the research and areas for future research, and discuss implications of my research for theory, policy, and practice. I review how core themes of the gift, fundraising/financing, and the history of the land animate the chapters and link them together. I end the chapter by asking how giftless transfers of resources and notions of the rightful share in practices such as basic income grants differ from philanthropy, and how such alternatives imagine transformation and other futures.

This Is LA, Not L.A.

Boarding a plane from New Orleans to Los Angeles, I spotted a white man in his thirties wearing a faded BRAD PITT FOR MAYOR T-shirt. Created more than a decade ago by the local Storyville apparel company, the shirts had a brief moment in the international media spotlight due to a "grassroots" campaign to "Draft Brad for Mayor" (Plaisance 2009). I use "grassroots" in quotation marks because local reactions to the celebrity benefactor were mixed, often tepid or trepidatious. While the local response was discordant, the national press praised Pitt's Make It Right Foundation after Katrina, lauding the generosity of his "radical experiment" (Little 2010) to rebuild the devastated Lower Ninth Ward by erecting environmentally sustainable homes.

By 2018, however, the tone had shifted and the national conversation seemed more reflective of local apprehensions. Homeowners complained that the homes built by the foundation were bad investments, plagued by design flaws, rotting drywall, and continual electrical problems. They also reported that the foundation itself was increasingly absent and inattentive, sometimes requiring homeowners to sign nondisclosure agreements before staff would agree to address problems. In the fall of 2018, several residents sued the foundation for unfair trade practices, breach of contract, and fraud for selling them "defectively and improperly constructed" homes (Zadrozny 2018). In turn, Pitt and Make It Right sued the lead architect for the problems with the buildings, and the legal battles continue.

The fact that Pitt and Make It Right are simultaneously lauded and derided is evidence of the complexity of the role of celebrity humanitarianism in shaping the "new" New Orleans. I highlight Pitt and Make It Right, arguably the most famous example of celebrity humanitarianism in New Orleans, for

FIGURE 1.5 A 2019 sighting of 2009's "Draft Brad for Mayor" campaign.
Photo by the author.

several reasons. First, it illustrates the importance of studying responses to
disaster over time: the story of Make It Right was different in 2006 than in
2015, and it diverged again by the time of the fifteen-year Katrina anniversary in 2020. In her eight-year ethnography that follows a family recovering
from the flooding, anthropologist Katherine E. Browne (2015) asserts that we
need longer-term studies to establish a more complete picture of recovery.
Previous research on disaster has focused on mitigation, emergency, and
short-term recovery, with significantly less consideration of long-term recovery (Burns and Thomas 2015, 24). My fieldwork occurred more than a

dozen years after the flood, providing different data from what is normally used. Attending to temporality is important, as it allows us to more accurately conceptualize and analyze interventions with more robust context as they unfold over time.

This exemplifies concerns about the politics and stakes of rebuilding—specifically, who leads the effort. In my field notes from 2017, I reflected on the "Draft Brad" campaign in relation to bumper stickers that emerged in the city in the early 2010s: "This is LA, not L.A." I saw the stickers on cars and slapped up around town, including behind the cash register at several bars. The phrase refers to Louisiana, abbreviated as LA, as opposed to Los Angeles (home of Hollywood). I understood the slogan to be aimed at the state's tax credit program for the film and television industry, but even more significantly I believe that the phrase gave voice to fears about gentrification and the loss of local culture following disasters.[15] What does it mean that Brad Pitt, a white Hollywood movie star, became a leader in rebuilding a historic African American neighborhood in New Orleans? As evidence of how privatized and individual charitable efforts dominated rebuilding efforts (Johnson 2011a), Pitt's leadership gives evidence to fears that New Orleans will start to look more like Hollywood than South Louisiana.

This reflects more general concerns about demographic change in the city. By some estimates, newcomers to New Orleans made up more than a quarter of the city's population by 2015, a decade after the flooding (Edge 2017, 251). The city has a conflicted relationship with the influx of young, white aid workers and reconstruction workers such as myself—variously referred to as intellectual carpetbaggers, transplants, and opportunists. For example, Black and African American teachers were laid off in mass firings and often replaced by young, white teachers with less experience. In 2004, 72 percent of educators in New Orleans were Black; a decade later, that number had dropped to 49 percent, and the number of Black local teachers was even lower (Felton 2016). There isn't similar research about nonprofit organizations and demographic change, but I suspect there are similarities. Many—if not most—elite, nationally recognized chefs in New Orleans were not born there, and most of the staff members of their foundations are also transplants.

Pitt's foundation also signifies an earnest desire to do good, celebrity branding, and a lack of expertise—all themes that animate this ethnography of celebrity chef philanthropy. Pitt told the *Times-Picayune* in 2015 (MacCash 2015): "We went into it incredibly naive, just thinking we can build homes—how hard is that?—and not understanding forgivable loan structures and family financial counseling and getting the rights to lots and HUD grants and so on and so forth. So it's been a big learning curve." This lack of expertise is pronounced in chef interventions as well. In my study, I found that chef humanitarians particularly lack competency in understanding historical and present-day oppression.

Through my research, I sought to understand how chefs' charitable institutions are created, practiced, and contested, and how their efforts are shaped by an intersectional politics of race, class, and gender. I studied the emergent philanthropic worlds of chefs by examining the geographies of these gifts, geographies that consider the history of the land, racial capitalism, plantation logics and legacies, and unfinished Black freedom movements. Unlike Brad Pitt, most of the celebrity chefs in this ethnography have positioned themselves as locals (even though most did not grow up in the city) who can "authentically" represent New Orleans's unique culture through its food. In these pages, I argue that the rebuilding of New Orleans hinged on the cultural importance of the city. Culinary culture was upheld as a central pillar for redevelopment and investment, which benefited chefs and helped position them as future leaders of the city's foodscapes. Restaurants became a saving grace in rebuilding efforts, and the successful return of the restaurant industry served as evidence that the city itself not only had survived Katrina but was thriving. Studying the proliferation of chef foundations illuminates the changing nature of development and humanitarianism, helps define the contours of advanced capitalism and ongoing disasters in an age of climate instability, and outlines the troubled contours of the "new" New Orleans.

CHAPTER TWO

Ambivalent Gifts

New Paradigms of Humanitarianism

> There are a million reasons why we give.
> —NURUDDIN FARAH, *Gifts*

In this chapter, I draw on theorizing about the gift, philanthropy, celebrity humanitarianism, and causumerism to provide a theoretical backdrop for understanding giving practices in New Orleans's foodscapes. As mentioned previously, I take a cue from anthropologist Erica Bornstein (2012, 12), who argues that academic distinctions between development, charity, and humanitarianism are limiting and should instead be seen as a "universe of giving." This chapter is divided into three main sections. I first consider anthropological and philosophical thinking about the gift and highlight how bias and inequalities shape the contours of giving and philanthropy. I next survey celebrity humanitarianism literature and review how other scholars have considered this phenomenon in New Orleans in the aftermath of flooding. In the third section, I tie my inquiry to scholarship on corporate social responsibility (CSR) and causumerism. In the conclusion, I link these theoretical concerns to local Black Lives Matter movements and my commitment to studying elites, wealth, whiteness, and racism.

Debate about the definitions of charity and social justice are useful as a launching point for this chapter. In historian Olivier Zunz's (2012) history of the development of the philanthropic sector in the United States, he argues that there is a significant difference between models of charity and the emergence of the "new philanthropy" after industrialization.[1] Zunz argues that philanthropy was preferable to charity: "Charity had been for the needy; philanthropy was to be for mankind" (10). Although Zunz's distinction may have been the case in contrast with historical precedent, I follow critics who argue that much philanthropy today still qualifies as charity in the form of programs and services for the poor or disenfranchised (Ahn 2007). Ahn and others argue that charity stems from the concept of "noblesse oblige," in which the rich are morally obligated to give to the poor. They contend that charity fundamentally requires social inequality, as a hierarchy must exist that creates a giver and a receiver; this is juxtaposed with social justice, which sets its goal as the erasure of inequity. Charity therefore alleviates the effects of inequality, while social justice aims to change the systems that create inequality. Here lies a foundational argument against private philanthropy: as foundations function through wealth created by capitalist endeavors, they will continue to preserve and serve the capitalist interests of their creators (A. Smith 2007, 4–5)—akin to Audre Lorde's (2007) assertion that "the master's tools will never dismantle the master's house." As Cynthia Sanborn and Felipe Portocarrero (2005, xii) put it, "Is it practical to think that those who have benefited from the unequal distribution of wealth are going to promote, or even permit, a change in this situation?" Silvia Federici (2012) warns that capital is learning that nonmonetary elements—common goods such as confidence, trust, and gift giving—actually matter to the success of markets: "We must be very careful, then, not to craft the discourse on the commons in such a way as to allow a crisis-ridden capitalist class to revive itself, posturing, for instance, as the environmental guardian of the planet."[2] In the conclusion to this chapter and throughout the book that follows, I explore the potentials and limitations of chef philanthropy to create substantive social change.

It is also useful to mention that positioning chef philanthropy within scholarship on private, public, and civil society sectors is difficult. Civil society is most commonly conceptualized as a part of society but distinct from markets and the state (Edwards 2014, 23; Lewis 2014). Civil society is the third sector, or nonprofit sector, and is largely based on a neo-Tocquevillian emphasis on voluntary associational life (Edwards 2014). However, I found the chef foundations in this research to be corporate, public, and private simultaneously. Of the nontraditional development actors established by LaFleur and Brainard (2009)—venture philanthropy, corporations, the poor, the public, and celebrities—chef foundations in New Orleans engage all but venture philanthropy. I interviewed a national venture philanthropy firm that has several partnerships with chefs who focus on foodscape issues, but I did not find any local chefs undertaking venture philanthropy in the context of New Orleans. To address these fluid boundaries, I follow Anna Lowenhaupt Tsing (2005). In her attempt to acknowledge disparate but simultaneous activist and economic accounts of resource extraction and environmental degradation, Tsing develops the concept of friction and specifically that of distress. Rather than try to neatly reconcile these various accounts, Tsing "puts the question of distress center stage rather than trying to avoid it" (viii). For example, Tsing explores how difficult it was to categorize and label the economic structures at play in Indonesia: "foreign was domestic," "public was private"—"even the staunchest of neoclassical economists admit that it was difficult to distinguish among domestic, foreign, and government ownership" (37). This informed my methodological approach, and thus my ethnography documents distress, contradictions, and complexity.

The Gift: Ambivalent or Impossible?

Sociologist Helmut Berking (1999, viii–ix) gives a historical-cultural account of the meanings, norms, and history of gifts, giving, and exchange, outlining the terrain of the gift as such: "To give means to acquire a power, to carry out a symbolic exchange, to initiate relationships and alliances, to attribute rights and duties, to objectify subjective meanings and systematically to classify alter egos. It means to dress up strategic orientations in altruistic motives, to make social challenges look like simple acts of charity, to honor and shame, to hierarchize and stratify, to solidarize, to knit forms of mutual recognition, to become equal and intimate." All-encompassing and simplistic definitions therefore do not accurately reflect the complexities of many different kinds of giving. Berking continually refers to the "ambivalent" system of giving and highlights the exchange element in gift exchange as "an interest-guided transaction which does not and cannot risk revealing itself as such. . . . Something is not exchanged for nothing" (26). In geographies of giving, the gift is shaped not only by social relations between people but also by place and time.

In his extensive anthropological study of giving, Marcel Mauss (2002, 2016) conceptualizes the gift as a three-part cycle of "the three obligations": giving, receiving, and reciprocating. Mauss stresses that the gift is always spun within a web of conflicting tensions, "a combination of interest and disinterest, of freedom and constraint" (Parry 1986, 456). In the foreword to Jane Guyer's translation, Bill Maurer (2016, xiii) writes that the gift is "a never-completed action involving always more than the transacting parties, a not-seamless coming together of perspectives or worlds or contending abstractions." Mauss's (2016, 183) interest in the gift was driven by a postwar-era sense of urgency: he believed that gift exchange is the kind of system "toward which we would like to see our societies orient themselves." Utilizing a gendered lens, Marilyn Strathern (1988, 191) argues that although anthropologists and other scholars focus on how gift cycles create relationships and societal integration, "we shall not get very far in the analysis of gift exchange without realizing that gifts quite crucially sever and detach people from people." Thus, gifts can form relationships *and* end relationships across gender and other aspects of inclusion and exclusion.

German Civil Code regarding conditional donations (Revocation BGB 530) states that "a gift may be revoked if the recipient, by committing a serious transgression against the donor or a close relative of the donor, is guilty of gross ingratitude" (Berking 1999, 26). Berking sees this as a rare but explicit acknowledgment of the inherent self-interest of donations. Agricultural scholar Wendell Berry (1981, 272) echoes this sentiment in reflecting on "the gift of good land," arguing that land is "not a free or a deserved gift, but a gift given upon certain rigorous conditions"—one of which is gratitude. I am interested in the requirement of gratitude in exchange for a gift, and examine the implications this has for donor-beneficiary relationships. I discuss this aspect of the gift in chapter 4 regarding beneficiaries of the Chefs Move! scholarship, referencing Lisa Smirl's (2015) research on how nongovernmental organizations (NGOs) responding to disasters demand or expect certain performances of gratitude from recipients.

In thinking about "the development gift" (Stirrat and Henkel 1997), critiques consider asymmetries in power in the social relations between states or other entities, such as NGOs, individuals, or communities. In discussing the large amount of activity in South–South development cooperation, Emma Mawdsley (2011, 257) stresses the importance of language as it is used to conceptualize power and the donor-recipient hierarchy: "For many in the South the word 'donor' is burdened with associations of paternalism, hierarchy and neo-colonial interference. Some of the (re-)emerging actors prefer to call themselves 'development partners' in a conscious promotion of a discourse of horizontal relations of mutual benefit, non-interference and respect for sovereignty, rather than the vertical hierarchy invoked by the terms 'donor' and 'recipient.' Similarly, they often prefer the term 'development assistance' or 'development cooperation' to 'foreign aid.'" Tomohisa Hattori (2001, 641) argues that "the primary effect of foreign aid is symbolic, i.e. to signal and euphemize (as opposed to actively reinforce, mitigate, or worsen) the underlying condition of hierarchy between donor and recipient. . . . What foreign aid does in a policy sense is secondary to a more basic role of naturalizing the social relation in which it arises." This risk of naturalizing inequalities is not unique to foreign aid but a concern across disciplines: relationships of giving must be attentive to the underlying hierarchies between donors and recipients and must seek to understand the hierarchical origins.

The paradoxical nature of the gift (*le don*) is examined in depth by philosopher Jacques Derrida (1992, 2002, 2007). Derrida wants to establish and examine the conditions that would make a "pure" or "free" gift possible (although Derrida does not use the terms "pure" or "free," for reasons that I aim to make clear here). The first condition he establishes is that of nonreciprocity, in which the cycle of giving must be broken or altered significantly for reciprocity to be nullified. Derrida thinks that this can be accomplished either by the giver being ignorant to the fact that they have given a gift or by the giver's "forgetting" that they have given a gift (the second condition). Likewise, the recipient must not know that they have received a gift (the third condition).

The second and third conditions require a temporal deferral that seems tied to Derrida's understanding of economy. Derrida's economy is broad and "refers not just to the circulation of goods and services, but also beyond that to the circulation of time, or rather to the way in which, through the medium of time, events and actions are related causally to each other" (Laidlaw 2002, 51). Thus, time would need to be disrupted, or circulation would need to be "interrupted" (Derrida 1992, 9), in order to enable the second and third conditions. Time is that which "undoes this distinction between taking and giving, therefore also between receiving and giving" (Derrida 1992, 3). Mauss believed that the gift carried with it a symbolic or spiritual linkage connecting everyone involved in the exchange; Derrida believed those links must be broken or undone, perhaps "forgotten." Marian Hobson (1998, 137), focusing specifically on Derrida's attentive use of language, highlights his assertion that *donner* (to give) is "not an exchange of an object nor is it an act," that it is "more than language and yet necessitates language." Derrida (2007, 148) states: "This 'giving' must neither be a thing nor an act, it must somehow be someone (masculine or feminine) not me: and not him ('he'). Strange, isn't it, this excess that overflows language at every instant and yet requires it, sets it incessantly into motion at the very moment of traversing it? This traversal is not a transgression, the passage of a sharply dividing limit; the very metaphor of overflowing [*débordement*] no longer fits insofar as it still implies some linearity." Based on the previous conditions, the final condition is that the gift cannot exist as "a gift" at all, because "as soon as it appears 'as gift' it becomes part of a cycle and ceases to be a gift" (Laidlaw 2002, 50). This cycle and requirement of reciprocity is what can make the gift "bad, poisonous (Gift, gift), and this from the moment the gift puts the other in debt, with the result that giving amounts to hurting, to doing harm" (Derrida 1992, 12).

Derrida (1995, 29) states that "a gift that could be recognized as such in the light of day, a gift destined for recognition, would immediately annul itself." This is what brings Derrida (1992, 7) to assert that the gift is "not impossible but the impossible. The very figure of the impossible." To Derrida (2007, 148), "the gift *is not*."

Caring for distant others is a common conceptualization of the humanitarian impulse and engagement. John Silk takes up the notion of distant caring, describing Derrida's "true" gift as "purely voluntary, unconditional, entailing no form of exchange or reciprocity" (2004, 232). Silk posits that "in practice this situation is approximated by the anonymous donor who gives to an impersonal organization" (232). Silk uses the adjectives "voluntary" and "unconditional" to describe the gift, and others use these terms too, such as Robert Payton (1988) in his often-cited work that defines philanthropy as voluntary giving, voluntary service, and voluntary association. My concern is that a condition such as *voluntary* does not reflect the relational aspects of human experience and actions, and risks assuming that subjects are autonomous and atomistic individuals who operate separate from a complex web of human (and even nonhuman) relationships. Although Derrida does not use the word "voluntary," the lack of a relational perspective is a charge leveled at Derrida's work on the gift more generally (Silk 2004). Here I think there is potential to draw on feminist theorizing about "relational autonomy" to understand both agency and social experience in a more holistic way (see Mackenzie and Stoljar 2000).

Silk's assertion that an anonymous donation to a large organization qualifies as a free gift is likely a common assumption. However, I find this to be a significant misunderstanding of Derrida's *don*. Derrida insists that both giver and receiver must not know that they have given/received a gift in order for a gift to be given. The gift is not automatically made possible through anonymous donation, because without the element of forgetting, the donor would still know that they had made a donation. This knowing nullifies the gift.

Philosopher Rosalyn Diprose explores the gift through the idea of generosity. The fundamental claim underlying Diprose's (2002, 2) analysis is that "generosity is not only an individual virtue that contributes to human well-being, but that it is an openness to others that is fundamental to human existence, sociality and social formation." Jörgen Skågeby (2013, 5) highlights how Diprose's understanding of generosity "includes an openness to others that goes beyond the notion that giving is limited to possessions within contractual exchange economies." Diprose's (2002) work emphasizes the corporeal nature (or requirement) of the gift. She follows Derrida's argument that the gift must be forgotten but argues that gifts cannot be unknown on the corporeal level: "Emphasizing the way that the gift does its work only by being forgotten and then through the dispersal of presence overlooks how, in practice, the generosity and the gifts of some (property owners, men, wage earners, whites) tend to be recognized and remembered more often than the generosity and gifts of others (the landless, women, the unemployed, indigenous peoples, and immigrants). It is in the systematic, asymmetrical forgetting of the gift, where only the generosity of the privileged is memorialized, that social inequities and injustice are based" (2002, 8). According to Diprose, sexual difference is an example of this systematic forgetting. Philanthropists in the United States have primarily been wealthy white men, and this is true in my study of philanthropy by elite chefs as well.[3] Conventional philanthropy overlooks systems of generosity in low-wealth communities or assumes giving is nonexistent (Wilkinson-Maposa et al. 2005). Susan Wilkinson-Maposa et al. (2005, vi) assert that "the poor should be seen as contributors to the supply side of philanthropy as well as the demand side." In a personal narrative from southern Louisiana, James Joseph reflects: "In the bayou country in Louisiana where I was born, the rivers of compassion ran deep. We were poor, but when we were hungry we shared with each other. When we were sick we cared for each other. We did not think of what we gave to others as philanthropy, because sharing was an act of reciprocity in which both the giver and the receiver benefited. We did not think of what we did for others as volunteering, because caring was as much a moral imperative as an act of free will" (Wilkinson-Maposa et al. 2005, vi–vii). The discussion about community cooks in chapter 5 reflects on Diprose's (2002) assertion that injustices arise when the gifts of certain people are forgotten while the gifts of certain others are memorialized. Other realms of giving, such as sharing and caring, are equally important frames in formalized philanthropy.[4]

Even though there is no "perfect" gift, the ideology or the belief in the free gift remains, preventing both donors and recipients from understanding their motives and actions (Osteen 2002, 21). If it is also true that "human beings are quite capable of simultaneously entertaining conflicting ideas about their behavior" (Osteen 2002, 16), then why is there still such a preoccupation with notions of altruism in giving? Business, and the intertwined development sector, have largely embraced or claimed their self-interest in development. (For an example, see A. Roberts 2015 on how investing in women is framed as good for business.) The same can be said of many philanthropists: "What's novel today is the outspoken way that powerful donors admit and even champion the fact that gift-giving is a useful vehicle for preserving privilege, something that disunites them from earlier donors" (McGoey 2005, 19). If a gift cannot be freely given, philanthropy done in the name of corporate self-interest may be trusted or at least better understood because it appears to be more honest. Erica Bornstein (2012, 16) urges researchers "to pay attention to the impulses that inspire people to engage in humanitarian action instead of solely paying attention to outcomes," as "specific eras articulate what makes something thinkable and possible at a particular time." My research considers these impulses in the time and place of New Orleans post-Katrina, and I detail the conditions and ways of thinking and knowing that made new configurations of chef humanitarian aid possible in the recovering city.

Celebrity Humanitarianism

The era of the New Poverty Agenda has seen the growth of public-private partnerships and nontraditional development leaders.[5] Writing from a feminist perspective, Elisabeth Prügl and Jacqui True (2014, 1138) summarize this new era of development as such: "In the wake of globalization, we are witnessing new roles of business as power has increasingly shifted away from legislatures towards a range of technocratic and private actors, and corporations are behaving more like states, building corporate patriotism, emphasizing 'soft issues' such as their value to society, causes such as poverty eradication, labor standards, environmental sustainability, gender equality, and delivering welfare services. In contrast, states are behaving more like traditional corporations, branding themselves, using business-speak, downsizing and privatizing."[6] My ethnography looks closely at celebrity humanitarianism as part of this new development era, which has thus far been understudied. In the introduction to the first issue of the journal *Celebrity Studies*, Su Holmes and Sean Redmond (2010, 1) assert a need to further develop celebrity studies through the exploration of "why and how celebrity is key to the way the social world organizes and commodifies its representations, discourses and ideologies, sensations, impressions and fantasies."[7]

There are conflicting attempts to define celebrity, from Luc Boltanski and Laurent Thévenot's (2006) theorizing about greatness and the importance of public opinion, to Daniel Boorstin's (1971, 58) assertion that "the celebrity is a person who is known for his well-knownness."[8] I follow Maxwell Boykoff and Michael Goodman (2009, 397) in understanding celebrities to be "those whose activities are more prominent and agency more amplified than the general population," with "an important and growing subset of celebrity . . . who have leveraged such privileged voices to raise public and policy attention to various social, political, economic, cultural and environmental issues." This definition, which focuses on what celebrities do and how they function, was useful as I looked at celebrity activism at different scales.

Critical engagement about elite philanthropy and "philanthrocapitalism" (Littler 2015) has proliferated (Callahan 2017; Giridharadas 2018; McGoey 2015; Reich 2018; Villanueva 2018), and an interdisciplinary literature on celebrity engagement in humanitarianism, aid, and development has grown rapidly in the last decade. Research in media and communication studies by Lilie Chouliaraki (2006, 2013) considers the way in which celebrity goodwill for "distant others" has implications for the public and the self regarding spectatorship and solidarity. Research in international development and international relations increasingly examines how celebrities function as development actors at various levels, including as ambassadors for NGOs or specific causes and as founders/directors of new organizations or campaigns (Budabin and Richey 2021; Brockington 2009, 2014; Cooper 2008; Dieter and Kumar 2008; Huliaras and Tzifakis 2010; Kapoor 2012; Richey 2016; Richey and Ponte 2011; Tsaliki, Frangonikolopoulos, and Huliaras 2011; West 2008; Wheeler 2013).

In chapter 3, I outline the specific conditions in post-Katrina redevelopment and investment that positioned chefs to become humanitarian leaders in New Orleans. Other scholars have sought to explain the emergence of celebrity humanitarianism, with Dan Brockington (2014, 37) using Colin Crouch's (2004) formulation of "post-democracy." Crouch (2004, 4) explains his post-democratic model in the following way: "Under this model, while elections certainly exist and can change governments, public electoral debate is a tightly controlled spectacle, managed by rival teams of professionals expert in the techniques of persuasion, and considering a small range of issues selected by those teams. The mass of citizens plays a passive, quiescent, even apathetic part, responding only to the signals given them. Behind this spectacle of the electoral game, politics is really shaped in private by interaction between elected governments and elites that overwhelmingly represent business interests." Brockington (2014, 37) argues that celebrity humanitarianism is therefore "part of the performance and display of elite-dominated post-democracies." Ilan Kapoor (2012, 1), drawing on Slavoj Žižek's work, also frames the phenomenon in terms of post-democracy, but with a more outright condemnation, arguing that celebrity humanitarianism is "significantly contaminated and ideological. . . . It is most often self-serving, helping to promote institutional aggrandizement and the celebrity 'brand'; it advances consumerism and corporate capitalism, and rationalizes the very global inequality it seeks to redress; it is fundamentally depoliticizing, despite its pretensions to 'activism'; and it contributes to a 'postdemocratic' political landscape, which appears outwardly open and consensual, but is in fact managed by unaccountable elites." Lisa Ann Richey and Stefano Ponte (2011, 159) argue that "the celebrity substitutes the state as the external guarantor of welfare, a new form of the social contract that underpins Brand Aid."[9] In these formulations, key questions arise about governance and the role of the state. In my research, I considered these questions with an emphasis on power, inclusion, and exclusion. A charge proposed by Michael Goodman (2013, 104) served as a point of departure for my research: "Before those ever accompanying choruses of 'at least they (that is, so-called caring celebrities, and corporations) are doing something' become even louder, our job is surely, first and foremost, to be doggedly engaged with, and critical about, what that 'something" is, where it has come from, how it is done, and what its impacts are." I critically consider these elements within the arena of foodscape interventions led by celebrity chefs.

Celebrity humanitarians are at the heart of consumer-based models of development, in which it is possible to "do good by shopping" through causumerism (Richey and Ponte 2011). Brockington (2009, 2) argues that "the flourishing of celebrity activism is part of an ever-closer intertwining of conservation and corporate capitalism," and I take up this framing in exploring the intertwining of development and corporate capitalism. Market-based approaches to humanitarianism and development have continued to grow, and celebrities are an effective conduit of these kinds of approaches. Following the early work of Leo Löwenthal (1961), who saw celebrities as "idols of consumption," Brockington (2009, 32) believes that celebrities are uniquely well-positioned to promote green products because attention is already focused on their consumptive lifestyles. I would argue that it is this positioning that also allows them to "sell" development interventions more generally, making projects more appealing to the public. Richey and Ponte (2011, 30–31) extend Brockington's argument further to claim that "while celebrities are well known for product promotion, advertising, and marketing efforts of various kinds, the emphasis on individuality as a product that can be consumed blurs the boundaries between celebrities and products. Celebrities themselves fall into commercial categories: they are objects of consumption."

Ethical consumption and causumerist practices contend that consumer spending can be directed toward humanitarian concerns and can be used to solve social problems (Lewis and Potter 2011; Ponte and Richey 2011).[10] Mainstream US food movement trends have had a significant focus on causumerism, such as calls to "vote with your fork" through buying sustainable, organic, or local food. Food is often positioned as a commodity or consumer good in advanced capitalist societies, and thus it is available for causumer mobilization. As I analyze in chapters 5 through 7, the primary public engagement strategy for chef foundations is causumerism through fundraising events.

Chouliaraki (2013, 84–86) outlines the major schools of thought that evaluate celebrity humanitarianism. Positive perspectives tend to lack disclosure of a theoretical framing, but Chouliaraki (2013, citing Marshall 1984) positions them within the positive theory of "the spectacle as the site of moral education." Empirically, positive perspectives tend to believe (1) that celebrities can function as effective mediators of the voices of distant suffering by personalizing a sense of shared humanity, and (2) that celebrities can revitalize not only beleaguered humanitarian organizations but politics more generally as celebrities become fresh public leaders that help shape humanitarian agendas (Bishop and Green 2008, 198–200). Skeptical perspectives tend to focus on questions of authenticity and situate celebrity humanitarianism inside a neocolonial framework or within a critique of the spectacle wherein this kind of humanitarianism is denounced as "an arrangement of power that reproduces the systemic inequality between those who are active and those who remain passive in the space of pity" (Chouliaraki 2013, 84). My perspective is inspired by Chouliaraki's (2013, 87) own assertion that we need to "move away from seeking authenticity in the 'truth' of the individual (a fallacy of essentialism) and to focus on how authenticity itself comes to be produced in the course of the celebrity's aspirational performances of humanitarianism." In chapter 3, I establish how celebrity chefs in New Orleans became "authentic" voices of the recovering city.

More case studies are emerging that provide detailed and diverse examples of celebrity engagement (see collection edited by Richey 2016). Some of this work specifically engages in gender analysis to unpack how performances of gender—and the symbolic meanings attached to these performances—both help shape the agenda of and manifest within celebrity projects (Mostafanezhad 2013; Repo and Yrjölä 2011).

Analysis of celebrity engagement in New Orleans is limited; Brad Pitt's Make It Right Foundation has received the most attention (Fuqua 2011;

Johnson 2011a). Sean Penn's rescue efforts in New Orleans were covered by the popular press, but most academic research focuses on his work in Haiti (Rosamond 2016). Geoffrey Whitehall and Cedric Johnson (2011) study Frank Stronach's Magnaville/Canadaville project (mentioned in chapter 1) in the collection of essays *The Neoliberal Deluge*. The collection frames rebuilding efforts in New Orleans in terms of neoliberal restructuring, and Johnson (2011b, xxxi) argues that the robust philanthropic and celebrity humanitarian activity post-flooding is reflective of the "expanding influence and scope of humanitarian-corporate complexes" of neoliberal disaster management. Johnson argues that the heavy response to Katrina is consistent with international trends in which "nation-states retain a vital role in post disaster rescue efforts" but that "the work of relief, clean-up, and reconstruction is largely undertaken by NGOs and for-profit firms."

Whitehall and Johnson (2011, 72) position Frank Stronach's Canadaville project as an example of "do-good capitalism" and a project in neoliberal citizen-making. They argue that racialized respectability politics and individualism drove this form of citizenship. Canadaville created positive publicity for Stronach as he was simultaneously undertaking a controversial lobbying battle in Florida to legalize his company's slot machines. The primary beneficiary of the project's good publicity was "benevolent neoliberalism": "by demonstrating that private institutions could respond quicker than government in moments of crisis, the project served as a powerful ideological justification of neoliberalization" (Whitehall and Johnson 2011, 71).

Academic scholarship about celebrity chef humanitarianism is limited, and most previous research has focused on Jamie Oliver in U.K. and Australian contexts (Barnes 2014; Dempsey and Gibson 2015; Piper 2013; Warin 2011). In chapter 3, I discuss public chef intellectuals (Eckstein and Young 2015) and culinary capital (Naccarato and Lebesco 2012) and show how these concepts manifest in New Orleans post-flooding.

CSR and Causumerism

Kathryn Moeller (2018, 24) explains how multinational corporations have embraced the idea of "doing well by doing good": "Consent for doing well is constructed through the other half of the corporate mantra — by doing good. In this particular historical moment, corporatized development sutures them together. As a practice, it enables doing well and doing good to occur in concert rather than in conflict with one another."[11] These approaches stem from corporate-produced knowledge that is business A. Roberts (2012, 2015).

Roberts's (2015) analysis about the corporate production of development knowledge has been useful, as I find that celebrity chefs make decisions based on bodies of business knowledge (see chapter 5).

Scholarship on fair trade offers insights for this research as it considers business and corporate engagement in social issues, often through causumerism. There are two areas that are most compelling: (1) that fair trade now increasingly works directly with corporations and is often positioned as a form of CSR, and (2) that fair trade was an early example (indeed, if not the first) of the now-commonplace use of hybrid market-based solutions to address social problems. Richey and Ponte (2011, 160) assert: "By developing 'sustainability' labels, social and environmental movements (later on in collaboration with industry) were able to give consumers the possibility of making informed choices that directly influenced the way coffee was grown and traded. Labels, in other words, helped turn consumers into causumers." Causumerism, as a market-based method mobilized to realize fair trade goals, is also often taken up in various forms by celebrity philanthropists.

Current scholarship considers the impact and implications of fair trade's mainstreaming and alleged "fair-washing" as certification standards are changed or loosened, and many multinational corporations have created their own in-house "fair" brands (see Doherty, Davies, and Tranchell 2013 for a history and an overview of debates; see also Fisher 2007; Jaffee and Howard 2010; Shreck 2005). Richey and Ponte (2011, 162–64) distinguish between "old wave" fair trade initiatives, which were established before 1990, and "new wave" initiatives. In rising new wave initiatives, "commercial success is 'built in' from the beginning," while declining old wave initiatives were more radical in their aim of trying to address inequalities in trade directly and challenging industrial agriculture by demanding organic alternatives. Fair trade movements have had some success in "re-embedding" moral and social relations into market exchange, but research finds that fair trade is susceptible to co-optation when powerful corporations, such as Starbucks and Nestle, become heavily involved (Jaffee 2012, 95). In fair trade, this co-optation takes the form of weakening or diluting of certification standards.

I consider literature on corporate social responsibility primarily in relationship to questions about wealth accumulation, labor exploitation, and environmental responsibility. Within scholarship on corporate philanthropy, there are attempts to differentiate between elite philanthropy by individuals, corporate CSR, and sponsorships (Gautier and Pache 2015). I highlight such differences throughout the book when evident, but overall,

TABLE 2.1 CSR activity matrix by location and type

		Type of CSR activity	
		Engaged	Disengaged
Location of CSR activity beneficiaries	Proximate	• Workplace conditions and policies at headquarters or own plants • Addressing environmental impact and carbon footprint at headquarters or own plants	• Cause-related marketing with beneficiaries in local communities of operation • Corporate philanthropy with beneficiaries in local communities of operation
	Distant	• Codes of conduct of suppliers • Addressing environmental impact and carbon footprint of suppliers and from trade/transport	• Brand Aid • Cause-related marketing with distant beneficiaries • Corporate philanthropy with distant beneficiaries

Figure from Richey and Ponte (2011, 129).

I agree that "these differences are too sharply drawn since altruistic intentions, self-interest and commercial motives feature in all forms of giving" (Marshall et al. 2018, 268). As mentioned in the opening to this chapter, in my findings regarding restaurant groups and affiliated chef foundations, elite philanthropy and corporate philanthropy are intertwined and sometimes almost indistinguishable as separate entities in practice.

Richey and Ponte (2011, 128) use the concepts of "engaged CSR" (also known as "proper CSR"), which refers to activities that "have a direct impact on company operations," and "disengaged CSR," in which activities are unlinked or only mildly linked to the company's functioning (table 2.1). Disengaged activities can have benefits, but "they do not challenge any of the tenets of normal business conduct—on the contrary, the more successful a company is, the more money it can donate—no matter how and where that profit was obtained" (Richey and Ponte 2011, 128). My question here was whether this sort of formulation relates to elite and chef philanthropy. A business executive accumulates wealth by various means and then later uses some portion of that financial success to engage in philanthropy. Thus, does the means by which wealth was created matter? If wealth created by any means—perhaps even in exploitative or unethical ways—eventually ends up "doing good" as philanthropy, does that erase or at least mitigate any harm done earlier in the process? These questions reveal troubled relationships between capitalism, global inequality, and the possibility of transformation.

Conclusion: Black Lives Matter and Elite Gifts

On July 5, 2016, Alton Sterling, a Black man selling CDs outside the Triple S Food Mart in Baton Rouge, was shot and killed by two white police officers. I was conducting fieldwork in New Orleans when news of the murder started spreading on social media. My spouse was called to photograph the story (Fausset 2016). We threw our clothes and Will's camera gear into the car and drove the hour and a half to Baton Rouge.

What followed were several months of upheaval. I bounced between protests in Baton Rouge and volunteering with chef foundations in New Orleans. While Will was working in Baton Rouge, I tried to support efforts by bringing water and supplies to those keeping vigil at the site of Sterling's murder, participating in protests myself, and working the National Lawyers Guild's emergency arrest hotline to assist the more than 200 protesters who were arrested in the weeks that followed (Toohey 2018). At a youth-led rally at the Louisiana state capitol, I had to leave early for an interview I had scheduled previously with a local chef back in New Orleans. When the rally ended and protesters were walking back to their cars, coworkers from Grow Dat—including several youth—were chased and corralled by police in armored tanks. Many spent hours hiding in backyards or inside welcoming strangers' homes while police in riot gear patrolled the residential streets near the capitol. My early departure meant I had narrowly missed what was described by friends as an absolutely terrifying experience.

The whiplash I felt traveling between the protests and the spaces of elite white philanthropy was extreme. The worlds, although geographically close, felt far apart. I often found it hard to bear chef philanthropy during the period surrounding Sterling's murder: attending lavish fundraising dinners and conducting interviews at the trendy hotel bars suggested by participants felt unconscionable. The disconnect I felt made me question the premise of my entire research project: Was I studying the right thing? Why give time and resources to this?

As my research continued to unfold, I found much that was necessary and important to study about chef philanthropy—not in the least of which was systemic racism and entrenched sexism within some of the foundations. I came to feel a sense of opportunity and responsibility: that researchers such as myself with access to white and elite spaces need to take advantage of such opportunities to "study up." I join the call for social scientists, including geographers, to become more willing to study wealth, elites, and racism.

This time of turbulence also gave me essential insights into the nature of the gift and social change. We struggled to raise funds from donors to make bail for protesters being held in Baton Rouge, the majority of whom were not wealthy and many of whom were people of color. Around this time in New Orleans, I watched hundreds of merry, drunken white donors at a foundation auction bid tens of thousands of dollars to have a celebrity chef cook a meal at their home. Let me say: I enjoy a good party and beautiful food. But I think what felt so confusing was the different understandings of how to make change in the world. *What needs to be changed and how?* Yes, chefs engage as humanitarians as part of their marketing efforts, but the chefs and donors I studied were *also* trying to do "good work." Like the protesters, they were imagining new futures, better worlds. I slowly came to the realization that the chef philanthropists and their teams that I was studying were not apolitical or socially disengaged; they were doing what seemed transformative or possible *to them*. Chefs were engaging in a configuration of politics and social change made possible only by the very strange mergers of advanced capitalism, legacies of white supremacy, and imagining a "new" New Orleans post-Katrina.

CHAPTER THREE

Marketing the City after the Flood

Remaking Foodscapes in New Orleans

Foodscape inventions led by private entities—particularly chefs—have been extensive since the levee failure. To understand why this phenomenon occurred, I first outline national trends that increased the prominence of celebrity chefs in New Orleans and across the country. I then consider the historical and cultural importance of culinary culture, chefs, and restaurants in New Orleans, and show how marketing the culinary world was central to post-Katrina rebranding and tourism campaigns. With this background in place, I document the chef-led interventions that have emerged in the city and establish how the post-Katrina disasters and processes of rebuilding provided the context for celebrity humanitarian interventions.

I posit that there are several intersecting reasons for the continued growth of chef-led philanthropic activity in New Orleans's foodscapes. The city's food culture and culinary traditions are unique in the United States and much celebrated (Beriss 2012); however, New Orleans is simultaneously marked by high rates of hunger, food apartheid, and diet-related diseases. Both the celebration of New Orleans's cuisine and a concern for the residents struggling to put food on their tables became justifications variously deployed by charitable projects. Investments in the cultural economy, combined with the sociohistorical importance of culinary culture, imbued chefs with a compelling form of culinary capital, which positioned them to become humanitarian leaders in the "new" New Orleans.

In this chapter, I limit my analysis to trends beginning in the 1970s and primarily consider the period since Katrina and flooding—2005 to the present. However, as I mention in chapter 1, the context for the changes in the "new" New Orleans are part of an extended timeline that requires a longer view. Specific to Katrina, historian Andy Horowitz claims an "unsettling truth that disasters have histories" and references a century of events and processes that caused the flooding (Horowitz 2020, 6). Woods (2017b, 217) asserts that elite political and economic interests—termed the "Bourbon bloc"—had adversely affected Black, poor, and working-class New Orleanians for hundreds of years before Katrina, resulting in a "disaster before the disaster." Woods documents key moments in political and economic development on local, national, and regional scales, and shows how practices like policing "contain working-class communities within particular geographical boundaries in order to facilitate the exploitation of labor and the accumulation of capital and power" (Camp and Pulido 2017b, xxi–xxii). Inequalities shaping the city's rebuilding and emerging in the "new" New Orleans are deeply related to unfinished Black freedom struggles in the United States: "Through the eye of Katrina, we see the old dry bones of both the Freedom Movement and the plantation oligarchy walking again in daylight" (Woods 2017b, 3).

Food and Water Aid Post-Disaster

In this section, I detail food and water provisioning in the immediate aftermath of flooding in New Orleans, with the goal of illustrating the initial context in which celebrities and chefs became active in relief and rebuilding processes. Hurricane Katrina made landfall in Southeast Louisiana on Monday, August 29, 2005. Subsequent storm surges and levee failures flooded up to 90 percent of coastal areas along the Gulf of Mexico and 80 percent of New Orleans. Between 1,245 and more than 1,500 people were killed. Property damage was estimated to be over $108 billion. Women and African American residents were disproportionately affected: African American neighborhoods were located in low-lying areas of the city, which were inundated with flooding (Fussell, Sastry, and VanLandingham 2010; Woods, 2017b, 217); and Black women were the slowest group to come back to the city (David and Enarson 2012). A decade after the storm, the city had 100,000 fewer Black residents (Allen 2015).

Christopher Cooper and Robert Block (2006, xiv) explain the salience of understanding the disaster as human-made and complex: "Hurricane Katrina wasn't the storm of the century; it didn't deal New Orleans a direct blow, and winds in the city were not as strong as in many outlying areas. City and state officials had managed to evacuate some 90 percent of the city in advance of the storm—a rate unprecedented in the annals of disaster response. Hurricane Katrina didn't present a double disaster—indeed, many of the floodwalls collapsed below their rated strength, in advance of the storm's passage." Beyond the failure of the levee infrastructure, Cooper and Block (2006, xiv) found that "accurate, real-time information" often "sat unused, unread, and even dismissed" by the officials who should have made sure the information went to the right people in the highest levels of government.

Tracing Homeland Security's emergency response, Cooper and Block (2006, xiv) argue that the provisioning of food and water was grossly inadequate.[1] The Federal Emergency Management Agency (FEMA) did not prepare enough food and water in advance, and the supplies that were prepped were staged in remote areas that were difficult to transfer to New Orleans as the crisis unfolded. FEMA's Camp Beauregard was a three-hour drive away and had been stocked with only a day's worth of food and ice. Earlier in the summer, New Orleans mayor Ray Nagin's administration had an area of the Superdome (home stadium of the Saints football team and a planned evacuation center) cleared for the storage of food, water, and other emergency supplies. However, the supplies were never stocked, and the storage area was empty when evacuees arrived at the stadium.

As flooding intensified, the Superdome swelled above capacity and was eventually closed to new arrivals. Evacuees sought refuge at the Ernest N. Morial Convention Center, named after the first Black mayor elected in 1978. The convention center was dry, and people had started gathering there unofficially; however, the center was not a planned evacuation location, and it did not have supplies stocked in advance. By Thursday night, it was estimated that between 20,000 and 30,000 people had come seeking shelter (Cooper and Block 2006, 205). FEMA's administration repeatedly promised that busloads of food and water were on their way to the convention center and evacuation areas across the region, but many supplies never materialized. Those that did arrive were a fraction of the amount of food and water that was needed. Emergency rescue teams—composed of state and federal agencies, the US Coast Guard, and volunteers—rescued tens of thousands of stranded persons and brought them to dry land, but "many of these rescue teams had no food or water to give these evacuees, who were tremendously dehydrated from having sat for hours on their roofs in the fierce summer sun" (Cooper and Block 2006, 180).

Celebrities and celebrity chefs were documented as participating in relief efforts and providing emergency food aid during this time. Actor Sean Penn traveled across the city in a rescue boat, while another actor, John Travolta (who is also a pilot), flew five tons of food and four hundred doses of tetanus vaccines into the area. Restaurants provided free meals to residents and relief workers. Drago's, a seafood restaurant in the suburb of Metairie, served "anyone who came to its doors" and distributed 77,000 meals (Fitzmorris 2010, 19). In a widely publicized example, chef John Besh, sometimes alongside chef Alon Shaya, cooked outside on propane burners to make red beans and rice for soldiers, relief workers, and residents in the nearby areas of the French Quarter and the Warehouse District. Besh told news outlets, "The first batch of red beans and rice I cooked was in a Walmart parking lot on Tchoupitoulas Street. It was the first time I ever fed a person who was truly hungry. Oh, I've fed hungry people before, but never people who were so hungry and had everything taken away from them. That changed my life" (Morago 2015). As the *New York Times* reported in 2007 (Severson, 2007) and the *Houston Chronicle* reported during the tenth anniversary of the flooding in 2015, "It's been said Besh fed New Orleans until it could learn to feed itself again" (Morago, 2015).

In one high-profile effort led by officials, chefs were proposed to be a part of formal relief efforts. Douglas Doan, in the Private Sector Office of the Department of Homeland Security, formalized a supply chain for the area with Walmart and began coordinating local chefs and restaurants to provide 26,000 meals for St. Tammany Parish (Cooper and Block 2006, 266). Doan said: "Louisiana makes the best food in the world. To be bringing in beanie weenies from Florida or peanut butter sandwiches from Ohio at a greater cost . . . is an outrage" (Dorell 2005). When Doan's plan was not approved by other officials, he publicly resigned in protest.

Food and water provisioning is just one area among dozens of others in which the government's response was deficient, as government at multiple scales failed to prevent the disaster and to adequately mitigate the harm inflicted on residents after the flooding. Jordan Camp and Laura Pulido (2017, 293) argue that the "feeble and incompetent" response of the federal government to the flooding needs to be understood as an outcome of the "evisceration" of federal social budgets over the preceding thirty years. The government's deficiencies "reinforced neoliberal nostrums that the state itself was the problem, which, in turn, purported to justify the elite's promotion of market solutions to social and economic problems" (293). It is in the context of this widespread governmental failure that celebrity chefs became leaders in rebuilding efforts. Charitable acts such as John Besh serving red beans in the street became symbolically important. In the following sections, I show how positive public opinion merged with material support and investment from the local and federal government to make chefs particularly well-positioned to intervene.

Food "Pulling Our City Back Together"

There were a few restaurants in the city—Drago's, little place on Clearview— they just fed people every day at no cost except to themselves. They just fed whoever came, it didn't make any difference. And a lot of people got by that way—a lot of workers, a lot of people didn't have food, food trucks came around. So I think it was a moment in time when people were at their best and they reached out and they helped. I think we were so beaten down that there was such a sense of appreciation and there seemed to be no difference at that time. We didn't feel the—the lines of class were gone, they were obliterated—we were all one single mess. I think it was a moment in time, a time of peace, an amazing thing truly. I think all of this [celeb chef philanthropy] was born from that, I really do.

—Interview with RHONDA, a John Besh Foundation donor

In the introduction to his memoir, restaurant reviewer and radio show host Tom Fitzmorris writes that he "wondered what force possibly could pull our city and our lives back together" after the flooding. To his "surprise and delight, that force was provided in almost unbelievable measure by cooks, restaurants, gumbo, poor boy sandwiches, soft-shell crabs, and our love of eating together" (2010, 11). Returning to the recovering city in October 2005, Fitzmorris describes a variously slipshod and decadent meal at John Besh's Restaurant August: spending hours waiting for service at the bar because the restaurant was understaffed; drinking Veuve Clicquot champagne during tearful reunions with neighbors and friends; eating seared foie gras with frozen french fries because the produce truck could not navigate the debris on the streets to make a delivery. Fitzmorris (2010, 173) writes, "That dinner was, for me, the confirmation of an idea that took root in my mind from the moment I arrived back in town: not only would the culinary imperative of New Orleans survive Katrina, but it would be one of the strongest forces pulling the city back together again."

In the quote that begins this section, Rhonda expresses gratitude for the outpouring of generosity that followed Katrina, and she says the flooding obliterated differences: "We were all one single mess." Eric Ishiwata (2011) documented the prevalence of this kind of "colorblind" thinking in which Katrina "impacted everyone." This uniform narrative creates a sense of community and shared struggle, but it also elides drastic differences in experiences and impact, which were very much about race, class, and gender. Only some New Orleanians survived, returned to the city, and ate at Restaurant August two months after Katrina.

In the immediate aftermath of the flooding, arguments for rebuilding New Orleans often hinged on the cultural importance of the city, referencing its food, music, and way of life (Beriss 2012). In this section, I detail how local government and private interests took up the mantle of New Orleans as a culinary superstar and heavily marketed it as a key component of the city's "cultural economy" (Gotham and Greenberg 2014). Campaigns such as "Forever New Orleans" and "In Louisiana, Culture Means Business"—a slogan of the Louisiana Cultural Economy Foundation—were part of the robust investments made in the cultural economy that positioned the city as a foodie travel destination and, in the process, created the context for the rapid and high-profile growth of culinary philanthropy in the city.

The concepts of tabula rasa and "blank is beautiful" animated much post-disaster discourse and planning in New Orleans and across the region. Louisiana State University ecologist John Day said that if there was an upside to the disaster, it was that "now we've got a clean slate to start from" (Bohannon and Enserink 2005, 1808), and Congressman Richard Baker proclaimed: "We finally cleaned up public housing in New Orleans. We couldn't do it, but God did" (Gotham and Greenberg 2014, 100). Here, Katrina's blank slate was considered a gift. Lynnell Thomas (2014, 129) argues that the "Fall in Love with New Orleans All Over Again" campaign (by the New Orleans Tourism Marketing Corporation in 2007) suggested "that instead of de-stroying New Orleans' vibrant culture and community, Katrina may have enhanced it," as ads claimed: "The food seems to taste better. The music sounds *more exuberant*. The art and ambience feel *more poignant*" (emphasis in original). Celebrity chefs echoed tabula rasa discourse. In speaking about the creation of his foundation, John Besh invoked a common settler colonial imaginary, comparing post-Katrina New Orleans to the Wild West: "We just made our own rules, and if you didn't, you went out of business. You had to act like a pirate just to survive" (Zuras 2016).

Tabula rasa presupposes that spaces of reconstruction are blank slates where building is seen as a fresh opportunity, separate from previous development. While some disasters may destroy the built environment completely, this is rarely the case. Tabula rasa risks invisibilizing key elements, such as (still existing) infrastructure that needs to be repaired or addressing the needs of residents who may be experiencing trauma or health problems (Smirl 2015, 167)—it is not a "blank slate" for them. As Kate Derickson (2014, 890) argues in her study of rebuilding along the Mississippi Gulf coast, "These were not blank slates but social geographies produced in the context of the racially segregated US South. The spatial politics of slavery and Jim Crow and their enduring legacy meant that the built environment and the urban fabric were not, as many tried to argue after the storm, postracial spaces that shed centuries of racialized distributions of wealth and property." The same is true for New Orleans.

It is significant that tabula rasa was a popular, widespread invocation: dominant framings of disaster are produced and are "immediately and inextricably politicized and used in different ways by different groups and for different ends" (Smirl 2015, 9). Kevin Gotham and Miriam Greenberg (2014, 196) find that members of the new regional growth coalition commonly made private comments that the "destruction of low-cost housing and underfunded schools, and the displacement of poor, black New Orleanians" presented them with a "clean slate."[2] The growth coalition saw the opportunity to advance a more "entrepreneurial" vision of New Orleans rooted in public-private partnerships (PPPs). Restaurants and chefs were a key part of this new vision.

Culinary Capital

In this section I explore the notion of culinary capital as developed by Peter Naccarato and Kathleen Lebesco (2012). Following Pierre Bourdieu's conceptualization of capital—economic, cultural, social, and symbolic—culinary capital establishes "how and why certain foods and food-related practices connote, and by extension, confer status and power on those who know about and enjoy them" (Naccarato and Lebesco 2012, 3). Culinary capital continues to expand and acquire new meanings for chefs as they occupy public spaces as philanthropists.

The status and power that is produced through culinary capital is not fixed, and Naccarato and Lebesco (2012, 2) stress the importance of focusing on practices and processes: "Rather than assuming that culinary capital circulates in a fixed and predictable pattern (for instance, that certain foods or food practices always confer culinary capital while others do not), we focus on the multiple and potentially contradictory ways in which it may function." This requires attending to how "value is assigned and reassigned to a range of foods and food practices on a continuous and ever-changing basis."

In their study of the Food Network and cooking shows, Naccarato and Lebesco (2012, 42) show how the programming promises viewers access to culinary capital, and how that access is imbued with possibilities of social and personal transformation. Food television "has promised its viewers empowerment through food. Such productive power, however, ultimately serves to advance the broader project of circulating prevailing ideologies of gender and class to viewers who embrace and seek to emulate the lifestyles portrayed by their favorite celebrity chefs." Learning from celebrity chefs becomes a "subtle yet effective" component of identity formation (66). I argue that the sociohistorical importance of culinary culture in New Orleans, combined with the roles celebrity chefs play in conferring culinary capital, positioned local chefs to become humanitarian leaders in the "new" New Orleans.

On a national scale, a rising interest in the careers of elite US chefs began in the 1970s (Beriss 2007, 159–60). Justin Eckstein and Anna Young (2015, 207) developed the term "public chef intellectual" (PCI) following Antonio Gramsci's conceptualization of the organic intellectual: "Put simply, the PCI educates the public on the art of cooking." Media studies scholar Signe Rousseau (2012, xi) argues that the prevalence of television, combined with health trends that position food and eating as risky endeavors (perhaps most evident in the "obesity epidemic"), has given celebrity chefs "a new kind of authority." Rousseau (2012, xi–xii) asks: "Why chefs and not all the government agencies and scientists (and charlatans) who have been advising people how to eat for centuries? Because amid the increasing media noise about how and what to eat, these figures have a competitive advantage when it comes to gaining our attention given that they combine the best of two worlds when it comes to food: entertainment and education." According to Rousseau, popular media, particularly television, has "the very strange power" to create a sense of trust in the viewer because the mediums appear to be transparent (61–22). Leigh Chavez Bush (2019, 26) engages the inverted term "chef celebrity" to identify a "more general phenomenon" of chef celebrity that "affects chefs, cooks, and food communities from the local to the global level."

Nationally, chefs have been progressively involved with various social issues, ranging from Alice Waters's Edible Schoolyard project for youth garden education (founded 1995) to José Andrés's World Central Kitchen disaster food aid nongovernmental organization (NGO) (founded 2010). Food policy work at the local and national levels has been championed by the Chef Action Network (CAN).[3] CAN partners with the James Beard Foundation to host the Chef Bootcamp for Policy and Change (founded in 2012). The boot camps take place several times a year (there had been eighteen sessions by summer 2019), training chefs on advocacy and food policy issues. Celebrity chefs are increasingly moving into charitable, philanthropic, and policy work across the United States. As argued in chapter 2, this follows ascendant global trends in celebrity public engagement, humanitarianism, and corporate branding strategies.

Sociohistorical Positioning of Restaurants and Chefs

> For as long as there has been a South, and people who think of
> themselves as Southerners, food has been central to the region's
> image, its personality, and its character.
>
> —JOHN EGERTON, *Southern Food*

The Egerton quote signals that food is essential to the discursive and material construction of the South and of what constitutes Southernness. Here I begin to develop the sociohistorical positioning of restaurants and chefs in the US South and New Orleans. Food scholarship has argued that food is "central to the Southern experience and understanding the area. Other regional cuisines might be able to make similar claims, yet it is clear that Southern fare provides a strong case study for the significance of food in defining a cultural identity" (Stokes and Atkins-Sayre 2016, 6).

There are robust debates about how and why food is essential to the cultures of the region, and my purpose here is not to transcribe those complex conversations. Rather, I outline the deep linkages between Southern food, regional identity, and race to stress why the study of foodscapes in New Orleans yields particularly salient insights into the power dynamics present in the reconstruction of the city post-disaster. As I mention in chapter 2, I join the calls for an explicit focus on race in studying food (Slocum 2013). Being committed to the histories and cultures of foods means engaging with histories of colonialism and enslavement, by the nineteenth century, New Orleans had developed an international culinary reputation, and Marcie Cohen Ferris (2014) argues that more recent regional ascendance of the "New Southern Food Movement" (Kelting 2016) began in the 1980s and was led by chefs. Chefs have featured largely in New Orleans's culture: they are topics of gossip, regular features at charity events, and commonly spotted running cooking demonstrations at farmers markets (Beriss 2007, 159). Beriss believes that the role of chefs and restaurants in the production and reproduction of New Orleans cultural landscapes and foodscapes is different from the roles held by chefs in other US cities: "One of the sources of this difference is that New Orleans has a long-standing food culture, a cuisine, built from local products, that is regularly produced in homes and restaurants and frequently discussed around local tables and in the local media" (2007, 153). Chefs such as Paul Prudhomme were known to claim that food in South Louisiana was different from food anywhere else because it "has an emotional taste" (158–59).

Chefs are culturally positioned as artists and artisans, which allows them to stand in as legitimate or trusted interpreters of local ingredients and as expert guides in the creation of local taste (Beriss 2007, 160). Beriss explains that "chefs and their restaurants often seem to stand in for the city where they work, so that one comes to think of some kind of necessary link between Los Angeles and the cooking of Wolfgang Puck, between Chicago and Charlie Trotter, and, of course, between New Orleans and Emeril Lagasse or Paul Prudhomme" (2007, 160). Chefs thus become positioned as "authentic" voices, with the right to speak on behalf of their associated cities. Local chefs were already synonymous with New Orleans; after the disaster, they became public figures claiming responsibility and authority to rebuild the city.

Rebuilding: "In Louisiana, Culture Means Business"

Gotham and Greenberg (2014, 22) trace the extensive and expensive "retooling of branding infrastructure" that happened in the city and argue that cultural redevelopment was key to rebranding New Orleans post-crisis. Disaster can create an "image crisis" for a city's brand, but tourism is widely considered a "driver of recovery and a long-term solution to crisis" (Gotham and Greenberg 2014, 188). Thus, officials decided to prioritize urban rebranding and invested heavily in marketing efforts. Plans for serious investment in the cultural economy were, in fact, already underway before the flooding. In 1999, the third and final goal (Objective 3.6) of Louisiana's Master Plan for Economic Development was to expand the tourism industry based on the state's scenic, recreational, and cultural assets (LEDC 1999). In July 2005, a month before the disaster, the Department of Culture, Tourism and Recreation published the first comprehensive study of the state's cultural economy, *Louisiana: Where Culture Means Business* (Mt. Auburn Associates 2005; see figure 7.1). The report recommended strategies that would enable rebranding the state as a cultural hub. The report outlined six areas of cultural economy: culinary arts, design, entertainment, literary arts and humanities, preservation, and visual arts and crafts (Mt. Auburn Associates 2005, 14–20).

The goals established in the report became all the more urgent in the context of rebuilding. The dedication of the government and private companies to the expansion of the cultural and tourist economies, largely service based, has precedent that began in the 1990s and early part of the 2000s. Woods (2017b, 240) identifies that the reemergence of the land-holding elite ("Bourbon restoration") enabled and required "the expansion of the low-wage economy and the numerous forms of dependency and desperation associated with it." By 2007, officials were sharing information about the Louisiana Cultural Economy Initiative nationally. That year the assistant secretary of the Louisiana Department of Culture, Recreation and Tourism gave a presentation at a conference in Baltimore that summarized the main findings of the *Louisiana, Where Culture Means Business* report. A slide in the presentation featured a portrait of a Mardi Gras Indian within a globe, signifying New Orleans' marketability for international tourism.

"Disaster tourism" was the first phase of rebranding, in which "initial crisis campaigns used powerful emotional appeals that foregrounded disaster and the capacity to overcome" (Gotham and Greenberg 2014, 202). Examples include the "soul is Waterproof" slogan and nostalgic imagery in the "Forever New Orleans" campaign. I argue that another period of disaster tourism branding occurred after the BP *Deepwater Horizon* oil spill in 2010. The State of Louisiana struck a $78 million deal with British Petroleum to go toward Gulf seafood: $48 million for safety monitoring and $30 million for the promotion of seafood consumption and tourism to the state (Associated Press 2010). Slogans in subsequent campaigns made sly references to the oil spill — "This isn't the first time New Orleans has survived the British" — and featured seafood dishes prominently: "There's no moratorium on shrimp po-boys."

Before the disaster, Beriss found that tourists were viewed unfavorably in the context of fine dining. In 2002, local residents who frequented Galatoire's restaurant claimed that "tourists were the demise of culture."[4] Regular customers expressed concerns that there was an effort to "rid the restaurant of its long-time patrons, with their tendency to linger for hours, and replace them with ill-dressed, but faster-eating, tourists" (Beriss 2007, 155). In addition to patronizing fine dining establishments such as Galatoire's, tourists have made "pilgrimages" to classic po-boy (sandwich) shops and will queue in line for more than an hour to taste the fried chicken at Willie Mae's Scotch House (Edge 2017, 250).[5] On bike tours of the Lower Ninth Ward, visitors are invited to drink beer and eat Vietnamese po-boys on a lawn in the heart of the neighborhood (Jaffe et al. 2019). In this context, tour guides use food to mediate tourists' sensory experience regarding "what urban poverty feels like" (Jaffe et al. 2019, 10).

I posit that the flooding tampered what would have been a more robust resistance to the promotion of culinary tourism. The expense of rebuilding paired with the fact that many locals had not returned to the city likely made the presence of "ill-dressed, fast-eating" tourists more palatable. Over the course of my research, however, the public conversation regarding the city's emphasis on promoting tourism became more critical. As I discuss in chapter 5, contentious debates about Airbnb and the company's role in neighborhood change and rising rents have flourished. Local food writer Ian McNulty (2019) mourned the 2019 deaths of chef Leah Chase and musician Dr. John in quick succession by asking what sort of future the city's cultural economy is crafting: "If tourists are the main market and buzzy trends make the strongest business case, New Orleans food and music will speak first to tourists and chase buzzy trends."

The second rebranding phase focused on utopian narratives (Gotham and Greenberg 2014). This branding strategy relies on long-standing ideas of cultural diversity in the city, alongside an effort to push new narratives about "greening" and sustainability—concepts that test positively with wealthy demographics of consumers, from home buyers to tourists (Gotham and Greenberg 2014, 208). Gotham and Greenberg argue that "as with most influential and resonant concepts, the discursive and semiotic power of these terms lies in their denotative simplicity and connotative elasticity, allowing room for vastly different interpretations and articulations" (2014, 209).

Utilizing greening and sustainability as branding concepts for tourism is unsettling when juxtaposed with Louisiana's primary economic driver, which is the petrochemical industry (Woods 2017b, 275). However, the state is not unaccustomed to such unlikely or ironic bedfellows, as evidenced by the annual Shrimp and Petroleum Festival, which has been held in Morgan City, Louisiana, since 1936.[6] More rhetorically, M. B. Hackler (2010) documents how policy makers framed local culture as "Louisiana's new oil" after Katrina: investments in the cultural economy would create wealth akin to the state's oil and gas industries. Lydia Pelot-Hobbs (2023) makes a direct link between the "extractive economies" of petrochemical production and tourism in the region.

Gotham and Greenberg find that the form of cultural diversity promoted is depoliticized and represented safely in terms of cosmopolitanism and multiculturalism. Here I add Kate Derickson's (2014) engagement with "banal multiculturalism," which more fully captures why Gotham and Greenberg are concerned about "depoliticized" and "safe" multicultural rebranding efforts. Derickson (2014, 895) draws on Mary Thomas's (2011) work to argue that while there are "robust" forms of multiculturalism that address and redress oppression, banal multiculturalism is "a way of rendering all cultures or forms of social difference equivalent, as though a slate has been wiped clean and historic forms of oppression and marginalization are no longer relevant. . . . Banal multiculturalism not only denies the current relevance of past injustices but works to mask or render less visible the way in which neoliberal accumulation regimes both rely on and further entrench racial difference and oppression." Other scholars have argued that tourism campaigns drew on "pre-Katrina tropes of racial harmony and tourist-sanctioned performances of blackness" (L. L. Thomas 2014, 128) in which Black culture is celebrated and commodified, packaged safely for tourists' consumption (Camp and Pulido 2017, 294). Lynnell Thomas (2014, 129) documents how tourism efforts (Katrina disaster bus tours, advertising campaigns, and so on) actively drew attention away from the disparities that were revealed by Katrina because "the reality of systemic racial and class inequality threatens the racial fantasy that propels the city's tourist image."

Fresh, local food—locally grown ingredients featured in traditional recipes—is an ideal venue to represent cultural diversity, greenness, and sustainability. The utopian narratives branding phase heavily utilized food, restaurants, and chefs, and foodscape utopian representations have continued well into the post-disaster period. In 2013, chefs John Besh and John Folse were featured alongside artists and musicians in full-page magazine advertisements as part of the "This Is My Louisiana" campaign (see figure 3.1). Led by the Louisiana Department of Culture, Recreation and Tourism, the chefs in these ads invited tourists to come and taste the state's thriving cultural economy.

As another illustrative example of this food-focused marketing push, I turn to a public event featuring John Besh. In January 2012, I attended the final meeting of the New Orleans Childhood Obesity Prevention Forum, which featured Besh as the keynote speaker. The forums were a series of research-gathering and strategic-planning sessions convened by the City of New Orleans, and the New Orleans Health Department's Fit NOLA initiative was launched after this final meeting. I attended the forums both in my capacity as co-chair of the New Orleans Food Policy Advisory Committee and as a researcher studying the "obesity epidemic," critical of the racist and sexist underpinnings of the so-called epidemic (Firth 2012).

John Besh took the stage to exuberant applause—which was quite surprising considering that previous meetings had been subdued and bureaucratic. Besh's enthusiastic speech sang the praises of local food and urban agriculture. Besh claimed that New Orleans was home to "seven times more urban farms than any other city of its size." At the time I doubted the accuracy of

FIGURE 3.1 Chefs have been featured prominently in tourism rebranding efforts post-disasters. Here Besh is identified as a "Louisiana Native," positioned as an authentic ambassador for Louisiana's unique brand. Image by Louisiana Department of Culture, Recreation and Tourism, 2013.

the statistic, as I had not seen any research tracking such data. More importantly, I was intrigued that Besh was platforming such strong support for urban agriculture. Shortly before this speech, Besh had launched Milk Money, the first initiative of his new foundation. Milk Money provided microloans of $500–$20,000 to local farmers "who have a marketable, delicious product, but are unable to afford the steps necessary to increase production and take their goods to local farmers' markets, grocery stores or restaurant kitchens" (John Besh Foundation website, discontinued, accessed 2015).

Food sociologist Yuki Kato argues that national public interest in urban agriculture peaked in 2012 (personal communication 2018). John Besh's excitement about urban agriculture was reflective of this trend, in which chefs were seen as essential partners in buying from urban farms and in helping promote local growers (see, for example, Somerville 2012). Thus, the marketing phase of utopian narratives aligned with heightened public interest in local and sustainable foods across the United States. Lily Kelting (2016) argues that a "New Southern Food Movement" has emerged, in which the South's "diverse, hyper regional, hospitable, and agrarian based" (Stokes and Atkins-Sayre 2016, 8) food appeals to national and international tourist markets. Scholars have noted that Southern cuisine, characterized by the traits Stokes and Atkins-Sayre describe, is well-aligned with national food movements calling for more locally grown and seasonally appropriate food: "Because Southern foodways are traditionally and strongly aligned with these larger food movement goals, Southern cuisine becomes a unique example of how Americans should be eating" (Stokes and Atkins-Sayre 2016, 8). Beriss (2012, 5) draws a distinction between the local food movement nationally and in New Orleans: "Since the 1970s, many chefs in American fine dining restaurants have promoted the use of seasonal and local ingredients, a movement that has since expanded into markets and home kitchens around the country. New Orleans is no stranger to this movement. However, when chefs and food activists in New Orleans promote local and seasonal foods, they most often do so by linking those foods to the city's history and people. Being a 'locavore' in New Orleans requires a knowledge of the city's identity and history, as well as an understanding of seasons and ingredients." Advocating for local food in New Orleans thus involves not only sustainable agricultural practices but also—or arguably even primarily—a commitment to the histories and cultures of traditional foods. Chefs have continued to be featured in tourism promotions: driving on Esplanade Avenue years later while listening to WWOZ, New Orleans's beloved local radio station, I suddenly heard, "This is Alon Shaya, and I love being a tourist in New

Orleans"—an advertisement for www.louisianatravel.com, sponsored by the Louisiana Office of Tourism and WWOZ.

The employment of utopian narratives branding was evident even more recently in the marketing for New Orleans's tricentennial in 2018. The New Orleans Tourism Marketing Corporation rolled out a massive "One Time, in New Orleans" campaign, a slogan I first came across during my fieldwork in late summer 2017. I was volunteering at the James Beard Foundation's Taste America fundraiser at the time and spent hours stuffing coupons for luxury cruises and private vineyard tours into black cotton tote bags with ONE TIME, IN NEW ORLEANS printed on the front in bright white curly script. Few guests took the bags home with them, and hundreds were loaded into dumpsters at the end of the night.

Throughout the tricentennial in 2018, the slogan appeared as "graffiti" on walls around the city, and I saw several full-page ads in in-flight airline magazines. The ads featured historical moments that framed the city as multicultural and politically progressive, such as "Dooky Chase's Restaurant fed the Civil Rights Movement" (see figure 3.2) A photograph of freedom marchers in 1963 sits next to a contemporary portrait of elderly chef Leah Chase (1923–2019) as she carefully measures vanilla. The tourist-viewer is invited to be part of this history, to come to Dooky Chase's Restaurant today and taste what Leah is making in that giant bowl. A project at Loyola University has been dedicated to documenting Dooky Chase's, and the oral histories collected emphasize the context of the restaurant: in the era of Jim Crow and legally enforced segregation, diners at Dooky Chase's were forbidden to patronize the acclaimed restaurants of the city (Loyola University n.d.). The tricentennial ad emphasizes that the freedom marchers were "peaceful." It does not mention the restaurant's role in the 1955 Godchaux Sugar Refinery strike or in lunch counter sit-ins, or when a homemade bomb was thrown at the restaurant in 1965. Dooky Chase's Restaurant—and Leah Chase—have been key in the struggle for civil rights in the city and across the South. What is important here is how a certain sanitized version of the restaurant's history was invoked for tourism marketing—progress presented without struggle.

Representing the Diverse City: Montage and Gumbo

In the rebranding phase of utopian narratives, a frequently deployed strategy used to represent "the post-race and post-class city was . . . montage—the seemingly infinite juxtaposition, listing, and mosaic of radicalized

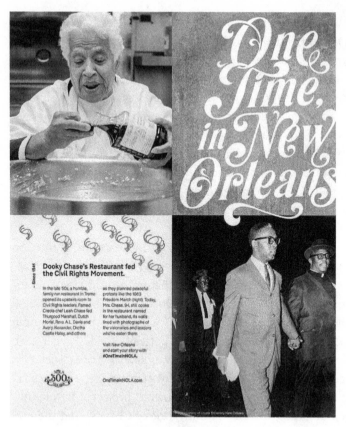

FIGURE 3.2 "One Time, in New Orleans." Tricentennial marketing
advertisement featuring Dooky Chase's Restaurant, chef Leah
Chase, and civil rights organizers. Image by New Orleans Tourism
Marketing Corporation, 2017.

aesthetic forms, sites, products, and experiences" (Gotham and Greenberg
2014, 210). "Exotic cuisine and all that jazz" (Toledano 2007, 32) has been a
core imaginary of the city long promoted by tourism officials (Beriss 2012,
12). In this sense, then, the marketing of New Orleans as an "exotic" place
to eat is part of a long, ongoing trend (see Heldke [2003] on the construction
of the "exotic" in eating).

I argue that "montage," as a representational strategy, has a locally and
culturally constructed manifestation: gumbo. Gumbo, a stew of meats
and vegetables served with rice, is frequently invoked as a metaphor of the
city. The examples are seemingly endless. In the "This Is My Louisiana" campaign, chef John Besh claims, "In Louisiana, we take the best from every culture and blend it all together for the perfect gumbo" (see figure 3.1). On *The*

World, Marco Werman (2013) claimed that the "language" of New Orleans can be summarized "in just one word: gumbo." Coverage of the tenth anniversary of Katrina described the demographic changes in the city—primarily the loss of Black residents across income levels and the establishment of larger Latinx communities—by using a gumbo metaphor: "New Orleans has always been a place that blended cultures. Now, as the city grows, newcomers are adding flavors to the gumbo" (Allen 2015).

David Beriss (2012, 9) explains the historical context of the idea expressed by Besh in the tourism campaign:

> Discussions of what constitutes New Orleans culture and cuisine usually start with the idea that it is the product of a mixture of techniques, ingredients, and recipes brought together by the diverse populations that make up the city. Native Americans, French and Spanish colonisers, African slaves, Germans, Italians, and Irish immigrants are usually cited as having contributed variously to making the city's architecture, accent, tastes, and foods. The result is described as a gumbo, a mixture in which the different elements form a delicious ensemble while still remaining, at least in some instances, identifiable. Versions of this story can be found in most of the city's cookbooks and tourist guidebooks, along with scholarly versions in the publications of historians and other social scientists. The idea of waves of immigrants contributing to the greater whole as they assimilate is a common American idea.

Food historian Jessica Harris explained the significance of the metaphor: "People have often referred to the culture of New Orleans as a gumbo. . . . It's a case where these parts make an extraordinary whole without totally melting. You know, if you have a good gumbo, you can still see the okra, you still know that that was Andouille, you're still aware of the fact that that was duck or chicken or what have you" (Werman 2013). Gumbo is invoked as a signifier of the city's diversity and resistance to assimilation to mainstream white culture. As Beriss (2012, 249) explains: "The claim, however, in New Orleans is that the mixture has created something distinct, both American and different. The society produced in this process is marked by the existence of a large population of free people of color and by a resistance to the sharp racial segregation that characterized much of the rest of the country." The various ingredients in gumbo are listed and juxtaposed with one another, creating a product or site for a tourist's experience of the diversity of the city. The prominent use of a food metaphor—gumbo—to symbolize New Orleans reflects the way in which the city has been branded as its food.

Humanitarian of the Year

In 2006, the James Beard Foundation declared the New Orleans restaurant community Humanitarian of the Year. In announcing the decision, the award committee claimed that the generosity of the restaurant community "carried the first evidence for many outsiders and for the few remaining locals, that New Orleans is a city worth saving" (*New Orleans CityBusiness* 2006). As David Beriss and David Sutton summarize (2007, 2) "Chefs became the heroes of the recovery." Post-flooding, chefs showed an outpouring of spontaneous goodwill. In the chapters that follow, I show how chefs' humanitarian work has changed significantly since that initial disaster-relief period as their philanthropy formalized and professionalized over the years.

New Orleans had limited philanthropic activity and few nonprofit organizations before Katrina (Woods 2017b, 280–81); after the flooding, formal charitable systems grew by leaps and bounds. Celebrity humanitarians and their projects took center stage, including politician Mikhail Gorbachev's Global Green, actor Brad Pitt's Make It Right Foundation, businessman Len Riggio's (of Barnes and Noble) Project Home Again, football player Thomas Morstead's What You Give Will Grow, and TV personality Oprah Winfrey's Angel Lane in Houston, to name but a few. Research about why this phenomenon has emerged is still largely unexplored, and I have chosen to contribute to this literature by specifically examining foodscape interventions.

Philanthropy by novices (which arguably describes much if not all of the celebrity activity I observed) can also be understood in terms of the regulatory vacuums that can occur at post-disaster sites: "Even where authorities are highly competent, organized and present, the multitude of humanitarian actors who arrive in a disaster site, the often overlapping and unclear channels of responsibility, and the overwhelming need of local populations provide a window where reconstruction standards and norms may be lowered, unfamiliar or unenforceable," creating "fertile territory for amateurs, students or ad hoc organizations" (Smirl, 2015, 167–68). Following Robert Burns and Matthew Thomas (2015), I argue that celebrity humanitarian activity can be viewed in the context of larger trends in privatization, a dominance of "non-local" rebuilding entities, and the growth of PPPs.

Burns and Thomas (2015) studied the relationship between disaster and political change in New Orleans, giving equal attention to pre- and post-

Katrina contexts, which is unusual in disaster scholarship. They argue that external forces, including national foundations, were the source of the resources that enabled changes in the city's political arrangements (8), resulting in a successful "top-down agenda" (153). Cedric Richmond, then a state senator, wanted displaced residents to return before any governmental reform was enacted, but he and others who supported this position were overruled as extralocal actors pushed through reforms, many that had originated before the storm (155). Burns and Thomas ask: "How much say, if any, do or should residents have in rebuilding and over the basic policies that govern their lives? In the New Orleans case, coalitions of various state and federal actors made important decisions about housing and schooling without input from residents, many of whom had yet to return. The mayor and the city council supported these choices" (154). Burns and Thomas feel hopeful about many of the reforms, as the city's "long history of patronage politics, corruption, lack of engagement by the civic elite and businesses, and multiple divides in public sector practices put New Orleans in line for possible political and government reconstruction along with the physical rebuilding" (24). However, they contend that "the list of winners and losers provides additional support to claims that reform is not neutral. . . . In almost every instance, either the poor and/or blacks bore the brunt of change" (161).

Celebrity foodscape interventions have been robust, and chefs and the restaurant industry have been the most prolific philanthropists. As previously mentioned, celebrity efforts in foodscapes range from Wendell Pierce's failed Sterling Farms healthy grocery outlets, to Ellen DeGeneres's sponsorship of a woman's vegan food truck, to Canadian businessman Frank Stronach's founding of Magnaville/Canadaville—a 900-acre sustainable agriculture community for almost 400 Katrina evacuees in rural Simmesport, Louisiana. Chef interventions are clustered in education, health, and labor/employment for food system workers—primarily focused on farmers/producers and workers in the restaurant industry. As mentioned earlier, California chef Alice Waters launched a local branch of her garden education program Edible Schoolyard. Locally based chef foundations have proliferated, including the John Besh Foundation, the Shaya Barnett Foundation, the Link Stryjewski Foundation, the Aarón Sánchez Scholarship Fund (which was housed under the Besh Foundation but is now an independent entity), and Kelly Fields's Yes Ma'am Foundation.[7] Emeril Lagasse launched his foundation before the storm in 2002, but Lagasse personally won the James Beard Foundation's Humanitarian of the Year award in 2013 for his foundation's work.

One high-profile chef effort was the reopening of Willie Mae's Scotch House in 2007. Argued to have the best fried chicken in the city, if not the country, owner Willie Mae Seaton won the Beard Foundation's America's Classic award just a few months before the restaurant flooded during the levee failures. In a campaign led by the Southern Foodways Alliance and chef John Currence, hundreds of volunteers and more than $200,000 in private donations helped rebuild the restaurant. Chefs Adolfo Garcia and John Besh catered meals for volunteers (Edge 2017, 248). After three years of work, several Beard Foundation–winning chefs assisted in the kitchen and dining room on the night of the restaurant's reopening.

Chefs "doing good" in the city is not without significant precedent, as chefs Susan Spicer and Leah Chase, among others, were long known for their community involvement and charitable work. Pre-Katrina, some of the most common forms of engagement were donating food to nonprofits for fundraising events and giving grants to local organizations. Beriss (2012) argues that African American chefs and Black-owned restaurants have been more likely to receive recognition for their charitable and community work than for the quality of their cuisine.

Here I note two indicative cultural practices in which "the gift" manifests in the social worlds of feeding practices in New Orleans more broadly: lagniappe and "giving a supper." "Lagniappe" is a Creole term that refers to a small gift, a bonus, or a little something extra. Customers might receive a lagniappe gift after purchasing goods, or a lagniappe appetizer or dessert might arrive at the table unexpectedly, free of charge. One of the childhood nutrition programs in the city sends "Lagniappe Packs" filled with food home with students over the weekend. "Giving a supper" is a local practice that has a long tradition in low-income African American neighborhoods in which women sell "plate dinners" to raise money for families or community (C. M. Williams 2017). Here, the language states that women "give" a supper: even though there is a charge for the meal, their cooking and aesthetically considered plating is understood as generous, and purchasing a meal is also an act of generosity (see chapter 5 for a discussion of who "counts" as a giver).

A reporter at the *Atlantic* claimed that for New Orleanians returning to the city in 2005 and 2006, the experience of eating out was "as essential as group therapy" (Kummer 2006). After the emotional dinner at Restaurant August described previously, Fitzmorris (2010) started tracking the number of restaurants in the city that were open for business. He published his findings, using the number of restaurants that had reopened as an indicator of the city's recovery and overall health. In his "Katrina Timetable: From a Culinary

Perspective," the final event on the timeline is the reopening of Mr. B's restaurant in the French Quarter on April 16, 2007, a year and a half after the initial flooding. The timeline ends with Mr. B's reopening because it brought the number of open restaurants in the city to 809, the same number that were operating before the flood.

The Restaurant "Renaissance"

The reopening of Mr. B's was taken as an indicator that the city's culinary world had survived Katrina. This had much broader implications and became evidence that the city itself had survived. The restaurant boom that followed the reopening of Mr. B's became part of a narrative that the city not only had survived but was thriving. However, generalizations about the recovery "miss out on the personal, complex intimacy of each venue and its significance to the local community," a point that Benjamin Morris attributes to chef Leah Chase (2010, 98). The focus on physical structures of restaurants does not take into account the symbolic, mnemonic, and social landscapes of food (Morris 2010, 99).

Southern food scholar Catarina Passidomo has been tracking the widespread celebration of what was heralded as a restaurant "renaissance" in New Orleans (Firth and Passidomo 2022). Media venues from the local *Times-Picayune* to the national *New York Times* lauded the city's recovery in culinary terms. *Times* food writer Kim Severson (2015) argued that "few would disagree that the New Orleans dining scene has not only come back, but the city is a much better place to eat than it was even before the storm." The same year the restaurant community was lauded for its humanitarian efforts by the James Beard Foundation, John Besh won Best Chef in the Southeast for Restaurant August.

A tourism official told Gotham and Greenburg (2014, 214): "[A] main theme in our work of branding the city had to do with the cultural renaissance the city was experiencing. The palpable energy of rebuilding that visitor's [*sic*] embrace. Explosion of new restaurants and culinary experimentation was taking place in neighborhoods across the city, ranging from high-end eateries such as Sylvain to neighborhood eateries like Dat Dog. John Besh is one of the celebrity chefs that the city rallied around to illustrate the culinary boom. And a big part of this story-line was how the scene was diversifying."

Culinary diversity was written heavily into the celebratory narrative of the New Orleans restaurant renaissance (see Fouts, forthcoming). Reviews highlighted how restaurants were using new recipes or nontraditional ingredients: "The joke used to be that New Orleans is a town of 5,000 restaurants and five recipes. The town still reveres its tradition, but restaurants that have been cooking New Orleans–style Creole dishes for more than 100 years have become sharper" (Severson 2015; see also Edge 2017, 246–53). Reviews mentioned emerging Honduran, El Salvadoran, and Vietnamese restaurants. The city's Latinx population, primarily composed of immigrants from Mexico and Honduras, grew during rebuilding efforts (up 40 percent from 2000 to 2013) and now makes up 5 percent of the population (Guzman-Lopez 2019; US Census Bureau, n.d.). With migration beginning in the 1970s, the city is also home to one of the most concentrated populations of Vietnamese immigrants in the country (Hiltner 2018). Even with this celebration of new forms of culinary diversity, the restaurants receiving the most attention in national reviews or in Beard Foundation awards have rarely been Latinx or Vietnamese owned.

Tunde Wey, a Nigerian-born chef who uses food as a venue for justice (see www.fromLagos.com/food), was enormously popular nationally when he opened up a small Nigerian restaurant in a new food hall called St. Roch Market.[8] The market was aimed at tourists, and Wey's Nigerian dishes did not correspond to visitors' expectations of Louisiana cuisine. Eventually the market's owners came to Wey and asked him to put a chicken sandwich on the menu. "I did it," he said, "but I was also like, 'Fuck this. I'm not here for a chicken sandwich'" (B. Martin 2019). Wey's restaurant closed shortly after. Thus, the pressure to offer "traditional" food that tourists expect reflects a reified and fictionalized idea of what constitutes "authentic" New Orleans cuisine.

Restaurants and Development in the CBD

Most of the prominent restaurants that reopened as well as the new restaurants that received acclaim are clustered in the French Quarter, Garden District, and the Central Business District (CBD), which was the site of heavy investment and development post-Katrina (Gotham and Greenberg 2014) (map 3.1). The majority of restaurants opened by the Link and Besh restaurant groups (both chefs with foundations) have been concentrated in the CBD, the area identified for heavy investment by city officials. The CBD was originally established in 1788 under the name Faubourg St. Mary on the site of the Gravier Plantation and slowly became the commercial and residential corridor known as the "American Sector" (S. Wilson 1998). Investment in the CBD declined after World War II, but preservation efforts began in the 1970s,

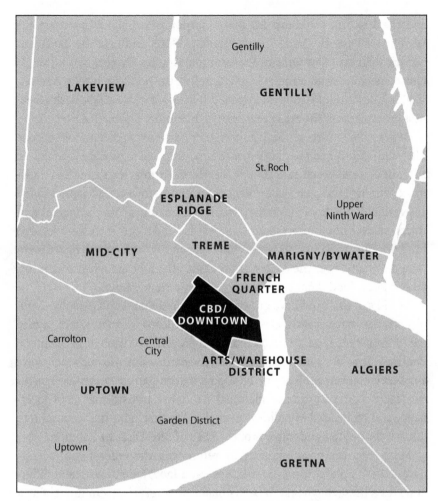

MAP 3.1 Reproduction of New Orleans Neighborhood Map by New Orleans &
Company (formerly the New Orleans Convention and Visitors Bureau) and
New Orleans Tourism Marketing Corporation, both of which are nonprofit
organizations promoting tourism. The CBD is black with white letters. The text
accompanying the original map read "There are many ways to divide up New Orleans
and depending on who you ask, you will always get a different answer. NewOrleans
Online.com has divided the neighborhoods in a way that we felt was most relevant
to tourists by grouping smaller neighborhoods into larger ones that are traditionally
more familiar to tourists." Original image by www.neworleans.com; reproduction by
UNC Press.

and the Historic Faubourg St. Mary Corporation helped designate the Warehouse District, Canal Street, Picayune Place, and Lafayette Square as historic districts (New Orleans Preservation Timeline Project 2019). Donald Link owned one restaurant, Herbsaint, before the flooding in 2005; by 2015, the Link Restaurant Group had opened four more in the CBD. Besh's business enterprises in the area grew even more rapidly during this time.

Besh's relief efforts in the Walmart parking lot expanded into an opaque PPP, with FEMA and possibly other federal agencies to provide food aid. In 2017, BRG (Besh Restaurant Group) Disaster Solutions registered as a trademark with the Louisiana Department of Revenue. However, I have not found any verifiable documentation that details information about the federal contracts, such as how much money was awarded and if contracts were secured for work during future disasters. BRG Disaster Solutions was never mentioned by name over the course of my research, and even when prompted, no one knew (or did not claim to know) that it even existed.

As PPPs of this kind have grown in the United States and globally, feminist scholars have examined their uneven gendered impacts.[9] In their profile of four PPPs that aim to increase the presence of women in business, Prügl and True (2014, 1156) suggest "that the partnerships do not simply solve a collective action problem or fill a governance gap as rationalists might suggest, but are part of a transnational, neoliberal transformation of governance and embedded in political struggles." In this light, it is important to unpack the politics and impacts of the PPPs of BRG Disaster Solutions.

Media sources have occasionally referenced the federal contracts as part of Besh's philanthropic work. Severson (2007) identifies them differently, as a lifesaving boost to Besh's business enterprises: "In hindsight, it turns out that the smartest move Mr. Besh made was quickly arranging a series of lucrative emergency catering contracts, feeding thousands of law enforcement, government and oil rig workers. The contracts, some of which lasted for a year and a half, made him enough money to bankroll the expansion of his businesses." Besh's food aid work is usually framed in terms of philanthropy, a gift he offered to the city he loves. In Severson's estimation, it was more fundamentally a savvy business strategy. Severson (2015) later reported that John Besh built his restaurant group by "securing federal contracts to feed workers rebuilding the city and working with his most talented chefs to open new restaurants in hotels that offered inexpensive leases." Besh's business indeed expanded rapidly during this time. In April 2005, several months before the storm, Besh purchased

Restaurant August, his first, from the restaurant's owner, who employed Besh at the time. By 2018, the BRG had opened, by my count, sixteen restaurants and bars. The rapid growth of the BRG was part of the proliferation of restaurants clustered in the CBD, an area targeted by the city for significant development post-flooding.

The kinds of restaurants that flourished and received great attention catered to upscale consumers and tourists, "two categories of eaters that have also seen notable growth in the decade since Katrina" (Firth and Passidomo 2022, 187). Which restaurants reopened, which remained closed, and who owned these restaurants? Were there places where tired residents rebuilding their homes could get a cheap sandwich as well as seared foie gras? The Southern Poverty Law Center found rampant labor abuses aimed at Latinx day laborers who were involved in rebuilding the city: 80 percent of workers reported having been denied pay (Southern Poverty Law Center 2007). As Sarah Fouts (forthcoming) explains:

> To speed up recovery in the following months after Katrina, the Bush administration temporarily suspended federal labor laws like the Davis Bacon Act (guarantees a prevailing wage for public works jobs), E-Verify (I-9 employee eligibility), and OSHA laws (worksite protections), while also suspending an affirmative action contract hire policy and allowing for an unparalleled amount of no-bid private (sub)contracts. With this extractive context set in place, tens of thousands of Central American and Mexican immigrants arrived to the region, making up almost half of the workforce that cleaned up and rebuilt under toxic conditions with few protections. As day laborers worked relentlessly, they fell victim time and again to an unregulated job market, receiving little to no compensation or protections.

What were the wages and labor conditions for reconstruction workers rebuilding the restaurants, and what were the wages for cooks, servers, and dishwashers? (See discussion of restaurant labor in chapter 6.)

In a broader sense, the focus on the restaurant renaissance ignores a wide swath of other indicators of the city's health, primarily addressing the question: Who was (back) in the city, and how were they doing? Dozens of other indicators could have been used to track the health and status of the rebuilding city. When considered alone, the restaurant indicator elides exploitation and displacement while contributing to the great inequality that is a hallmark of the "new" New Orleans.

Conclusion: Legitimizing Uneven Redevelopment?

Local chefs, imbued with unique formulations of culinary capital, became leaders in rebuilding efforts due to the sociohistorical importance of culinary culture and widespread governmental failure during and after Katrina, which eroded trust in the state. The rebranded landscape of the "new" New Orleans "has served to frame, reify, and (to a degree) legitimize the controversial, contested, and uneven political and spatial interventions of crisis-driven urbanization" (Gotham and Greenberg 2014, 22). This "unevenness" of rebuilding is most evident in tourist areas: "By 2009, tourists would come to the city, would never leave the French Quarter or Garden District, and would think that things were back to normal. But locals knew better, and many had to pass through or leave from decimated neighborhoods each day as they went to work in the recovered parts of town" (V. Adams 2013, 120). The website of the New Orleans Convention and Visitors Bureau claimed a year after the flood: "The most celebrated and historic core of the city—including the Faubourg Marigny, French Quarter, Central Business District, Warehouse and Arts District, Magazine Street, Garden District, Audubon Park and Zoo, and St. Charles Avenue—not only remains intact, both physically and spiritually, but is thriving" (L. L. Thomas 2014, 129). Meanwhile, residents still trying to recover referred to wealthy areas along St. Charles Avenue as the "Isle of Denial" (V. Adams, 2013, 74). Lydia Pelot-Hobbs documents how surveillance increased in "tourist zones" and how gendered, raced, and classed policing practices have displaced "populations deemed a threat to the sanitized image tourism capitalists seek to promote" (2023, 9). Low-cost investment after the flooding penetrated the high-risk landscape, creating a new layer on the historical map of inclusion and exclusion for the city, which offered wildly profitable opportunities for some.

Woods (2017b) writes that the ruling "Bourbon elite" aim to make invisible or naturalize the disposability of Black lives, while mainstream news media and tourism industries capitalize on that same Black disposability. In the decade after the flooding, the demographics of the city shifted significantly. New Orleans had been a majority Black and African American city; by 2015—the tenth anniversary of the storm and levee failure—the city was whiter and more affluent than it was before the storm, with at least 100,000 fewer Black residents (Allen 2015). New Orleans's restaurant boom and culinary imaginary (through representations such as gumbo) were mobilized as part of the depoliticized and easily digestible versions of multiculturalism and diversity—a manifestation of "banal multiculturalism"—which became a driver of uneven redevelopment. Ironically, it is this uneven redevelopment that threatens the diversity and sustainability of the city. This aligns with other research and claims from activists that New Orleans is now inhospitable to many of the very people responsible for the city's history and deep cultural roots: primarily poor and working-class people of color. The diversity heralded as a "renaissance" in the kitchens of New Orleans elides the exclusion of Black and African American communities in the city.

CHAPTER FOUR

The Fundraiser

Financing Celebrity Chef Philanthropy

Although a prominent spatiotemporal configuration of contemporary giving practices, fundraising events have not been significantly studied. I argue that fundraisers are not simply a means to an end to raise money but essential to the practices and purposes of elite chef philanthropy. I focus on the John Besh Foundation (JBF, founded in 2011), since it ran in-house programming and was a knowledge hub: three additional chef foundations within the Besh Restaurant Group (BRG) were launched in less than two years in 2016–17: the Shaya Barnett Foundation, the Aarón Sánchez Scholarship Fund, and the Yes Ma'am Foundation (chef Kelly Fields). My findings show that other foundations outside the BRG are interested in or have already outlined their intention to expand their own programming, as I discuss later in the chapter in reference to the Emeril Lagasse Foundation.

Chef foundations fundraise extensively through events, which are key to both their income generation and operational activities. As one director of a chef's foundation said: "You only raise money through events—all the work I do now is going to pay off on Nov 5 [the date of an annual fundraiser]." Annual local fundraising events in the decade after Katrina included the Lagasse Foundation's Boudin, Bourbon and Beer Festival and Carnivale du Vin; the Link Stryjewski Foundation's Bal Masqué; and the Besh Foundation's Fêtes des Chefs. Foundations also run numerous smaller fundraising events, such as crawfish boils or Dinners on the Farm at Grow Dat, as I'll discuss in chapter 5.

Not surprisingly, food is key to these events. The promise of a meal that is variously traditional or unique is mobilized strategically depending on the target "foodie" (Johnston and Baumann 2015) audience.[1] Fundraisers are performative sites of "ceremonial humanitarianism," a practice that "mobilizes the discursive resources of language and image in order to construct the boundaries of political community in ways that may either confirm our existing sense of belonging or extend this sense to encompass the zone of distant suffering" (Chouliaraki 2013, 107). Marketing often hinges on the exceptional and ephemeral nature of these events, creating a sense of urgency and exclusiveness. However, I argue that fundraisers need to be conceptualized in a way that is equally attentive to their consistencies and repetitions as sites of ceremonial humanitarianism. In this chapter, particularly in the section "Donor Experience," I highlight the boundaries of political communities which are created or re-created during fundraisers.

Most elite chef initiatives in New Orleans call themselves foundations, but this is perplexing, as a significant portion of my fieldwork was spent observing the fundraising activities of these organizations. "Foundation" is a broad term with no legal definition nationally (some states place their own restrictions), but in the United States, it has traditionally been used to denote endowment-based entities.[2] The Internal Revenue Service, which authorizes and oversees the tax-exempt status of 501(c)(3) organizations, distinguishes between private foundations and public charities as such (IRS 2018): "Generally, organizations that are classified as public charities are those that . . . have an active program of fundraising and receive contributions from many sources. . . . Private foundations, in contrast, typically have a single major source of funding (usually gifts from one family or corporation rather than funding from many sources) and most have as their primary activity the making of grants to other charitable organizations and to individuals, rather than the direct operation of charitable programs." The John Besh Foundation, Link Stryjewski Foundation, and Shaya Barnett Foundation, among others, are not endowed entities. They do not function as private foundations as outlined by the IRS, or as public or community foundations. Instead, they function as charities that fundraise and run their own programming, as would any 501(c)(3) charity or standard nonprofit organization. Most chef foundations do not engage in significant grant making, if at all.

In general, the legal status of foundations forbids their engagement in the political process through political "action," but the realm of education is permitted if it is "politically neutral" (Zunz 2012, 5). Foundations were established as "public good" institutions that are therefore exempt from taxes. As questions about the definition of "the public good" are inherently political or ideological, philanthropists more broadly have been at the heart of many contentious and partisan debates. Tax-exempt status, believed to foster giving, is also controversial: "Foundations are made partly with dollars which, were it not for charitable deductions allowed by tax laws, would have become public funds to be allocated through the governmental process under the controlling power of the electors as a whole" (Ahn 2007, 65). Thus, the concern is that money that would (or should) enter into the government system as tax revenue stays in private hands and is distributed according to the goals of private foundations.

Geographies of giving are shaped by the history of the land—the gift is specific to particular articulations of temporal and spatial social relations. The perspectives of staff, donors/attendees, and beneficiaries illuminate how fundraising events are racialized, classed, and gendered. Fundraisers are sites of financial gain for foundations; sites of branding and meaningful charitable work for chefs; sites of pleasure and ethical consumption for attendees or donors; and sites of opportunity, intense racialized histories, and contested representations for beneficiaries. I highlight how beneficiaries experience public fundraising events, an area that is currently understudied, and I develop how beneficiaries view and understand the gift.

I argue that the gift is continually reconstituted and contested in the spatial and social legacies of racial inequality in the United States, which stems from the genocide of Indigenous people and enslavement on the land where foodscape projects—and the fundraising that enables them—now take place. These troubled legacies continually reconstruct white philanthropists as givers and beneficiaries of color as receivers. Chef philanthropy is part of the restaurant world, which enables them to successfully raise money through events: restaurant expertise—business-based knowledge—enables effective fundraising. I explore how this also risks reproducing and rearticulating the inequalities and exploitations of the restaurant industry.

"A Delicious Excuse"

On a Saturday in May 2017, I make the hourlong drive across the shallow but massive Lake Pontchartrain on a series of elevated highways that connect the City of New Orleans with the suburb of Slidell. I am scheduled to volunteer for a JBF fundraiser at Besh's house as part of my ongoing research with the foundation. In Slidell, I reach an unassuming gravel road across the street from a strip mall, and as I turn onto it, I feel that I have suddenly been transported somewhere rural and remote. I bump along the uneven surface in my rusting Toyota Corolla: the muffler roars and all four hubcaps have been missing for years. The Besh family home emerges against the bright blue sky: a "shored up" (structurally elevated to protect against flooding) three-story estate, painted white with dark shutters. An elegant porch runs along the full length of the facade, and a wide staircase flanked by potted ferns leads straight from the circle drive to the front door. A fountain spurts on the grassy front lawn (figure 4.1).

FIGURE 4.1 Arriving at the Besh family home for a crawfish boil and the Chefs Move! scholarship awards ceremony. Photo by the author.

I have arrived here to volunteer at a crawfish boil, a quintessential culinary event in South Louisiana. The boil is part of the Besh Restaurant Group's Johnny + Friends pop-up series, billed as an opportunity to "join legendary Southern Chef John Besh, *Garden & Gun*, and a host of culinary masters for a series of unforgettable culinary experiences" to benefit the John Besh Foundation.[3] Omni Hotels and Resorts promoted exclusive accommodation packages to encourage tourists from across the country to attend, and *Garden & Gun* magazine declared it "a delicious excuse to visit the Crescent City" (Sivewright 2017).

Although not mentioned in the marketing materials, I am here today because the foundation will announce this year's Chefs Move! scholarship winners. I've been volunteering with the foundation throughout the application and interview process this spring, and I am eager to see which young people have been selected to attend school this fall. Chefs Move! is one of two projects run by the foundation; the other, Milk Money, assists in financing microloans to local farmers (see chapter 6 for a closer look).

I turn my car into the circular gravel drive in front of the house, and the first person I see is John Besh himself, walking toward a shiny sports car parked behind me that I think might be a Porsche. I remember that Ruth, one of two employees at the Besh Foundation, gave me specific instructions about parking, and I am not supposed to be in this circle drive. I blush but give Besh a quick nod, which he returns, and I quickly pull back out onto the rocky road. I find an area designated for staff parking, which had been cut out of the surrounding pine forest. The lot was muddy, and at the end of the party, a series of tow trucks would arrive to pull cars out of the muck.

Walking back to the Besh house, the party is already beginning to unfold on the lush lawn and gardens behind the stately house. It is a striking building, and it immediately reminds me of the homes of plantation owners along the Mississippi River, now popular tourist destinations on River Road (Alderman, Butler, and Hanna 2015). A peaked white tent has been erected over a stage and sound system. Half a dozen tables with snacks and desserts surround the perimeter of a swimming pool. A line of guests dressed in pastels and floral prints is forming at the main bar, and a quick-moving team of servers in dark aprons fill glasses with an iced tea–based cocktail. Long rows of tables with white-and-red-checkered tablecloths will soon be covered with piles of steaming crawfish, dumped out directly after boiling from giant metal baskets.

Fundraising with the Besh Restaurant Group

Hoping to spend as much time observing the foundation's activities as possible, I had asked Ruth if I could assist with setup before guests arrived. Ruth told me they would not need help with setup or takedown, and subsequently Melanie, the foundation's director, asked if I would like to come as a free "comp" and bring my spouse along to attend as a guest instead of volunteering at all. The offer of this gift to me, the ethnographer, speaks to both my positionality and to how chef philanthropy operates. As a white cis woman who has lived and worked in New Orleans for eight years, I would "fit in" as a guest, merging easily with the crowd. Ruth's and Melanie's insistence that they did not need any volunteers to throw a 350-plus-person event was my first indication that this fundraiser would be different from my past experiences at nonprofit organizations. I coordinated fundraising events at both of my previous nongovernmental organization (NGO) jobs, and I was heavily reliant on volunteer help at both of them. Once, in the early hours of the morning after Grow Dat Youth Farm's annual Hootenanny fundraiser, a board member and I spent several hours cleaning up trash after all the other volunteers had gone home, exhausted after working a ten-hour shift. Since the organization could not afford the risk of being charged an additional cleaning fee by the venue, it was up to the two of us to shovel paper plates into giant black rubbish sacks at 2 A.M. Witnessing the seemingly flawless and picture-perfect party unfolding in front of me now, I grasp for the first time that the event is being thrown not by the Besh Foundation (with its full-time staff of two employees) but by the BRG.

The development of the BRG in the decade after the flooding earned John Besh the status of "an exemplar of civic-minded entrepreneurial success" (Price 2016). In 2016, the BRG had an estimated annual revenue of $60 million. By one count, the BRG had opened sixteen restaurants concentrated in the Central Business District of downtown New Orleans, which, as discussed earlier, was targeted for redevelopment and investment after the disaster. With 1,400 employees, the group was one of the largest employers in the city at the time of the crawfish boil.

Today, my official volunteer assignment is helping at the front desk: a folding table erected along the front circle drive. The responsibility is light: I check-in guests, point them toward the bar and restrooms, and sell T-shirts. Most attendees arrive by official shuttles that are running between a parking lot in nearby Slidell and another going to and from the official hotel partners in New Orleans. As they disembark, guests show us receipts on their phones or hand us printed Eventbrite Johnny Sánchez + Friends tickets. Some list a ticket price of $130, and others appear to be free or complimentary. There is no actual guest list, because, as Ruth explains, anyone who has managed to find the "secret" location of Besh's house is supposed to be here.

Ruth oversees me and two other white women who are affiliated with the BRG, both in their early thirties or younger. One woman works in the main BRG office in finance, and the other is chef Alon Shaya's assistant, Alison. Alison is helping launch Shaya's emergent Shaya Barnett Foundation, and she tells me that she has learned a lot from the Besh Foundation about how to start the new organization. She regularly seeks advice from Melanie and Ruth, and helping at the event today is, presumably, part of Alison's ongoing education.

Just a few months after the boil, Brett Anderson (2017) at the *Times-Picayune* published an investigative report detailing allegations against John Besh and a "culture of sexual harassment" throughout the BRG. Sexist and ageist hiring patterns at BRG were identified in Anderson's reporting, and

I found evidence of the same practices at the foundation. At both the BRG and the foundation, slim young women were hired into roles that required close interactions with corporate leadership, particularly John Besh and Octavio Mantilla, co-owner of the BRG.[4] Marisol, a former director of the foundation, experienced extensive sexual harassment as the organization's leader, which included unwanted touching and pressure-laden requests for sex from Besh. Emery Whalen, then an executive of the BRG and Marisol's superior, said that "keeping chef happy"—at whatever cost—was a requirement of the job. A Chefs Move! winner experienced ongoing sexual harassment while undertaking the required yearlong internship at a BRG restaurant. After graduating from culinary school, interning at a BRG restaurant is mandatory for all Chefs Move! winners. In chapter 6, I examine sexual harassment at the foundation and the incidents mentioned here more closely.

White Men and Troubled Food Histories

An announcement is projected over the loudspeaker. Some of the crowd stops what they are doing and gathers around the white tent and stage (figure 4.2), while others continue eating and drinking in small groups near the pool. John Besh takes the stage to welcome the crowd. He situates the geography of the gathering as Native American, saying that Indigenous Choctaw people created the burial mounds visible along Bayou Liberty and that they gathered in the area: "People [have been] cooking and eating here long before the Europeans came here, many years before the Africans got here." Besh explained that he sees today's event as part of that long lineage of people eating together on the land. In his brief comments, Besh reveals some of the tensions of addressing food histories in the US South:

> I think New Orleans is the only indigenous food in America, period. We have a culture and part of that culture comes from our African heritage: there's no mistaking that. So what we're trying to do is to make sure that everybody has a shot at becoming a top tier chef. And education is that step. You're helping people, you're helping educate our neighbors and the people around here who will sustain this great culture. What we're worried about the most is having this culture white-washed to the degree that it no longer is special. Every one of you in your own way is contributing here to changing people's lives.

FIGURE 4.2 Gathering around the white tent for the Chefs Move! awards ceremony. Photo by the author.

In interviews, Besh has reiterated these claims, saying that he and cofounder Jessica Bride started Chefs Move! because they were concerned about the presence of "white suburbanites" in the New Orleans culinary scene post-Katrina/levee failure: "We're going to start to whitewash this culture if we're not careful" (Zuras, 2016). African and African American foodways in Southern culinary traditions have long been invisible or rendered unimportant in mainstream culinary culture. Scholars such as Jessica Harris (1989, 1995, 2011) and others (Carney 2009; Opie 2008; Sharpless 2010; Tipton-Martin 2015) have traced the complex racial histories of Southern food. Harris continues to call for others to "study the silences" (Pinchin 2014). Michael Twitty wrote frequently on the topic online in *Afroculinaria* and in his book *The Cooking Gene* (2017). In an interview, Twitty reflected: "Some of our most delicious food came to us through strife and oppression and struggle. Are we willing to own that and are we willing to make better moral choices based on that knowledge?" (Mansky 2017). In Besh's comments and in the creation of the foundation itself, I hear Besh trying to address that question but struggling to do so.

As mentioned previously, Catarina Passidomo (2017, 432), drawing on Byrd (2015, 104), expands on Twitty's comment: "'Authentic Southern food,' if such a thing exists, is most accurately a product of the violences of colonialism, Indian removal, enslavement, and cultural and resource exploitation by the white elite. Authenticity, then, must account for both appealing and less appealing elements of a cuisine or a culture." In a study of gastrodiplomacy in cookbooks, Passidomo (2017) is concerned that white chefs engage a rhetoric of a diverse and multicultural South but that their practices reestablish white racial superiority.

Besh's comments follow what Passidomo observes: in his *rhetoric*, Besh claims a desire to address the effects of racism in restaurant culture, but as I show in this chapter, his *practices* and the practices of the foundation, regardless of intention, often reinscribe white superiority. I believe that even as he claims to be concerned about the "white-washing" of African foodways, his passive language does its own white-washing: Europeans "came here," and thus he does not say that they were settler-colonialists who forcibly removed Indigenous people; and Africans "got here," which erases the violences of the transatlantic and domestic slave trade.

Besh claims that the history of African foodways has been obscured, and he next offers a solution: "So what we're trying to do is to make sure that everybody has a shot at becoming a top tier chef. And education is that step." Judging the efficacy of specific programmatic interventions is not part of my research agenda. However, what I can assert is that the "solution" Besh utilizes—to send aspiring chefs of color to elite culinary schools—is significantly different from other approaches and solutions offered by community and non-elite chefs, the focus of chapter 5. While formal culinary education might have positive benefits for the winners, it does not solve many—if any—problems of entrenched racism (let alone sexism or classism) within the BRG or the broader culinary world. At the BRG, there were few people of color in leadership positions at the foundation, at corporate headquarters, or in kitchens at the restaurants. Several people I interviewed claimed that there were no Black New Orleanians in BRG leadership positions at all. I am left with the question that my friend and colleague Jabari Brown asked regarding enduring inequalities in the restaurant world: "What if lacking credentials isn't the problem?"

Racialized Performances: Ceremonies and Beneficiary Experience

After Besh's welcome, representatives from *Garden & Gun*, the International Culinary Center, Aarón Sánchez (chef of Johnny Sánchez, a BRG restaurant), and Melanie take turns at the microphone. Their comments are brief, providing basic information about the foundation and its scholarships. Sánchez announces that today marks the first time a scholarship will be given to a Latinx recipient through the Aarón Sánchez Scholarship Fund, which at the time was housed under the Besh Foundation. He explained why he started the fund:

> We need to give back to the industry which has allowed us to have a fancy spread like John has [laughter from the crowd] — Porsches are flowing around. Find your mission, make sure that you are mentored, make sure you have structure and discipline — don't do it to be a TV chef like what has happened to my life [a woman in the crowd sarcastically yells: "It sucks!" and others laugh]. I mean, do it for the right reasons: do it because you're passionate, because you care about making people happy. And that's what we're doing here in essence, all of us in our own ways.

Sánchez ends his comments by thanking the guests for their help in making the scholarships possible. All speakers stress their gratitude for the generosity of today's attendees.

Melanie then quickly announces the names of this year's four scholarship winners. White noise hums in the loudspeaker. Each winner pauses for a quick photograph on the stage. A woman in the crowd near me exclaims in a stage whisper, "Aaw, I think I'm going to cry." My reaction is different: the ceremony feels strangely antiseptic and impersonal to me. Melanie casually remarks that one winner is quite young, but other than that, there is no personal information about who each winner is or why they were selected. It's all over in less than two minutes.

The awards ceremony was quick and simple. However, in multiple interviews with seven past winners, the majority highlighted that such public performances were complicated for them, and most spoke about concerns regarding representation. Tajee, for example, was born and raised in New Orleans and won the Chefs Move! scholarship when he was in his mid-twenties. Tajee is African American, and he says that most of his family identifies as Creole. We met for an interview before his nightly shift at the restaurant inside a new hotel in the CBD. Tajee was wearing a Besh Foundation T-shirt, the same one we were selling at the boil: a light gray material with the foundation's trademark logo. His long black bag of knives sat on the side of the table during our interview. I asked Tajee about the biggest challenges he had experienced with the foundation and being a Chefs Move! winner:

> Staying—it's not a challenge to stay true to what I believe, but having to sometimes, sometimes—maybe to question, to know if I am truly going the right way, doing the right thing. Am I being represented in the right way, you know, with the image I'm building for myself? (Q: Do you have an example?) [Tajee pauses, takes a breath, chuckles] Sooooo, I recently did a commercial that will be played during one of their fundraisers, in an attempt to gain more funding, you know, get more funding. As an African American, to me, it wasn't a problem: business is business, connections is connections. You use me, I use you. You're getting that repping, I'm getting exposure. Win, lose, gain. But just the sense of—am I, am I, selling myself out? Am I being used as a puppet, so to speak? Am I being used as [pause] a token? And in my image as an African American is that question, you know: Will other African Americans look at me on average and think I'm just another Uncle Tom or something?[5] And the reality is that no, I'm not. (Q: What conclusion did you come to?) I'm not. Business is business, and what I'm doing with this platform I'm building for myself proves that. And what Chef Besh is doing—he's not, I don't believe that. His image is not betrayed. That's not what I'm doing, and that's not what I perceive of what I've been doing with the chef, so [trails off]. But those are the kind of questions that do come up. (Q: And you have to think about them?) You have to think about them, you have to think about them.

As discussed in chapter 2, one of my research questions draws on theorizing about "the gift" and aims to understand how beneficiaries conceptualize reciprocity and to see if they attempt to engage in it. Marcel Mauss (2002) conceptualizes the gift as a three-part cycle called "the three obligations": giving, receiving, and reciprocating. This third component of Mauss's cycle—reciprocity—is of particular interest in relationship to beneficiaries. Berking (1999, 26) claims that gift exchange is "an interest-guided transaction which does not and cannot risk revealing itself as such. . . . *Something* is not exchanged for *nothing*" (emphasis in original). In the preceding passage, Tajee describes a sort of transactional reciprocity in which "You use me, I use you. You're getting that repping, I'm getting exposure." As Tajee continues, he stresses that there is also another dynamic at play, in which he questions, "Am I selling myself out? Am I being used as a puppet, so to speak?" Tajee's comfort with "using and being used" is complicated by a larger question in which he cannot seem to reconcile whether or not he's a "puppet."

In the context of humanitarian aid, "a repayment in kind is obviously not intended by the donor. Here, repayment is something more ephemeral. It is the feeling or knowledge that the gift is being used, and most importantly appreciated in the way that it was intended" (Smirl 2015, 134). In her study of housing reconstruction in post-tsunami Aceh, Indonesia, Lisa Smirl (2015) found that NGOs that had sponsored homes demanded certain responses from beneficiaries. Beneficiaries were unhappy with the design and quality of the homes that the NGOs had built, and as the homes did not fit their needs, many recipients decided to "make do" and use them as rental properties for income generation instead of living in them. Smirl (2015, 135) finds that "when NGOs perceived that the intended beneficiaries were abdicating their obligation to repay [in the way that donors and NGOs expected], they felt morally wronged and manipulated and expressed contempt for the moral character of the beneficiaries."

At the end of the interview, Tajee asked if he could speak more about this, admitting that his concern is not just with how African Americans may perceive him but also white people. He spoke about his concern about the "image that is portrayed":

> For example, for an African American to even have that option to look at my image that I'm building and to think that maybe I'm a sell out in a certain way. On the other hand, the Caucasian may look at me and see me as just a charity, yadda yadda yadda. For an African American to look at me and say, "Oh, you're a sellout." But I took an opportunity: Why did your mind bring you to that? And that's where it needs to switch. And in the same sense of the charity "you just taking free money"—but why did it come to this? Why did this person need to create this opportunity for me to take?

In Tajee's questioning "why did it come to this?" I hear him positioning the image of him, as a Black man standing beside a white man—Besh, his benefactor—in a sociohistorical context. That context is a complicated one, with alternative readings depending on the viewer: it is a history that might make a Black viewer see him as "sellout," while a white viewer might see him as "just a charity." In asking viewers about why things are the way they are, Tajee is demanding acknowledgment of long legacies of historical exclusion, systemic racism, and inequality. Those are the reasons why there was a "need to create this opportunity for me to take."

Chanelle, an African American woman and another one of the early winners, echoed Tajee's concerns of appearing to be "a charity case" when standing next to Besh onstage during a previous event. She framed much of our interview in terms of there being "three strikes" against her: being Black, a woman, and young. She described facing racism, sexism, and adultism—the assumption that she lacked the experience needed to succeed in a culinary career due to her youth. Once, after a fundraising event when she stood onstage with her child while Besh gave a speech, she heard a white donor making a comment to another woman that a little boy had been "hanging off" Chanelle while she was onstage "like a monkey." Chanelle, visibly upset at the memory, told me, "See?! That's how these white people view us: as monkeys."

Importantly, Chanelle stressed that the story was not a criticism of Besh personally—that it was not *about* Besh. All interviewees echoed Chanelle's sentiment that the problems they were sharing with me were not a personal attack on Besh, like Jolissa, another winner, who declared, "It isn't personal against him" while discussing criticisms of the foundation. None of the winners I interviewed reported sexual harassment, abuse, or overt racism from Besh directly, even if they had experienced it in other BRG contexts as part of their internships (see chapter 6). Winners variously reported that he was a source of inspiration, a mentor, or that they did not have much contact with him at all.

It is intentional that beneficiaries are present and highly visible at donor events. The awards ceremony used to be held at a local BRG restaurant and was smaller and media focused, but the switch to the crawfish boil at Besh's home was designed with donors in mind. Ruth explained: "As more people are donating, they want to know what's going on. I think it got to this point where so many people were like 'I want to *see* the winners, and I want to be involved and I want to see what I'm donating to.'" Ruth emphasized the word "see" as she spoke—highlighting that donors want to see *who* they are donating to. "Seeing" the recipients promotes a racialized articulation of the need to give for white donors, and as discussed in the vignette from Fêtes Fest that opens chapter 1, this also helps guests to "feel better" about attending exclusive and expensive events.

The Big House

The awards ceremony took place in the backyard of a home built in the architectural style of a plantation owner's residence. The design of Besh's home references planters' estates from the mid-1800s, often called "the big house" by enslaved persons (Vlach 1993, xv). As Martha Colquitt, enslaved on a plantation in Georgia, described in a Federal Writers' Project interview: "Our Big House was one grand fine place. . . . It was all painted white with green blinds and had a big old porch that went all 'round the house" (quoted in Vlach 1993, 10). The largest plantation estates were concentrated in three areas, one of which was the lower Mississippi River valley, which ran from Memphis to New Orleans and encompassed the River Road plantations (figure 4.3). While there were an estimated 46,000 plantations in the US South in 1860, only 2,300 were representative of the large-scale "manorial ideal" of the plantation estate of popular imagination.[6] Vlach (1993, 8) reflects:

> How such an unrepresentative place as the great plantation estate came to dominate the self-perception of the South is a matter about which there has been considerable discussion. . . . Both the farmers who owned only a few slaves and those who owned none were impressed by the lavish plantations inhabited by the gentry, and they looked upon them with a mixture of admiration and envy. The deference with which the few great planters in any county were regarded is related no doubt to the messages that were visually conveyed by the design of their estates, crystal-clear indications of a landlord's dominance that required the submission of black laborer and visitor alike.

The symbolic value and material importance of the plantation estate described by Vlach did not end with the Civil War and emancipation but has taken on new meanings over time. According to historian John C. Cell (discussed by Hale 1998, 93), representations of continuity before and after the Civil War were essential to racial segregation's success as the primary mode of social organization during Reconstruction and beyond. Grace Elizabeth Hale (1998, 85–119) argues that the plantation home was a key representation and symbol that ensured such continuity. Jessica Adams (2007, 54) explains: "During the Lost Cause, the 'white home' became a symbol that connected antebellum racial hierarchies with postbellum society."

Tajee demanded that we ask why there was a "need to create this opportunity for me to take." I hear answers to Tajee's question in the work of both

FIGURE 4.3 The Big House at the Whitney Plantation Museum on River Road, along the Mississippi. Unlike other plantations marketed to tourists, the experiences of enslaved persons in plantation agriculture are the focus of the museum, and the Big House is visited last on tours. Photo by the author.

Woods and Katherine McKittrick. Woods (2017b, 228) writes that powerful antebellum planters accelerated their wealth accumulation by limiting property taxes, which guaranteed a weak state, widespread poverty, and dependency—trends that continue to shape the social and spatial realities for white and Black New Orleanians today. McKittrick (2006, xxii) proposes that "geographies in the diaspora are accentuated by racist paradigms of the past and their ongoing hierarchical patterns." No white attendees or Besh staff mentioned the event location in terms of the history of plantation estates; in fact, I often heard how "perfect" the setting was. In contrast, when I first showed images from the crawfish boil during a public talk at Tulane University, a photo that featured Besh's home was met with gasps of disbelief from the audience. During the question-and-answer portion, a woman of color remarked, "Look at the optics of that house: that tells us everything we need to know."

Jessica Adams (2007, 4–5) writes that "the strange and contradictory possibilities that slavery released into the realm of the normal still shape social spaces." The woman's comment during my talk illustrates Tajee's, Adams's, and McKittrick's contentions: we are in postbellum society, but the continuities of antebellum racial hierarchies, the "ongoing hierarchical patterns" that McKittrick writes of, appear not only as the "optics" of the big house but in the power structures of the ongoing legacies of racial inequality in the United States that stem from enslavement—power structures that construct white "givers" and Black "receivers."

Class Performances: "Those Kinds of People"

Melanie ends the ceremony by announcing a live auction led by a chef opening up the newest BRG restaurant in Houston. Melanie encourages the crowd to get out their pocketbooks "to help make sure that we can continue to grow this foundation so that we can support more people like the wonderful recipients behind me." The live auction begins at a bid of $2,500 for a painting of a crawfish by a local artist and a dinner for ten guests at Aarón Sánchez's home.

Live and silent auctions at fundraisers for chef foundations can raise huge amounts of money. The most money ever paid for a single bottle of wine—$350,000—occurred at an Emeril Lagasse Foundation live wine auction a few months later. Previous research on elite fundraising events stresses that auctions are an important component of events that are (seemingly) more informal and casual. Diana Kendall (2002, 68) notes that formal or black-tie events usually benefit institutions that serve wealthy individuals, such as elite universities, medical schools, or the arts, specifically opera, the symphony orchestra, or ballet; informal/casual events, on the other hand, typically benefit people who are lower class. Kendall (2002, 69) finds that even with casual dress and attempts to bring in middle-class attendees, "there is an expectation that those who attend will spend money on raffle tickets and expensive auction items because it is for a good cause." At the Besh Foundation's Fêtes Fest live auction, a frustrated woman illustrated this expectation, as she stepped away from auction proceedings into the corridor and exclaimed to her friends: "Oh my god! They need to have a middle class auction!" She had repeatedly bid on items but lost out as they doubled or tripled in price.

A local chef who owns several restaurants also expressed fatigue over in-person solicitations happening at high-end chef foundation events:

> These guys were charging $1,000 a ticket. Now they've lowered it to $300 this year—it WAS a $1,000 a ticket. It's funny. So the first year, they actually invited us, "Chef come! It's our first event, we want you to be there." They invited a bunch of chefs in town. . . . But then you get there and it's like, "Ohhhhh, if you want to sponsor" [interrupting himself] There were four of us, so you already spent four grand ($4,000) to go, and then they're like, "Ohhhh, if you sponsor one of the kids for five grand ($5,000) you can—" [interrupting himself again] I'm like, "Whoa, whoa! There's other people in the city. You're trying to take all my money!"

In interviews with the foundation throwing the fundraiser the local chef was referring to, the director said they were now experimenting with offering different types of events at lower ticket prices. Just as I found with Dinners on the Farm at Grow Dat (chapter 5), new chef foundations are constantly shifting their fundraising events to try to find better ways generate revenue.

As the JBF auction hums in the background, I watch hired photographers working their way down a prepared shot list of various combinations of scholarship recipients posing with the chefs. Guests look on from afar while the four winners (two young women, two young men—one is Latino and the others are Black or African American) are congratulated by a small crowd off to the side of the tent. They unfold and put on the crisp white chef coats they had been handed onstage: two rows of buttons run down the middle, and to the right is a Chefs Move! or Sánchez Scholarship Fund logo, and to the left is the winner's name in black cursive.

A few family members are with the recipients, snapping photos and exchanging hugs. I am surprised to see relatives, based on previous events in which families were excluded from attending. Marisol, a Latina in her mid-twenties and a recent MBA graduate, was recruited by Emery Whalen (then the foundation's director) into a leadership position at JBF several years before. At that time, there was an unwritten policy that family or guests of the winners were not invited to the awards ceremony. When she was overseeing the same event two years before, Marisol described her anger at the exclusionary practice during one of the planning meetings:

Emery said, "No, we don't invite the family members." And I was like, what do you mean? This is like when you graduate college, it's a huge thing. You want your family members there. If I'm inviting the mayor of New Orleans to celebrate with these two people, why the hell would I not invite the mother or the father or whoever is important?! And they were like, "No, we just don't." And I was like, "I think we need to, particularly with Marcus, we need to invite the family because this is like his high school graduation." And Emery said, verbatim, "We don't know the type of people they'll bring."

In asking Marcus about the awards ceremony, he said that he had been told he was going to a final interview with Besh for the scholarship. Instead, he walked into a surprise party at a BRG restaurant in the CBD:

> It was a room full of like fifty people, decorated, and Chef Besh and the cofounder Bride, and they're like, "Congratulations, you won the scholarship!" And then everyone else starts clapping and they present us with our Chefs Move! coats with our names on it and it's all official and they hand me a mock-tail because I'm seventeen at that point. And I'm shaking with the glass in my hand while everyone is speaking because everyone is looking at me and I'm just like, "Oh, I won . . ." (Q: How did you feel?) I felt very overwhelmed. I could not speak. My face went like flat. People were talking to me and it was just going over my head. I don't really remember it.

Marcus was only seventeen at the time he was selected, and he attended this large event with media present without any family or friends in attendance. Marisol remembered being worried about him and his participation in the program in general: "I could see everything that was going on and I just thought of myself when I was seventeen or eighteen and I would not want to be thrown into this machine. I kept in touch with his mom and I tried to bring her in to everything." Marisol attempted to include Marcus's mother, believing that she was aware of the power dynamics at play and therefore could be an additional protective force for the young winner.

Marisol's concerns about age and possible exploitation were echoed by Gaines. Gaines won the scholarship when he was in his early twenties, and I first spoke with him five years later: "I feel like I've matured. . . . I was an idiot back then. But now my entire mind is opened and now I'm more educated on race and gender equality, and more educated about the world. I observe everything now." Gaines told me he feels a need to speak out now, and he is more willing to share feedback with the foundation that might be critical or challenging for them to hear. Gaines also felt it was important to share his concerns with new scholarship winners—as reflected in his intentionally wearing a STAY WOKE shirt at Fêtes Fest.

It took Marisol pushing the point and asking why multiple times for Emery to give a less vague and more direct answer about the policy of winners not being allowed to have guests at the awards ceremony. Marisol stressed the significance of family members being excluded from the awards event and said that Emery's explanation of why revealed distrust in recipients and a deeper racism: "This defines the way they saw these students. They were never equals. They're still 'those kinds of people.'" She said she found Emery's response racist and "gross," and she cites it as one of the many reasons that she resigned after being in her role for less than a year.

The Boil

By late afternoon, the party is bustling. Children in swimsuits splash in and out of the pool, taking turns pushing one another on a giant inflatable duck through the fountain spraying in the middle. Staff in aprons jog swiftly between offstage and onstage, darting in and out of storage areas, replenishing tubs of ice, whisking away bags of rubbish. A young girl, blond and barefoot on the lush green lawn, scoops cherry red ice from a sugary snowball in a Styrofoam cup. A man, likely her father, stands above her, watching, hands on his hips, wearing leather loafers, maroon shorts, a crisp blue button-down shirt, a blue ball cap and shades. Far from the house along the woods, a middle-aged white couple lounges on slatted wooden chairs next to a slab fire pit. They quietly smoke cigarettes and drink cocktails, looking out over the crowd (figure 4.4).

Ruth keeps insisting that I should "take a break and have some fun," so I decide to join the guests hunched over the long communal tables teeming with piles of bright red crawfish (figure 4.5). Crawfish boils—group gatherings to eat "mudbugs"—occur frequently across South Louisiana at this time of year, when the tiny crustaceans are first coming into season (Gutierrez 1992). The tradition is Cajun, but now transcends many race and class lines in the region.[7] At today's boil, though, the guests are almost entirely white, and the ingredients have a gourmet flair. Crawfish are traditionally accompanied by boiled "fixings"—typically sausage, corn, and potatoes. This boil prominently features asparagus and sweet potatoes, unusual fixings alongside the humble crawfish.

FIGURE 4.4 A middle-aged white couple on slatted wooden chairs next to a slab fire pit, smoking cigarettes and drinking cocktails, while the winners try on their new white chef coats and are photographed in the background. Photo by the author.

Sliding into the line of eaters, I find that it is fairly easy to spot tourists: while locals snap off crawfish tails, suck the heads, and pull out the tender tail meat with their teeth in a series of deft movements, others seem to be struggling and often ask for help and advice. In South Louisiana, this insider–outsider distinction based on the skill necessary to eat crawfish is considered a marker of cultural and ethnic boundaries (Gutierrez 1992, 103). Alternatively, boils can be an important ritual of inclusion, in which newcomers across race and class lines are welcomed to share the boil and are proudly taught how to eat crawfish with local knowledge known as "Cajun know-how" (Gutierrez 1992, 103).

I chat with the eaters around me. I wave to three or four alumni (former scholarship winners) that I have been getting to know through interviews. They are some of the only people of color present, which is strange for a crawfish boil. Not only is New Orleans majority African American, but it is also a city with long-established Black middle and upper classes and philanthropic

FIGURE 4.5 Guests lined up at long tables to enjoy iced beers and crawfish, with asparagus and sweet potatoes as fixings. Photo by the author.

community. Other research has found that when fundraising events are held by white-led organizations, they are likely to be attended primarily by white guests (Kendall 2002, 57–58). The working-class people and people of color who are present are most likely to be servers and cleaners (Kendall 2002, 57–58). The wealthy white crowd was cultivated further by the event's focus on attracting tourist attendees (rather than locals) and by Slidell being the location, a majority-white suburb.

I meet a reporter from *Garden & Gun* magazine, one of the event's sponsors. The man standing opposite me works for a coffee company in Chicago, and he has been based at BRG restaurant Willa Jean this week, conducting some kind of product testing and promotion. His wife flew into town to join him today, and she echoes a sentiment that I have heard more than a dozen times: that it's a perfect day. No one mentions the foundation unless I prompt them, and no one knew in advance that Chefs Move! winners would be announced today. I say hello to Kristin, whom I had interviewed recently, the affable director of the new Link Stryjewski Foundation, started in 2015 by chefs Donald Link and Stephen Stryjewski. I knew Kristin before starting my research through her previous work with local farmers. In interviews with her and other directors of chef foundations, I was told that everyone working at chef foundations makes an attempt to get along, even though there is obviously competition. One director said, "It's nice because we are all relatively new in our positions," reflecting how recently most of the entities have emerged.

Gender, Generosity, and "Foundations"

Guests told me at the boil and in follow-up interviews that they found John Besh to be "generous." Guests were paying $130 a ticket to attend, and I don't believe that Besh did any of the cooking or serving that day himself; instead, staff from the BRG undertook the majority of the labor. This might be surprising considering his chef status, but it also fits within more standard models of elite fundraising events in which the majority of physical labor is undertaken by working-class people, predominately people of color (Kendall 2002, 57). Judging by the list of event sponsors, the crawfish boil might have been administered by a separate company entirely. Considering these factors, I aim to better understand Besh's association with generosity.

Besh has a ready smile and a friendly, approachable demeanor. Deborah, a donor, told me that when she met Besh and Sánchez, she was surprised that celebrities would be so friendly, and that she could tell the chefs "genuinely" wanted to connect with them: "I didn't get this feeling that it was a celebrity stop by—I didn't get that feeling at all. It was the real thing." Besh is also heavily associated with the foundation that bears his name, which implies that he is a philanthropist, giving away at least a portion of his wealth through the foundation. This sense of generosity is also cultivated in gendered ways related to domestic space. Besh ended his speech by calling out to his wife Jenifer in the crowd and thanking her: "Jen, thank you, baby, for putting up with me and especially the Mexican [referring to Aarón Sánchez; crowd laughed] and letting me invite 350 of my closest friends to join us. Jenifer and I welcome you here." Besh welcomed guests and emphasized that his goal was to share his domestic space with his "closest friends."

Harris and Giuffre (2015, 20) trace how culinary spaces are gendered, citing a strong public–private divide in which men who cook inhabit public spaces and engage in paid labor, and women who cook inhabit private spaces, undertaking labor that is largely unpaid (see also DeVault 1991). They find that "men and women cooks operate in distinct venues (restaurants vs. homes), with different levels of skills (professional vs. amateur), and with very dissimilar goals in mind (expression of creativity vs. caring for the family)," which upholds the separation of men as professional chefs and women as amateur cooks (Harris and Giuffre 2015, 27). The stakes of maintaining these divides for male chefs are high, as the higher percentage of women in a profession, the lower the pay (Harris and Giuffre 2015, 8).

Tracing the roots of "southern hospitality," Anthony Szczesiul (2017, 169) argues that hospitality rituals were strategically developed in the antebellum period by the planter class. Hospitality as an ethos and set of practices was cultivated by the elite as a way to support their continued mobilization of social and cultural capital post-emancipation, "a reproductive and legitimating tactic that enhanced and extended their own power and influence." As Szczesiul (2017, 170) explains:

> The southern hospitality myth helped legitimate white supremacy and privilege long after slavery, helped shape American cultural memory of the slaveholding class in a laudatory way, and provided future generations of white southerners with an effective branding strategy for some of the modern South's most important economic endeavors. At the same time, modern iterations of the southern hospitality myth inevitably erase the fact that it was the slave's degradation and labor that paid for the master's hospitality. But these contemporary iterations of southern hospitality cannot be entirely separated from the past of slavery, for they achieve their recognizable meanings only within the framework of this long history of repetition of citation.

Historically, hospitality has been a productive enterprise, and it continues to be. John Besh's hospitality at his plantation-style home is evidence of how "material spaces and places underpin shifting and uneven (racial, sexual, economic) social relations" (McKittrick 2006, xiii).

At the fundraiser, the emphasis was on hospitality rather than haute cuisine. This aligns with Besh's larger branding efforts, which shifted over time—from his association with fine dining at Restaurant August to being a "family man" on television. His 2011 cookbook was titled *My Family Table: A Passionate Plea for Home Cooking*, and his TV show on PBS, *John Besh's Family Table*, was filmed in his domestic kitchen.[8] Despite the fancy fixings, hosting a crawfish boil, which is eaten communally, further emphasized that the event was about hospitality and relationships, not gourmand excellence.

One aspect of what guests report experiencing as "generosity" was Besh's crossing of stereotypical and gendered culinary boundaries. Women's presence in domestic kitchens in food preparation is so expected and ordinary that it is considered "invisible labor" (Harris and Giuffre 2015, 20). But for men, occupying these roles and spaces is exceptional and conceivably helps to make their presence feel generous rather than expected. Although it was not consciously acknowledged as such, part of what guests positively responded to was a sense that Besh "gave up" some of his masculinity by being warm and inviting others into his private sphere; crossing such boundaries can be perceived as a generous act.

Simultaneously, Besh was able to retain or establish masculinity in several ways. First, serving meat and having it cooked and prepared outside are both key ways in which men's masculinity in the United States is asserted within the highly feminized realm of food being cooked "at home" (Nath 2011; Lax and Mertig 2020; Sobal 2005). The process of cooking and serving crawfish is also a traditionally male role in the region (Gutierrez 1992, 89, 98). Crawfish are brought to the site of the boil alive and then are killed through the boiling process, which has masculine cachet. Additionally, Besh's public declaration of love for his wife emphasized his heterosexuality and was in line with branding strategies that position him as a loving husband and father—appropriate gender roles for a white Catholic man in southern Louisiana. By thanking his wife for "allowing" him to host the boil, he reestablished that this private domestic space is her domain, not his—he is a bit of a guest here as well.

This characterization—and brand—of Besh as a "Christian family man" was dominant at the fundraiser but was challenged soon after as allegations of sexual harassment became public. During the satirical and often lewd Krewe du Vieux parade in 2018, at least four John Besh–themed floats rolled down Frenchman Street. Besh was the target of both humor and ire in floats such as "Predators"—a riff on the film series (figure 4.6). Tyrannosaurus rex

FIGURE 4.6 A Krewe du Vieux Carnival float names John Besh, here as a dinosaur wearing a white chef's coat, a "Predator" in the wake of the #MeToo movement. Photo by the author.

dinosaurs in a cage were labeled with the names of various celebrities that had recently been accused of sexual harassment or assault as part of the #MeToo movement. One "predator" had the name John Besh in cursive script on a white chef's coat, in the same style as the coats that the Chefs Move! winners were presented with at the fundraiser.

I argue that there is another aspect of generosity circulating in chef philanthropy, one that is invoked by the use of the word "foundation." Philanthropic consultant Courtney Harvey (personal communication,

2016) has noticed a national increase in loose usage of the term, and my findings indicate that this trend is particularly pronounced in chef-based initiatives in New Orleans. Harvey is unsure of why this trend is developing. There are several possible explanations for the use of the term "foundation" even though these are non-endowed organizations that are reliant on fundraising. In future chapters I show how knowledges and practices circulate among local chef foundations and how they influence one another. For several years as it was being developed, chef Alon Shaya's project was called the Shaya/Barnett Initiative, but in 2018 it made the switch to "Foundation." As many of these foundations are directly linked to the BRG, replication is likely a reason use of the word has become so prevalent. It is possible that there is a misunderstanding about the term and what it designates. Regardless of whether or not it is intentional, use of the term "foundation" does two things: it suggests that the chefs hold significant wealth, and it signifies that they (and their restaurants) are generous entities who are sharing the wealth of their success.

Harris and Giuffre (2015, 89) contend that "being a chef is not a high-earning career. Unlike the multimillionaire chefs who are presented on television, in the real world, chefs often work for not that much money." A leader from the James Beard Foundation who advises chefs on their activism and philanthropy agrees, saying that chefs organizations usually have to fundraise, because even successful restaurants run on tight margins with modest returns. Nationally, chefs and head cooks had a median annual wage of $45,950 in 2017 (US Bureau of Labor Statistics 2017a). In New Orleans, the annual mean wage of chefs and head cooks was $43,710 in 2017 (US Bureau of Labor Statistics 2017b). Chefs and head cooks are defined by the Bureau of Labor Statistics according to these responsibilities: "Chefs and head cooks oversee the daily food preparation at restaurants and other places where food is served. They direct kitchen staff and handle any food-related concerns" (2017b). Earnings are higher for chefs who hold executive management positions in their restaurants or are chef-owners, although owners may hold significant debt. Thus, regardless of a chef's actual wealth, starting a foundation positions a chef socially as being both wealthy and generous. Donor Rhonda said that Besh "may be selling more cookbooks [as a result of his philanthropy], but I think he was going to sell cookbooks anyways. I think the reason he can do this is because he's already at that level." As Marisol said, "I think philanthropy is a very chic way of saying 'I've made it.'"

Donor Experience

As the festivities draw to a close late in the day, dozens of guests gather at the circle drive as they wait for the shuttle buses to return. There is a line of people who want to purchase T-shirts before they depart, and their slurred speech and difficulty locating wallets indicate that the alcohol has been flowing freely all afternoon. In all, we sold between $700 and $900 worth of Besh Foundation T-shirts. I am honestly shocked, as I have done this task for Grow Dat dozens of times but rarely sold more than a few. In addition to tickets and the auction, selling T-shirts appeared to be another mechanism to capitalize on consumption and consumer spending. Several people tell me that the shirt will be given as a souvenir to friends or family back home, or that it will serve as a personal memento of a wonderful day. It leaves me wondering what work the shirts will do: Will they serve as a marker of proximity to fame? Perhaps it is more socially acceptable to proclaim or boast about associating with a celebrity due to the presence of the word "foundation," which signals altruistic intent. Do buyers feel a sense of altruism or activism that they are "doing good" by shopping?

While they're waiting for the bus, I strike up a few conversations and learn that some guests have traveled from far across the country. Deborah, whom I mentioned earlier, is in her late sixties, and she came with her daughter Sarah from outside Cleveland, Ohio, to attend the event. Deborah is warm and friendly, and she tells me that they are a "foodie family" who love watching Besh's television shows. Sarah knew that Besh had recently had a birthday, and she brought him a Cleveland T-shirt as a gift. Besh and Sánchez came to the table where they were eating crawfish, and Sarah gave him the shirt. The whole interaction went "swimmingly" and left Deborah "starstruck": "They were there really to be with the people. That's what I liked so much, that's the feeling I got. That they were there to really be with that group of people. They were focused, they got how important it was for everybody to be there together."

While Deborah's experience centers on her short but direct interaction with this celebrity chef, these kinds of encounters are rare. Chef foundations such as Besh's appear widely in the public realm, and activities seem approachable and transparent through friendly public personas, the medium of television, and an active social media presence. However, as Robert J. Thomas (1993, 81) points out regarding the study of elites, "Visibility is not the same as accessibility." In trying to study chef Jamie Oliver's foundation in London, my phone calls and emails outlining my research interests were not returned. I emailed my professional network of food NGOs and restaurants to see if anyone had connections to the foundation, and I even reached out to a few weak leads through LinkedIn—I never heard back from anyone. After months of dead ends, I went to Oliver's Fifteen, a workplace-training restaurant, and struck up a conversation with the bartender. Eventually I was able to speak with a staff person at the foundation. Access for researchers needs to be considered, as more celebratory analysis regarding the increasing presence of the private sector in aid and social provisioning claims that philanthropists are more responsive and democratic than governmental institutions.

Deborah found out about the boil through an advertisement in *Garden & Gun*. She considered purchasing a full vacation package offered by Omni Hotels but decided instead to buy the $130 tickets individually through Johnny + Friends online and then book her own accommodations. She estimates that hotel and airfare cost more than $1,000. She questioned whether that money should have gone directly to the foundation instead: "I mean, is that money better spent donated to the foundation? Let's say, I had a ball! I went for a good time—I had a great time. It was worth it to me. But as far as a big monetary donation to the foundation that day—we didn't make one."

We speak several times over the next six months about her experience that day. Later on, our conversations shifted to her sense of betrayal upon learning about Besh's predatory behavior. She told me that her daughter said it was naive not to know "that kind of thing happens all the time" in the restaurant industry, but they were both surprised that Besh specifically would be a perpetrator: "I could see it with other chefs, but not Besh!" Closer to the time of the boil, though, our follow-up conversations centered on the magic she felt: "I would say I belonged there. And though I didn't know a soul and had never been there, I felt from the beginning of getting off the shuttle and walking into that backyard that, 'Yeah, I belong here.' It just felt right." I asked Deborah what felt right or what was done to make her feel so comfortable:

Well, first of all that setting in the yard! Take me out to a great backyard any day and my blood pressure is just like normal, my breathing
is wonderful, there's just no stress. I didn't even feel uncomfortable
laying my purse down at a table and not knowing who else was sitting
there. It was just very comfortable. Plus the bottles of that vodka, what
was the name of that vodka, like Fat Cat? (Me: Cathead?) Yes, that's it,
Cathead, you're right. So that was sort of the signal that you were there

to relax . . . you were just welcomed and . . . made to feel like you were part of this group.

The ease and welcomeness that Deborah describes signals that the event was designed for her and for donors like her. Chefs Move! winners, in contrast, often expressed discomfort with the awards ceremony, and as stated previously, their families and friends were excluded from attending events. Ruth's explanation that the boil was developed because people "wanted to see the winners" further underscores this point. Other research finds that humanitarian interventions "tend to reflect the desires of the donor, not the recipient" (Smirl, 2015, 169; discusses housing and Brad Pitt's Make It Right project in New Orleans).

Is this an awards ceremony or a fundraiser or something else? If you are a guest or donor, it is a chance to meet John Besh and enjoy a delicious crawfish boil. If you are a staff member of the foundation, it is both an awards ceremony and a fundraising opportunity. If you are the former director Marisol, it is one of the reasons that you quit your job. If you are a new Chefs Move! winner or an alumnus, it is an awards ceremony, a networking opportunity, and part of an ongoing association with an organization that holds the potential to both provide access to resources and reinscribe racist histories. Thus, the boil was not an event *for* the winners.

I further argue that it was not an event *about* the winners. I did not meet any guests who knew that there would be an awards ceremony, and in subsequent interviews, donors expressed minimal knowledge about the Besh Foundation. As Smirl (2015, 136) describes: "To present someone with a gift is to go through a process by which the giver determines what the recipient needs and wants, and, in doing so, must formulate an image or idea of what constitutes the 'other.'" Donors may have only begun to understand themselves as such (as donors) after attending the event. Then, in formulating the image or imaginary of recipients, donors often made assumptions about the class backgrounds of winners, using terms like "poverty" to describe them. While some winners come from poor and working-class backgrounds, not all do. Unlike the earliest winners, several of the recent beneficiaries were upper middle class and had attended elite and expensive private schools. This was a topic of debate among former winners on the foundation's Alumni Council when they were involved in the selection process: Should applicants who have financial need be prioritized? Despite alumni protests, foundation staff stressed to me that the award is based on talent and merit, not need.

Conclusion: Business-Based Knowledge and Expertise

For a more traditional nonprofit, throwing a huge event is outside their expertise and budget, and fundraisers are unlikely to resemble their day-to-day service provisioning or programming. A few months after attending the crawfish boil, I served as a volunteer at a Dinner on the Farm, one of a Grow Dat's new strategies to increase earned income, which I discuss in chapter 5. My field notes from that night are filled with descriptions of the stark contrast between the smooth operation of the chef foundation's team (from the Link Restaurant Group) and Grow Dat's bumbling attempts—including my own—to pretend that we knew what we were doing. We spent more than an hour stringing up (and breaking) lights over the dining tables, only to realize they had been hung backwards. While pouring glasses of an expensive wine I couldn't pronounce, I mentally willed my arm to stop shaking—it did not. While I frantically took notes during the rapid description of the food we'd be serving (duck confit with local muscadines), the staff from the Link Restaurant Group appeared to be somewhat bored and barely paying attention.

Chef foundations tap into practices of hospitality and draw on industry knowledge in ways that deeply align with their for-profit work and daily operations—the "how" of this kind of philanthropy is both imagined and enacted within business-based practices and procedures (see Moeller 2018 and A. Roberts 2015 for related findings from the context of the Nike Foundation's Girl Effect). In corporate social responsibility efforts, there is a push for greater alignment between a business's standard operations and its philanthropy (Amelia Brandt, personal communication, 2017). Such initiatives aim to create continuity between a business's for-profit imperative and its philanthropic work, following a logic that businesses should "do what they know best" in all areas of engagement. This push for continuity is commonly conceptualized in terms of the intervention: that businesses should target areas of need that are closely aligned with their work. Chefs show this kind of alignment, intervening on broad food issues like food policy, and even on very specific industry issues, like culinary job training. My research in New Orleans shows that chefs are aligning their businesses and philanthropic efforts not only in what they do but also in how they do it.

Selling tickets to raise money for a cause is not a new strategy, as traditional NGOs in the United States have used special events like annual galas for years. However, aspects of this emerging model are unique or are at least emphasized in instances of chef philanthropy. Chefs use restaurant resources in tangible ways regarding staffing, infrastructure, and products, and draw on the restaurant industry's knowledge and experience. The director of the Lagasse Foundation described its events in this manner: "The way we do stuff is off the charts. These are food and wine events at the highest degree. When you come to our events you don't get a ten dollar bottle of wine, it's a two hundred dollar bottle of wine that you're drinkin'—I mean, boutique. It's awesome." He stresses the foundation's excellence in how it manages its events and also in the quality of its provisioning. At the Besh crawfish boil, one of the drink stations by the pool showcased a new Stumptown iced coffee drink. The attendant enthusiastically told me about the product and shared a detailed narrative about its development. I met several other people throughout the day who were affiliated with food and beverage brands: such events also become marketing opportunities to showcase product lines.

While the privatization of disaster aid in New Orleans and elsewhere has been noted by concerned scholars, there is insufficient ethnographic research on the topic, particularly that which is attentive to donor and beneficiary experiences within philanthropic configurations. In-depth consideration of chef-led philanthropy is salient and urgent, as private organizations operate largely without external oversight or systems of accountability. Foodscape projects, and the fundraising that enables them, must consider the land and legacies of oppression—particularly settler-colonial expansion and enslavement—that continue to shape the social realities of the gift.

CHAPTER FIVE

The History of the Land
Grow Dat Youth Farm and Caring Chefs

This chapter concerns raising money and doing "good work for good food" in foodscapes. Around 2015, my former organization Grow Dat Youth Farm began partnering with celebrity chefs and their foundations to raise money. In the first half of this chapter, I share my findings about this new initiative, Dinners on the Farm (also called Farm Dinners). Illustrative of attempts by nongovernmental organizations (NGOs) to develop partnerships and associate with celebrity humanitarians, Grow Dat's Dinners on the Farm aimed to utilize the culinary capital held by celebrity chefs to generate market-based revenue for the nonprofit. I discuss Grow Dat's History of the Land, a workshop and pedagogical lens, in relation to Farm Dinners and show how place-based histories have influenced my analytical perspective. As I found at the John Besh Foundation (JBF) crawfish boil fundraiser, raising money cannot be separated from the history of the land. Who belongs at the farm? What does it mean to have elite white adults purchase expensive tickets and be served a meal in a diverse youth-focused space? How are old narratives reproduced, edited, and resisted at Farm Dinners? To assist in answering these questions, I provide a partial history of the land in City Park where Grow Dat is located. Legacies of exploitation, exclusion, freedom, and transformation are threaded through the land's history and its development into a youth farm today. I continue to develop the argument that we must carefully consider place, history, and power in order to understand the gift and its manifestations in foodscapes.

In the second half of the chapter, I broaden my scope to study chefs who do not have foundations. I work to understand how other chefs (some of whom self-identify as cooks) attempt to "do good" in foodscapes. I begin with an introduction to Roseline at the Village, a chef who has also partnered with Grow Dat, and I show how her engagement at the farm and in foodscapes reflects a development agenda (Woods 2017a) that differs from that of elite chef humanitarians. I next discuss findings from interviews with elite chefs who have decided not to start foundations and with women who left careers as professional chefs to work for community organizations. The chapter ends by discussing the pressure on chefs to engage in charitable causes (or the expectation that they will) and ties this demand to professionalization and formalization trends in which chefs start their own foundations and NGOs. Themes of fundraising and marketing run throughout the chapter.

Part I: Dinner on the Farm

> I think one of the biggest things about those dinners is that beautiful setting and the experience. Pinterest and Instagram have really branded that sort of outdoor, pretty lights, fresh food, the table cloth on the lawn thing with chefs—to me, that is hot. Everyone wants that photo. They want the experience. They want the photo that documents the experience.
> —CLAUDIA, Farm Dinner guest

A marketing email about Grow Dat's Dinner on the Farm advertised: "Each dinner will begin with a half hour of cocktails and passed hors d'oeuvres followed by a farm tour focusing on our program, growing practices, and the stunning ecology of our growing site. After the farm tour, guests will sit down to a beautiful, locally focused meal paired with wine" (email, February 2018). Claudia's comments about the appeal of such an "Instagrammable" event reflects how culinary culture has become part of an (inter)active mediascape in which consumers "double as media makers": as co-creators or prosumers (Bush 2019, 16). To produce the dinners, a chef donates their time to prepare a meal that features vegetables, fruits, and herbs that were grown on-site as part of Grow Dat's youth leadership program. Guests sit outside at long tables that flank the bayou, under lights strung from tall metal poles and branches from Granny Oak, a towering live oak tree estimated to be more than 300 years old (figure 5.1). During a dinner with the Link Stryjewski Foundation, the chef's team constructed an open grill and filled it with meat. Grow Dat staff marveled at an alligator, a rare sighting at the busy farm, lurking near the smoking grill on the bank of the bayou.

Dinner on the Farm was launched in 2015 as a method of generating revenue in which "guests" purchase tickets to a series of fall and spring dinners. The fact that attendees are conceived of as "guests" rather than "donors" illustrates how this funding strategy is different from standard nonprofit fundraising: instead of being a donor making a charitable contribution to Grow Dat, being a guest signifies hospitality, mimicking language from the restau-

FIGURE 5.1 Grow Dat staff and volunteers set up lights, rented tables, and white linens for Dinner on the Farm along the bayou, under Granny Oak. Photo by the author.

rant industry. As with restaurants, being a guest requires the purchase of a meal and an experience. Calling attendees "guests" reveals other complexities about the dinners, which I discuss further throughout this section. Purchasing a Farm Dinner ticket also supports Grow Dat, but in a less direct way than making a donation, and the motivation to attend the dinner (the presence of a celebrity chef) also differs. Calls to "Vote with Your Fork," as championed by Michael Pollan (2006), combined with a national interest in urban agriculture (as discussed in chapter 3), created a promising environment for such dinners to capitalize on causumer spending trends and boost the organization financially. The dinners were launched and managed by Dawn, who oversaw Grow Dat's social enterprise initiatives. Dawn previously worked for a national for-profit company that produces farm-to-table meals at farms across the country, and she was brought on for her expertise in executing such events.

Since its inception in 2011, Grow Dat aimed to have a portion of its operating budget funded by earned revenue, rather than by grants or donations exclusively. Each year since, approximately 12 to 20 percent of the organization's revenue has been earned income, primarily from produce sales. The farm's CSA (community-supported agriculture) box scheme has been particularly strong as a source of revenue. Different initiatives over the years have tried to increase the organization's earned revenue, including consulting, field trips for schools, cooking demonstrations, and yoga classes. Farm Dinners were devised to be part of this earned-income stream.

I served as a volunteer server at several Farm Dinners while conducting participant observation, and I interviewed guests and staff members from both the chef foundations and Grow Dat. In interviews with attendees, questions about the featured chefs received more time and attention than other questions. Guests focused on telling me about their personal interactions with the chef. For example, "I had seen Donald Link several times at his restaurants and had met him through my son. When I saw him [at the Farm Dinner], he got up from his table to come over and say hello—he's just that type of guy, just like a regular person!" In contrast, Grow Dat staff described their interactions with Farm Dinner chefs as limited, and overall they seemed to have minimal interest in celebrity chefs.

Luis, the sole Farm Dinner chef who was a person of color (POC), was the only chef that most staff members could reference by name; however, he was known because he had led a workshop during the youth program. When I asked, "Is the celebrity chef important to the Farm Dinner?" a young Black staff member responded: "I don't feel that way. I work here, and the chef is not important to me. But it might be important for a funder. I don't know the chefs, they are not from my community." For him, these chefs (exclusively white other than Luis) were not celebrities that he knew and cared about. They were personally irrelevant, but he knew they might be appealing to "funders," his term to describe guests coming to a dinner. I highlight this to draw attention to how disparate the worlds of Grow Dat and gourmet restaurant culture can be, and to the fact that so-called celebrity chefs are only celebrities to some people: celebrity is shaped by race, class, and location. An African American woman who won the JBF's Chefs Move! scholarship echoed this sentiment, saying with a laugh that she had to google Besh online when she was applying because she had never heard of him.

To launch the first Farm Dinners, Dawn eagerly approached local chef foundations, as they seemed like ideal partners. Chef foundations have dedicated staff that Dawn could coordinate with, and she assumed that they would have funding available to produce the dinners on Grow Dat's behalf.

Dawn also saw potential to cultivate deeper partnerships between chef foundations and Grow Dat: the plan was to establish ongoing and long-term interactions between the institutions outside of the dinners, creating more meaningful relationships that would challenge giver–receiver hierarchies. Such an approach has been successful in other partnerships, as with Tulane service-learning students. Tulane undergraduates spend a school term or more with Grow Dat—they attend workshops led by youth program leaders, are managed by the team in agricultural farm tasks, and are trained in VISIONS anti-oppression curriculum. Grow Dat has been working with VISIONS since 2012, and I have personally been training and facilitating in the model since 2016. VISIONS Inc. is a women- and persons-of-color led nonprofit that was founded in 1984 by three Black women and a white Jewish man. The VISIONS approach is "built on the understanding that change to any system must occur at multiple levels and address multiple variables of difference, including race and ethnicity, gender, class, sexual preference, and others. VISIONS recognized it was not enough to open doors to diversity at the institutional level alone. Instead, one must also address barriers to inclusion at the personal, interpersonal, and cultural levels as well. This approach revealed the attitudes, unconscious biases, and behaviors that prevent people from succeeding in organizations and pointed out what needed to change to make success for everyone a possibility" (www.visions-inc.org /who-we-are.html). Engaging in VISIONS activities with Tulane students is designed to challenge unequal power dynamics implicit in the standard dichotomy between givers and receivers.

As a first step in the new partnership, foundation staff and the affiliated restaurants were invited to a series of agricultural workdays on the farm. The volunteer days fell rather flat, however, and Dawn's plans for a more robust partnership were not further developed. Jesse (they/them), one of the farmers managing the first volunteer day, said the participants from the restaurant left the workday early. Jesse had sensed resistance to undertaking the task: to dig an irrigation ditch, an essential but rather unglamorous job. The volunteers were disappointed that teenagers were not at the farm (they attend school during the day). Jesse said the volunteers used language like "giving back to their community," "teaching children in the city how to farm," "teaching them how to eat healthy"—all of which Jesse took as evidence of a "shallow understanding of what Grow Dat is actually doing, and also that they were only interested in a particular kind of experience." The volunteers held limited conceptions about the nature of their presence on the farm, reflecting stereotypical ideas about what "charity" is or what "giving back" should look like. Grow Dat has hosted hundreds of volunteer groups, and this is not an unusual dynamic. Visitors to the farm need to see themselves as learners rather than experts; without that, partnerships fail to be a more mutual exchange. Despite Grow Dat's attempts to set clear expectations and explain the farm's ethos from the beginning, some groups are disappointed that the farm does not provide them with the "charitable" experience they were expecting.

What was more unique to this attempted partnership was a tension that developed between Grow Dat and chef foundations regarding fundraising: Were dinner guests potential donors for Grow Dat or donors for the chef foundations? Dawn felt uneasy when chef foundations requested the attendance list from the dinners with guests' contact information. Grow Dat had hoped that partnering with foundations would create a more robust relationship between the institutions. Instead, Dinner on the Farm became a shaky negotiation between a nonprofit organization trying to earn money and chef foundations that were also trying to earn money. Dawn shifted to working primarily with independent chefs rather than foundations, as the model made more sense with chefs who do not have fundraising needs for their own NGOs. In my findings, however, independent chefs are more likely to be white women and chefs of color (both men and women) who operate smaller businesses and thus often lack the resources necessary to undertake charitable events like the Farm Dinners (see later discussion under "There's No School for This").

Earned Revenue and Market-Based Fundraising

As a fundraising strategy, the dinners have had mixed results. Guests I interviewed praised the experience, like Claudia, quoted at the opening of this section. Claudia, who works for the mayor's office, stressed that "everyone" desires the outdoor "branded" experience of the dinner. Other guests, such as the woman I sat next to at the Shaya Farm Dinner mentioned earlier, tied their ticket purchase directly to causumerism, fulfilling a desire to "give gifts that are doing good." However, the popularity of the dinners varied: some sold out, while others did not. Even with volunteers, sponsors underwriting alcohol and rented equipment, and chefs/restaurants donating labor, the expenses required to orchestrate each dinner were significant. Funds raised above the cost of the dinner have sometimes been minimal. Dawn expressed concern that the market would be exhausted at some point in the near future, and that there is a limit to how many tickets could be sold in New Orleans.

Over the course of my fieldwork, the financial team at Grow Dat came to see Farm Dinners as an opportunity for cultivating donors rather than earning revenue. Grow Dat's strategy changed over time: the primary goal of the dinners shifted from generating income to establishing relationships with potential donors. One of the farm's leaders explained his hope that "Farm Dinner guests can be involved and integral to our work beyond the dinner." Despite snowball sampling, networking at dinners, and Dawn sending out emails to all guests on my behalf, I had difficulty securing interviews with attendees. The guests with whom I was able to secure interviews all had previous connections to Grow Dat: a Tulane grant writer who had helped garner funding for the farm, an enthusiastic member of the CSA box scheme, and a woman who had helped design and build the farm's office spaces—she had been given a free ticket from a board member to attend. The fact that I had difficulty connecting with any "new" people who had purchased full-price tickets suggests that Farm Dinner attendance does not create an automatic deepening of an attendee's connection with the farm, as executive leadership had hoped. However, the long-term impact of Farm Dinners has not yet been measured, so the question remains as to whether they harness new donors.

As part of the organization's founding staff team, I participated in planning sessions that determined that earned income should be a component of Grow Dat's funding. This thinking was largely inspired both by a sense of limited resources—that donors and foundations could or would only give so much, particularly as post-Katrina funding sources waned—and by research findings suggesting that organizations risk becoming beholden to the requirements and desires of powerful foundations or individual donors. INCITE! (2007, 232) summarizes the hazards of foundation control and advocates for diversified funding: "Foundations, overall, exert far too much control over organizations and, ultimately, over our movements for social change. Luring social justice activists with the promise of financial support, they also determine the rules of engagement. Meanwhile, we become trapped in the cycle of apply, apply, apply—threatened with proposal rejections or even promised money being pulled if folks do not understand or agree with our vision." It was not the organization's goal to be funded entirely by earned income, but rather for earned income to be part of a diverse portfolio of funding sources. In light of this aspect, Grow Dat has been conceptualized as both a social enterprise and a social entrepreneurship project. Grow Dat's founder Johanna Gilligan won the Urban Innovator Challenge at Tulane University and was nominated "Business Woman of the Year" for a local magazine.

A market-based fundraising approach seems to have fewer strings attached than funding from donors or foundations, but the reality is more complicated. Through participant observation and in multiple interviews with eight staff members, it became clear that significant conflict surrounded Dinners on the Farm. One staff member said the chefs' presence on the farm was representative of a "white, male/masculine, fine dining culture—a bro, fratty, meat-centric culture," which, they argued, is fundamentally antithetical to Grow Dat's approach to *growing* food. Another staff member shared his wish that the farm be funded by the state so that Grow Dat didn't have to fundraise in the first place. He believes "voting with your fork" promotes an illusion that "we can just shop our way out of the problems of capitalism." Simultaneously, however, he believes that there *are* ethical implications to how we spend our money, "that shopping at Walmart is not politically neutral." Thus, he stressed that what he thinks is important is making sure that shopping—causumerism—is not the primary solution. As a leader of the youth program, he said he actively invites these kinds of conversations and encourages staff and young people to think critically about the nonprofit industrial complex, capitalism, and social change.[1]

The History of the Land

Fundraising happens within historic and contemporary power dynamics, both spatial and social, and constitutes their continual construction and reconstruction. The history of the land is essential to understanding the spatial and social implications of the Farm Dinners. My analysis is informed by the History of the Land workshop Grow Dat has been developing since the organization's inception. The workshop was first conceived by Jabari Carmichael Brown, with support from Leo Gorman (both Brown and Gorman are also on Grow Dat's founding staff team), and has continued to be developed by program manager Kevin Connell. It is a key lesson in the leadership program's curriculum, and it is now led for student field trips and with adult visitors to the farm as well (figure 5.2). Using popular education methods, the lesson explores the history of the land on which the farm resides, asking questions such as: How have people changed this land? How has that affected the ecosystem? How should the land be used? The lesson plan explains that "understanding how this land has been used in the past can help us understand why it looks the way it does today (soil quality, vegetation, infrastructure), or why things happen the way they do (i.e., flooding during storms). It can also help us think critically about how the land should

FIGURE 5.2 Adults visiting the farm participate in the History of the Land workshop. Here Granny Oak hosts information about some of the Indigenous Nations who lived on and were removed from this land. Photo by the author.

be used in the future" (Brown et al. 2016). In Grow Dat's understanding, the social and the ecological are not separate. I have been involved in ongoing history of the land work with Brown, Connell, and Theo Hilton, and in the next section, I draw on our research together (Brown et al. 2020); Brown, Gorman, and Connell's lesson plans (2016); and historical material about City Park from Jochum, Knight, and University of New Orleans History Department (2019) to situate the history of the land.

The long row of Farm Dinner tables under the twinkling lights along the bayou are set up on land that has a history even older than Granny Oak's. The land was a cypress swamp (figure 5.3), filled with regal bald cypress trees and their attendant gangly "knees"—woody protuberances of debated purpose sticking up above the waterline. The area would flood seasonally with the ebb and flow of the Mississippi River. The Choctaw name for the land is *Bulbancha*, "land of many languages," and as the name signifies, many Indigenous nations lived in the swamps for thousands of years, including the Chitimacha, Acolapissa, Houma, Bayogoula, Washa, Chawasha, Atakapa-Ishak, and the Biloxi. Nearby in southern Louisiana, a small part of the Chitimacha's ancestral land is still held by the tribe, and the region is home to 17,000 members of the Houma Nation today.

By the late 1700s, the Allard Plantation was established on land stolen by white settlers, and the Allard family enslaved people in order to transform the landscape for their use. Enslaved people drained the cypress swamp, usually through hand-dug drainage canals, and cultivated crops for the Allard's financial gain, growing sugarcane (the most common crop in this part of Louisiana), indigo, cotton, corn, and rice. While Allard is the only plantation mentioned in historical materials distributed by City Park, Kalie Ann Dutra from the University of New Orleans's Midlo Center is currently conducting research and finding evidence of multiple plantations within the park—now more than a dozen.

Although often overlooked in historical memory, Black people living close to the land in the US South were—and are—essential to freedom movements. Monica White (2018, 4) argues that Black farmers "fought for the right to participate in the food system as producers and to earn a living wage in agriculture in the face of racially, socially, and politically repressive conditions, using land as a strategy to move toward freedom." Freedom movements have not been limited to those holding the title "farmer," however. In practices of both survival and resistance, enslaved persons foraged, hunted, fished, and raised livestock on the land (M. M. White 2018, 11–14). White draws on Judith Carney and Richard Nicholas Rosomoff's (2009, 122) scholarship, which documents how the earliest arrivals of enslaved Africans faced "the real prospect of starvation" and "in their struggle to stay alive . . . drew deeply upon the agricultural expertise and the crops of their own heritage, while adopting the knowledge systems and plants bequeathed to them by Amerindians." Without the knowledge and practices of enslaved Africans (seeds brought across the Atlantic, agricultural skills

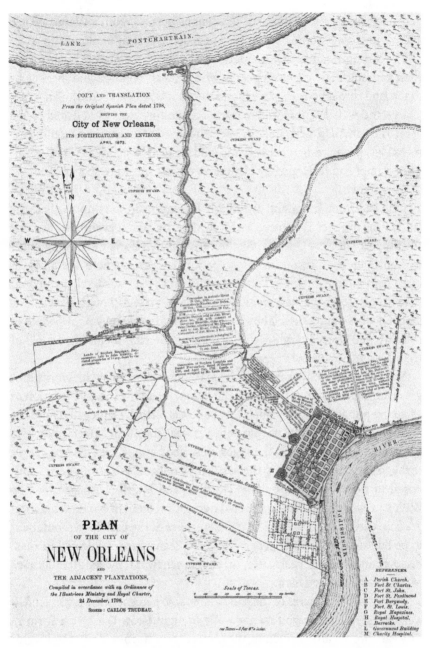

FIGURE 5.3 *Plan of the City of New Orleans*, 1798. The trees (which look like small circles) indicate the prevalence of cypress swamps, including the entire area that is now City Park—approximately the center of the map north to Lake Pontchartrain. Original Spanish plan dated 1798, copy and translation April 1875. Drawn by Alexander Debrunner. Printed by H. Wehrmann, No. 90 Exch. Alley, N.O. Courtesy of Library of Congress Geography and Map Division.

and relationships fostered with Indigenous people), both enslaved people and white settlers would have starved to death in the early colonies.

The cypress swamps that surrounded Allard Plantation were home to maroon communities, enslaved people who escaped bondage and lived close to the land throughout US slavery and the Civil War (Diouf 2014). San Malo, a large and well-documented maroon community, was established in the area. The San Malo cultivated the earth and lived off the swamps, selling cypress logs, produce, handicrafts, and wild game in New Orleans (Hall 2019). The swamps, undeveloped by plantation capitalism, were spaces of refuge and resistance.

John McDonogh bought the Allard Plantation in 1845 and willed the land to the cities of Baltimore and New Orleans, and it eventually became the property of New Orleans. By the early 1900s, efforts were being made to transform the plantation into a park. The bayou where the alligator lurked among the duckweed during the Farm Dinner was likely hand dug, as are the systems of lagoons throughout the park. Although slavery was illegal by this point, such labor was usually undertaken by poor people of color as well as recent white immigrants to the city, including people of Irish descent.

Many development projects in the park were taken up by the Works Progress Administration in the 1930s and 1940s, including the construction of a massive public swimming pool. City Park was formally segregated until the late 1950s, and only white people were allowed. Tom Dent, a Black man who grew up in New Orleans in the 1930s, described biking with his best friend through City Park and being thrown out by police: "We weren't even supposed to ride through the park" (Jochum and Mizell-Nelson 2019). The WPA pool was closed during the civil rights movement to avoid forced integration. City Park donated land at the entrance of the park for a monument to be built to Confederate general P. G. T. Beauregard, dedicated in 1915; just over one hundred years later, the monument was removed after decades of organizing and activism.

By 2005, over 500 acres of the park—almost 40 percent of the park's land—was occupied by four golf courses. We brought Grow Dat Youth Farm to City Park in 2012 after launching the project at Hollygrove Market and Farm. The site negotiated at City Park was seven acres on one of the former golf courses, which had been abandoned since the flooding. Tulane University, Grow Dat's fiscal sponsor at the time, signed a cooperative endeavor agreement with City Park for a lease. Each year the farm pays rent to the park, with in-kind payments representing the bulk of the contribution. Young people of color in leadership positions at the farm are part of a long tradition of Southern Black farmers working the land for collective freedom.

Dinner on the (Farm) Land

Legacies of exploitation, exclusion, and freedom are threaded through the history of the land and its development into what it is now: a youth farm dedicated to inclusion, food justice, and environmental stewardship. Most of the complex dynamics of the Farm Dinners have a spatial dimension, and I imagine that many would look drastically different if the dinners took place off-site—if they were held at the featured chef's restaurant, for example. In chapter 6, I highlight common problems in the restaurant industry, including endemic sexism and the industry's dependence on a racialized, low-wage workforce. Jabari Brown has contended that at the Farm Dinners, chefs and guests bring their previous restaurant experiences onto Grow Dat's land. In these "gourmet culinary imaginaries," wealthy white guests bring with them the practices of racism, sexism, and classism, which are normalized in elite restaurants: white men are "in charge" as chefs, "attractive" white women (conforming to stereotypical gender presentations and beauty standards) are visible as servers and hostesses, and people of color are servers or are made invisible in backrooms and kitchens.

Reinforcing Brown's idea and related to my findings about JBF donors, several Farm Dinner guests told me that they would have liked to have youth present at the dinners, echoing the desire to "see the winners," as discussed at the Besh crawfish boil. One interviewee wished that "more of the participants would have been at the dinner," assuming that some of the Black staff at the dinner were actually youth crew members. Young staff of color were "read" as program participants, echoing an assumption in the white donor imaginary that young people and people of color would be the recipients of such a program, not the program's leaders.

Almost every staff member discussed how drastically the demographics and dynamics of the farm change during the dinners: there are no youth present, and the guests attending appear to be almost exclusively white, wealthy, gender binary, and gender conforming. This is a stark contrast to the inclusivity and multiculturalism that is central to the youth program's ethos. A gender nonconforming farmer and youth educator said it was strange to sit down at the dinner and suddenly "feel out of place" at their workplace—an environment where they normally feel they can be themselves. Staff attire at the dinners became a topic of serious reflection: What exactly did it mean to "look nice" for the Farm Dinners? Whose definition of "nice" was being used? Staff discussed how the concept is coded by race, class, and gender, and debated how to dress and show up as themselves in the strange white, heteronormative space the dinners created. As one leader summarized: "The Farm Dinner is not cheap and the audience is exclusive." The demographics of the dinners—the same demographics that are supposed to bring in financial resources—significantly altered a space that is youth-centric and committed to diversity and inclusion.

At one of the first dinners, Chris, a young Black staff member, was seated at a table with an older white married couple. Over the course of the evening, the man implied that Chris had been flirting with his wife. Chris recalled:

> She was sitting across from me and we were having an in-depth conversation. He didn't directly say "You're hitting on my wife" but he was emphasizing "This my wife! We're married!" all of these subtle hints. I guess I might have been rubbing off on him in the wrong way, but that was not my intention at all. I was just involving myself in dialogue with everyone at my table. . . . I went to the bathroom, and we met at the bathroom. He was telling me more about what he does, that he partially owns a restaurant. He said, "My wife's on the [park's] Board, *you* were talking to her earlier—ha ha ha," that kind of thing. I'm like, "Oh, okay, that's fine" [Chris mimics moving away from the man, pushing his chest and shoulders backward, putting his hands palm out in front of his lower chest]. Nothing overly aggressive. More like subtle, very subtle. It was one of those moments when you're like, "Did I read that wrong just now?"

Chris was surprised by the accusation: "It was funny to me! Because I'm like nineteen and this guy really thinks that his thirty-seven- or like forty-year-old wife wants me right now?! That's so crazy. So it was just funny to me that he would even believe that that was possible."

Chris said he had been trying to do his job as a fundraiser for the organization by speaking about the farm and "involving myself in dialogue with everyone at the table." However, his engagement was perceived in line with old racist tropes. In our interview, we spoke about historical patterns in which white men have positioned Black men as threatening to white women. Accusations, such as the one suggested by the man at Chris's table, are loaded. The brutal lynching of young Emmett Till came sharply and painfully into my mind while Chris was describing what happened. Chris spoke about the concept of "safety" at length, and told me that he knows when he is safe and unsafe. He distinguished this as different from how white men experience feeling uncomfortable: "Historically, white men feel that when they are uncomfortable, that there is like the same reaction as if a person of color is uncomfortable—where they want to pull out of the situation. But when it's white men or white people in general, [that's] just the feeling of being uncomfortable—versus like this gut feeling, or knowing that this situation is about to get out of hand [for a person of color]."

Chris believed that the situation was satisfactorily resolved—the couple said goodbye to him as they were leaving: "I didn't feel any hard feelings. I just thought it was a really awkward, a really funny moment." However, he decided that it was important to share the incident during the debrief session about the dinners with other staff. He wanted to discuss it and try to understand it with the team, and to see if there was a way to prevent it from happening again. In interviews, other staff stressed that this was considered a serious incident of racism. In response, it was decided that staff members would be seated together in pairs, creating a support system for those attending. Chris's experience also helped settle an ongoing debate whether or not youth from the program should attend the dinners. Some staff argued that it would be a beneficial youth development experience, an opportunity for youth to practice public speaking and to learn about nonprofit fundraising. Chris's experience, however, combined with the presence of alcohol around minors, settled the debate that youth should not attend.[2]

Concerns about whiteness and exclusivity also inspired staff to develop strategic interventions for the Farm Dinners. Guests are likely unaware of— or uncritical of—the fact that their meal is happening on land of Indigenous erasure, former plantations, and a segregated park. Could the dinners be an opportunity to educate wealthy white adults about this history? Could the dinners better align with Grow Dat's methods and mission, with guests seeing youth leadership and environmental stewardship on the farm through the lens of the past?

In response, I observed Grow Dat institute a series of workshops between the cocktail hour and the seated meal. Three options were offered to guests: a farm tour about agroecological practices, the History of the Land workshop (figure 5.4), or a discussion about VISIONS' "Guidelines for Effective Cross-Cultural Dialogue." Some staff members were thrilled about this change, seeing potential for more radical education and for building relationships with elite individuals—not necessarily so that they would become donors but so that they might become allies. Others continued to express mild

FIGURE 5.4 Jabari Brown (far right) cofacilitates a History of the Land workshop with Farm Dinner guests before they are seated for the meal. Photo by the author.

annoyance that they had to give time and resources to the Farm Dinners at all. The debates at Grow Dat about Farm Dinners have wider resonance: How do you best redistribute wealth in a society with a long history built on maintaining inequality for capital creation?

Chris didn't have a "gut feeling" that the interaction had crossed the line to become a serious threat. He reasserted several times that "I haven't felt not welcomed because this is *my* space." There is deep historical significance to Chris's assertion "this is *my* space," invoking land-based Black freedom movements and rupturing the white supremacy that has often shaped land tenure in City Park and across the region, supremacy that can be reproduced in situations such as these. Chris saw the couple as guests in his space, which, despite many other power dynamics, was essential to feeling that the situation was physically safe for him. The risk of reinscribing the white supremacist dynamics of restaurants (that elite white diners would be served by working-class women and people of color) and of the land (that it was a sugar plantation, that the park was segregated) feels threatening to staff, but these attempts also never fully succeed, as they are destabilized and rescripted by new realities that configure power differently on the youth farm.

Part II: Knowledge and "Doing Good" in Foodscapes

In this section I broaden my scope to consider other foodscape interventions, and I compare the work and perspectives of community organizations and community cooks to that of elite-led culinary philanthropy.[3] I look particularly at elite chefs who have decided *not* to start foundations. In dialogue with my findings on the importance of fundraising in chef philanthropy, my discussion seeks to understand how these chefs fund their charitable activities. The remainder of the chapter aims to determine what knowledges are drawn on in informal and non-elite interventions, and considers how culinary capital operates differently in these contexts. In this section, I continue to respond to Rosalyn Diprose's call to acknowledge *all* givers by paying more attention to community food activists and the charitable work of non-celebrity chefs, who are often designated as "cooks."

At the 2019 Oxford Food Symposium held in England, Roberta Wedge asked, "What's the difference between a cook and a chef?" The audience correctly replied "gender," and Wedge quipped, "about fifty thousand pounds [GBP] a year" (Wedge 2019). This exchange demonstrates the importance of boundaries—both symbolic and material—between chefs and cooks. As mentioned earlier, Harris and Giuffre (2015, 18) argue that boundary work has been essential to raising the status of the chef occupation and that women's exclusion has been key, as the higher the percentage of women there are in a profession, the lower the pay. Men work as professional chefs, while women are primarily cooks, both domestically and in restaurant kitchens.

In interviews, participants variously described themselves as cooks, activists, chef teachers, and chef educators. I found that people sometimes use "cook" politically, as a form of resistance to or rejection of mainstream chef culture. Ayomide is a Black man from West Africa who doesn't use the chef title: "I think 'chef' conjures particular connotations of a certain kind of approach to food and also a pedigree that I don't have. . . . I also don't buy into it, I'm not personally bought into the model of 'chef' as a description for me. Other people, it works for them, but not for me." To him, the title "chef" is a marker of vocational training, credentials, and approach. In his own practice, Ayomide uses food as a vehicle to convene larger conversations about power and oppression, particularly racism, sexism, and nationalism.

Thus, although he frequently cooks food and is considered an accomplished chef in his own right, the title of chef doesn't capture the purpose behind his cooking.

The following exchange with Nikki, a white woman who owns a small Cajun restaurant, illuminates another aspect of what the chef title signifies:

NIKKI: The best restaurant model in the city, of people being paid
    what they're worth in the industry, is Paladar.
ME: What's their story?
NIKKI: Everybody gets paid the same. And everybody splits the tips.
    No matter what role you're in. And who is the chef at Paladar?
ME: I don't know.
NIKKI: Exactly.

Nikki believes that not being focused on a single chef is one of the main elements that makes a restaurant a great place for workers. To Nikki, celebrity chef culture is part of the "old boys' club," a network of white men in positions of power that serves to keep those men in such positions. In our exchange about Paladar, the presence of a known chef—or lack thereof—is indicative of a restaurant's *values*. This is salient in the context of celebrity chef culture: What changes about the culture of a restaurant when a famous chef is, or is not, the focus? I came to see pushback against the chef title as a rejection of the values associated with both celebrity culture and foodie culture.

Welcome to the Village: Community Chefs

Pontchartrain Park is a historic Black middle-class subdivision in northeast New Orleans, created in the 1950s by African American designers during the Jim Crow era. Driving around the golf course and massive live oaks, I pass actor Wendell Pierce's house—evidence of another celebrity humanitarian project. After the flooding, Pierce launched two charitable initiatives, one to open healthy grocery outlets called Sterling Farms, and another to rebuild Pontchartrain Park with eco-friendly and sustainable housing. Even though the housing initiative failed to take flight, he, as promised, moved into the model home, the only structure that was built.

Roseline and Sylvester had invited me to their home in Pontchartrain Park for our interview. Lush elephant ears and purple flowers spill out onto the sidewalk in front of their ranch-style house. The house serves as a de facto community center, with a studio, an art gallery, and an Airbnb.

A variety of handmade jewelry was for sale in the front room, and Roseline teaches vegan cooking classes out of her kitchen. The sound of the screen door swinging open and closed occurs throughout the audio recording of the interview—the house was bustling with activity. A young cook, arms laden with produce, entered the kitchen; a repair team was fixing a bathtub; several children from the neighborhood ran in and out of the foyer. Roseline said naming their home The Village referenced their "village style of living" in community.

When I started interviewing chefs who were community engaged but not famous or did not have a formal foundation, Roseline was the first person I contacted. I met Roseline several years before, when she cooked for a Grow Dat Community Lunch. Community Lunches are held once a week during Grow Dat's summer leadership program. Although they also center around a meal at the farm, I mention them to highlight how they are significantly different from Farm Dinners. Each week, a different chef or cook donates their time (Grow Dat provides the ingredients) and partners with a crew of teenagers on the farm to cook a meal together. The crew invites community members to attend, and the youth lead a facilitated discussion on food justice while everyone eats the free lunch together. For their Community Lunch, Roseline and several of her young chef apprentices cooked and served a vegan meal with one of the youth crews. At the end of the meal, crew members asked for photos with Roseline and her team, urging them to come back to the farm again. Meeting Roseline again in The Village's living room for our interview, Roseline spoke slowly and took breaks to breathe oxygen, a treatment for what she called her "uninvited guest"—cancer.

This first community chef interview with Roseline and Sylvester was significantly different from the dozens of interviews I had previously conducted with chef foundations and food philanthropists. They requested we meet at their home instead of at an office or a hotel bar in the central business district (CBD). Children and young people were present in the space. Roseline switched easily from reflecting philosophically on racial capitalism to telling me about the African art on the walls, her international travels, and the stones that she was wearing (primarily opal that day). Rather than feeling as though I was an inconvenience on someone's packed schedule, the couple thanked me repeatedly for my interest and asked if they could record a video of our conversation for their own research and archives (Sylvester worked the video camera, and his voice joined our dialogue). Roseline gave me hours of her time, more than three hours in all, even though it was a considerable effort for her to speak in her current state of health. After our extensive conversation, she sent along several pages of additional written responses to the interview questions I had sent her in advance.

Roseline and Sylvester were quick to challenge me when they thought I was asking the wrong questions or when they disagreed with my assertions or assumptions. For example, Roseline questioned my interest in what I had called "charitable engagement," dismissing it by explaining, "We don't view what we do as charity: we view it as sustainable education, sustainable sharing, communal living, and fellowshipping." She later pushed back against my conceptualization of nutrition as individualistic, saying that in her work, she is "striving for wellness and balance in our personal lives and simultaneously working for the same in our community. Because collective responsibility is just as important as personal responsibility and success." At the start of our conversation, I framed my research in terms of "foodscapes and philanthropy in post-Katrina New Orleans." Twenty minutes later, Sylvester redirected the conversation to come back to that introduction: "'Post-Katrina' as you say—I want to address that. Essentially, we call it 'post-levee breach.' It's important that people be as accurate as they can about circumstances that happened, specifically traumatic events so that you can root source it back and you can heal from it. If you're working from a falsity at the root, at the foundation, then you're not going to be able to heal yourself." He then joked: "All this disrespect of someone by the name of Katrina, she's probably a nice lady, she's probably a really decent person. [Roseline chuckled] There's probably a lot of Katrinas out there suffering from having the burden of being blamed for a man-made mess, just like the most recent situation in Houston."[4] In this pushback, Sylvester and Roseline assert that the devastation that happened in the city (and continues to happen in the long wake of the flooding) was a human-engineered disaster. Their comments emphasize both the gravity of misdiagnosis and the expediency of accurate identification: with a falsity at the root, problems will not be fixed and healing cannot occur.

Much of the difference of our experience can be attributed to crossing from the world of formal food philanthropy into the informal realm of community food work, and from moving from studying organizations to researching individuals and smaller groups. Another explanation is racial and cultural and reflects a different development agenda. I moved from white cultural spaces to a cultural space that was created by and centered on people of color. Roseline and Sylvester are Black and draw inspiration from African American and African diasporic traditions. Prior to visiting The Village, I had been interacting almost exclusively with white people and in institutions run by them (I hesitate to say institutions "created by white people" because the labor and wealth of the restaurant industry is largely produced and reproduced by people of color). In his scholarship on development agendas, Woods (2017a) charts a Black Southern development agenda emerging from African American traditions of explanation, development thought, and social action. Woods (2017a, 27) argues that these aspects merge to create a unique agenda that emphasizes social, economic, and cultural justice, and The Village stems from such a development agenda, reflecting alternative visions of the future than the white-led formal institutions I studied.

I later heard grumbling from friends who are active in fair housing efforts about an Airbnb promotional video featuring Sylvester. In it, Sylvester explains that renting their guest room allows him to work as an artist: "I was a starving artist before this. I've actually got a full belly right now." Short-term rental companies have been controversial and contested in the city, primarily due to the prevalence of full-time rentals that are not owner occupied (Johnson 2015, 192–193). Thus, critics were worried that stories such as Sylvester's were being used by Airbnb to distract from the deleterious impacts of whole-home rentals. During my visit, Sylvester explained that hosting tourists was part of an ethos of hospitality at The Village and was an opportunity to "show visitors a *real, Black* New Orleans." Here, Sylvester differentiates between the imaginaries of Black culture promoted for tourism downtown and the *real* places where Black lives unfold outside the tourism center (see Reese 2020 for a parallel example in the context of Washington, D.C.). He is also illustrating a strategy of some New Orleanians to navigate the post-Katrina economy, attempting to access the wealth being created by the cultural economy, and directing tourism money away from its concentration downtown in the French Quarter and the CBD.[5] As a backdrop, only 27 percent of businesses in the New Orleans metropolitan area are Black or "minority" owned (McCline et al. 2015, 2), and few businesses in the tourist center downtown are Black owned.

"There's No School for This"

Chapter 4 argued that formalized chef philanthropy stems directly from business-based knowledge and practices. In this section, I examine the various knowledge sources utilized by chefs and cooks who do not have foundations: Why do they trust the sources they do, and how do they use this trusted information? How do individuals understand the information they are engaging with, and how do they make it meaningful or put it into practice?

At the urging of several Grow Dat staff members, I interviewed Chef Luis. Luis gave a hog-butchering workshop at the farm during the youth leadership program and was resoundingly received as "cool," "a really nice guy." Luis is Latino, grew up in New Orleans in a Central American family, and now owns several restaurants in the city. He invited me to one of his restaurants in the CBD for our interview. It was mid-afternoon, and the restaurant didn't open until dinnertime, but our table had already been preset with plates and an array of stemmed glassware. Luis is warm and answered my questions with a sense of excitement, but I spent the first quarter of our interview preoccupied with the worry that I would knock something expensive off our tiny table.

I explained my interest in how and why he does "good work," and the first thing he told me was this: "There's no school for this. There's no place to really learn what the right thing and what the best thing to do is." Over the course of our interview, Luis explained that he learns primarily by replicating what other chefs are doing:

> I look at what other people — Emeril, he's in my industry, so I know that he started doing a lot of stuff so I kind of looked at that and I kind of honed down what I like to do, "Okay, that makes so much sense, that's a great model to follow." I think in life, you're always looking for the great mentors — even though they don't know that they're your mentors — you kind of want to emulate people you respect and people that you think are doing the right thing. And then Donald Link is another guy. They've come in really strong and they've made a huge impact in a really short amount of time. So I kind of like look at them and see what they're doing a lot. They're helping out the youth farm [Grow Dat], they help out at programs for youth, they help out all these different people.

In looking at the charitable engagement of Emeril Lagasse and Donald Link, Luis describes thinking, "Okay, that makes so much sense, that's a great model to follow." Luis framed Emeril and Link as "mentors," and throughout our interview he spoke of other famous chefs in ways that positioned them more as peers, calling one celebrity chef his "brother" and telling me that he "hates" another. Luis follows a trend I found within the practices of chef foundations: of watching and replicating what other chefs are doing philanthropically. In Luis's case, he has not started his own foundation (I explore why in a subsequent section), but he "emulates" what Lagasse and Link are doing by engaging with the same organizations they do. However, a director of a chef foundation I interviewed expressed a downside of replication, lowering his voice as he asked, exasperated, "Three chefs with foundations [Link, Lagasse, and Besh] doing the same kind of things in New Orleans?!" All three of these foundations are focused on youth and culinary education. The director said this is why he wants to expand his foundation's programming to locations outside New Orleans.

Replication is related to the idea of vetting. Chefs and restaurants receive constant requests for support. One chef from a prestigious multigenerational Creole restaurant said he worries about aligning with organizations that do not share his family's values, and thus they are always looking for better ways to evaluate who they partner with. When one celebrity chef begins working with an organization, it has a legitimizing effect, and other chefs may feel more secure in offering their support to that organization. Jane, a white chef with several successful restaurants, is also concerned about vetting and the risk of accidentally supporting a "bad" organization. Instead of looking to other chefs, however, she tries to do her own research: "Personally, if I'm going to give money—when something happens like Puerto Rico, Houston— and now we're all wary about the Red Cross.[6] So I go to Charity Navigator, I try to read—that's what I mean by trying to 'vet' something. I think it's a trustworthy website, but I've never really talked too much to nonprofit people about it [what they think of Charity Navigator]." She seemed concerned about whether Charity Navigator is a source that nonprofits themselves want used as a form of evaluation.

When chefs were asked about where they get information about their charitable work and who they trust to provide information, relationships were the predominant theme. Luis's comments are indicative of this broader trend, as admired or respected peers was the most common response. Nikki, who owns the Cajun restaurant, highlighted that she is inspired by "friends who do small, sustainable things." Holly, a white woman from the Dickie Brennan Restaurant Group, said that in her marketing background, what Luis described (that he copies what he sees other chefs doing) is referred to as the "steal, steal, steal!" principle. She thinks this "stealing" is responsible for the rapid growth of chef foundations in the city, as well as for the popularity of fundraising galas, a common nonprofit fundraising strategy. Holly and her white coworker Julia are critical of the gala model and events, particularly when chefs are asked to serve food off-site. A common event structure in New Orleans involves restaurants bringing food to a nonprofit's fundraiser and then serving small plates or appetizers to guests—one chef referred to this as a "dine around" event. At these events, several chefs may be featured, or there could be dozens of different chefs or restaurants present. Julia described these events as burdensome for staff and resources, and that they dislike "playing in the same sandbox as everyone else." Thus, the Brennan Group has prioritized fundraising for nonprofits in-house, within the walls of their restaurants. Lindsay, a white co-chef at an upscale restaurant in Uptown New Orleans, was also critical about the prevalence of event-based and "dine around" fundraising in the city: "In New Orleans, while people are doing great work, I just don't think we need to have a party for everything we do. Just write these people a check! Okay, everybody donate everything they're doing to donate, and we can have one big party and we can just ball it out. If that's what you really need. But it's almost like you need to be convinced? It makes me sick." Lindsay questions why donors need a party at all, let alone many culinary fundraisers constantly happening across the city—why don't they just make a donation directly to the nonprofit?

Lindsay's quote brings up another theme that emerged in other interviews: that charitable events serve as marketing opportunities for restaurants. She explains her conflicted feelings of participating in these events: "Am I being philanthropic? Sure. Am I also hustling my ass off trying to get more diners in my door? YES. It's a room full of a bunch of rich white people! 'Come, spend your money at my restaurant!'" When she serves food at a charitable event, Lindsay is being philanthropic and simultaneously advertising her restaurant. This dynamic became even more complicated for chefs with foundations at Grow Dat Farm Dinners: guest chefs were not only advertising their restaurants but hoping to cultivate donors for their foundation. This set up a dynamic of direct competition between the host nonprofit (Grow Dat) and the guest chef's foundation.

Debbie is a chef who now works full time cooking for the large regional food bank. During the flooding in Baton Rouge and surrounding areas in July 2016 (mentioned in chapter 1), Debbie made red beans and rice for 5,000 people per each recipe batch.[7] She never left the food bank's kitchen, but many chefs went to Baton Rouge, and some served the food she had cooked (see figure 5.5). Debbie said chefs show up for these kinds of aid responses because "it is a good picture. It is a really good Instagram. And since I'm not selling anything anymore, I don't really need that. So I'm happy to let them take that glamour shot and I'll just work." Debbie is in her sixties now and became politicized in the 1960s–70s through Cesar Chavez's work and the farmworker boycotts. Debbie argues that the recent growth in chef philanthropy is the result of the rising importance of social media for

How New Orleans chefs fed 50,000 meals to flood victims in a week

James Cullen (left), Lisa White of Willa Jean and Robert LeBlanc (right) of Cavan, Meauxbar, Sylvain and Barrel Proof, make food for Louisiana flood victims. (Photo by Judy Walker)

FIGURE 5.5 Media coverage in the New Orleans Times-Picayune (online) of chefs providing aid after the 2016 flooding in and around Baton Rouge. Image by Walker, NOLA.com.

branding: "With the advent of social media and how everybody is a lot more visible, I think that chefs and entrepreneurs and corporations and pretty much everybody has understood that this is a cause-related marketing thing. That you look good when you give back. And it might not be the closest thing to your heart, but it sure is good for business." Chef Luis said he feels he can be more selective regarding his charitable engagement now that his restaurants are more established: "When I first started out as a business owner, we would kind of go for the high-profile stuff—oh, because we want to try to get our name out there, obviously we're trying to promote the restaurant." For both Luis and Debbie, there is no debate here about the purpose of visible charitable engagement for chefs: it is "obviously" "good for business."

Personal relationships with other chefs or elite customers can limit or direct philanthropic engagement, driving it in different directions. Luis said, "One of the things I learned as I got older, I want to support things that I believe in, not so much 'Well, you know so-and-so comes in here and they're on the board.' And that's kind of a big consideration because you want to keep everybody happy and help everybody that you can." Chefs can feel a sense of obligation to their important or frequent customers and want to reciprocate the gift of their patronage. Here, Luis describes how that obligation can direct chefs to engage with issues or organizations in which they have no interest.

Several small restaurants and chefs expressed their desire to do more community engagement but said they are economically limited in what they can do. Grow Dat had approached Nikki about Dinner on the Farm. Despite her excitement, she could not afford it: "I don't have any money. I don't know how most of these people can come in and donate the money and everything else and write it off in some way, but I'm like [whispering] 'this could tank me.'" While Nikki would like to support Grow Dat and other nonprofits, she cannot participate in the same philanthropic systems as the formal chef foundations. White male chefs have privileged access to capital and resources; the success of their businesses pave the way for the prominent spaces they occupy as philanthropists. Within this model of giving, only certain chefs qualify and participate as humanitarians.

Not all chefs look to peers within their industry for advice or inspiration. I asked Debbie, the former restaurant chef-owner who now cooks for a large food bank, if she trusts other chefs. She said that chefs, although they are her professional peers, are not a consideration in her charitable work: "I'm very wary of that. Even if I admire someone's culinary skills, I'm not sure I would look to them for political insight or views of the world." Overall, celebrity chefs were mentioned as a source of trusted information only by their peers—the most elite chefs and the largest restaurants groups.

Debbie and Ayomide, both accomplished chefs, reported that they draw on the perspectives of close friends who work in sectors other than food. Debbie said, "I have a very small group of friends who I trust, I really do. I certainly trust my husband, and there are probably six other people who I *listen to* [emphasized], you know? Who I think have valuable insight. Not necessarily about what I do but about the world and the way we live in it." Ayomide, who also relies heavily on friends in other fields to help him "workshop" new ideas, explained that skepticism drives his process of starting new projects: "I have an orientation which is usually skepticism of what is conventionally accepted. So I start there. I just research along those lines." Ayomide and Debbie both believe that valuable insight comes from those who are outside the culinary world. This follows Ayomide's "skeptical" orientation in which outsiders are perhaps less likely to hold the same assumptions or perspectives as those working within the same industry.

Leaving Professional Kitchens for Community Food Work

Women enroll in culinary school at the same rate as men, but post-education, men are more likely to work as professional chefs and hold the most prestigious positions (Harris and Giuffre 2015). Men are more likely to be hired and promoted, and the prevalence of sexual harassment creates discriminatory work environments in which women are systematically devalued (Harris and Giuffre 2015). In interviews, Nikki referred to restaurants as the "old boys' club," in which white male chefs consolidate power by partnering with and supporting other white men in their industry. Analyzing food media, Harris and Giuffre (2015) found that media representation favors and rewards male chefs. They note a gendered differentiation in media coverage between "good chefs" (women) and "great chefs" (men). Men are represented "as creators who master the kitchen, innovate cuisine, and build empires, while women chefs are depicted as being food producers who re-create traditional or homey dishes and are not highly invested in their careers unless guided by a man" (Harris and Giuffre 2015, 47–48). Restaurant reviews and competitive awards are informed by media coverage, and reviews and awards can make or break a chef's career.

Of the women who do make it into professional chef jobs, Harris and Giuffre (2015) find that many women leave, often citing incompatibility of work with home life and care responsibilities. Women chefs who left professional cooking jobs highlighted long hours, inflexible and difficult work structures, and lack of benefits—particularly in childcare and health care. Many chefs said they were not able to meet expectations of being the "ideal worker" and the "ideal mother" simultaneously (Harris and Giuffre 2015, 169–70).

Women who leave chef positions take jobs that are still within food systems, including working as culinary instructors, cooking in corporate contexts like catering, running small food businesses, and buying or preparing food for grocery stores. Several participants in my research left chef positions to take up cooking roles with nonprofit organizations. Sarah, a queer white woman in her mid-thirties, described a cycle of "burning out" in the restaurant industry: "I was just working at festivals and having fun, but also—I feel like the way a lot of chefs come around to 'doing good' is you get kind of burnt out by just like feeding the masses in this way that doesn't feel that satisfying or that worthwhile. It's just like a bunch of drunk people partying at festivals and you're like feeding them tacos. So I hit a little cynical phase and I was like, 'What can I do?' And that's how I came around to teaching." Sarah describes becoming cynical about the everyday realities of "feeding the masses." After her latest cycle of burnout, Sarah began using the title "chef teacher," and she has taken on roles as a cooking educator in several organizations over the past eight years. As I discuss more in chapter 6, Sarah continues to push her culinary teaching efforts to align with labor organizing and racial justice movements in foodscapes. Debbie, after more than twenty years of working as a chef and owning two restaurants in Chicago, started directing a food bank kitchen. Expressing her lifelong commitment to supporting social change, Debbie saw cooking at the food bank as a way to blend her desire to help others with her love of cooking.

Formalizing Doing Good: Chef Foundations

Early in my research, a leader of the Southern Foodways Alliance and a board member of a chef foundation proposed that the phenomenon of the rapid growth of chef foundations could largely be understood as an "exercise in control." Restaurants and chefs receive constant requests for charitable engagement. They are asked to donate gift cards for auctions or to be given out as prizes, approached to cook on-site at fundraising events (such as "dine arounds"), solicited as board members, and asked to champion causes or events. Jane, the chef mentioned earlier, estimates that she receives ten requests a week, amounting to more than 500 requests each year. The Dickie Brennan Restaurant Group, with four restaurants in the French Quarter, reports similar numbers and sometimes more. For Jane, one-third of the requests are donations for a range of 200–1,500 portions of food for events, and two-thirds ask for gift cards or in-kind donations for auctions. Both the Brennan Group and Jane report that they get a surprising number of requests from organizations that are not local but are trying to put together a New Orleans–themed trip package. Organizers of the James Beard Foundation's Chef Bootcamp for Policy and Change (see chapter 3) have found that the average restaurant they work with gives out about $50,000 in donations each year.

Most restaurants don't have a formal system to process the stream of requests, such as dedicated staff who are assigned responsibility to oversee charitable donations, or a set rubric for making decisions about who to support. In this context, starting a foundation allows chefs to clarify their philanthropic mission and dedicate resources toward establishing formal operations and procedures. Luis explained that his lack of infrastructure hurts his ability to meaningfully interact with many charitable organizations: "My office is my car. I just sit in my car and I don't have an office anywhere. I just sit at home, I sit on my computer, I don't have an HR person, I don't have any of that stuff." It is therefore challenging for him to interact with nonprofits unless they "set up a system" for him to plug into. Chefs also stressed that they would like to find more long-term and meaningful ways to engage, rather than just showing up once a year for an event or donating a gift card, which feels even more anonymous and disconnected. As mentioned earlier, Grow Dat has tried, with varying levels of success, to develop more robust partnerships with chefs or chef foundations.

I asked Luis why he has not started a formal foundation: "You know what, I don't want the tail wagging the dog. . . . I don't want an office, I don't want bureaucracy. I don't want to have somebody calling me and I have to show up. I don't know, that really doesn't motivate me. I love the freedom that I have." Luis said he learned hard lessons when he had six restaurants open at the same time, and that he now knows he does not want to have to manage that much again.

Starting and running a foundation of the kind that is prevalent in New Orleans—one that is not endowed, has considerable fundraising responsibilities, and runs programming—is a considerable logistical endeavor that requires skill, funding, and ongoing labor. A leader of the Chef Bootcamp program at the James Beard Foundation told me that she has been asked by a "remarkable" number of chefs if the foundation would be willing to take over or absorb their foundation, which it is unable to do. She described chefs as "action oriented," which means they often want to start their own initiatives. However, as they lack adequate infrastructure to run a nonprofit, their organizations risk being unsustainable and having to shut their doors. Rather than creating a new organization that will compete with other organizations to raise money, she said she advises chefs to donate to an established organization or find ways to partner with them.

Mandy, a Black woman who runs a Food as Medicine program connected with a POC-led community growing project in the Lower Ninth

Ward, also expressed frustration with the trend of chefs and other philanthropists starting new projects rather than supporting organizations that are already active:

Everybody talks about philanthropy and how they want to give back. "Yeah, if ya'll become famous and make a whole bunch of money and ya'll want to give back, hey, that's wonderful." But my community never sees it. You want to give back? We have a great program. Support our program. Cause we're already doing what you want to do. Don't take what you're doing and do it yourself and then you get all the funding for it. No! Partner with us, and we can show you how to do it right. That's big thinking. We've been doing this for three years now. We're already doing what you're just jumping into.

Others expressed similar frustrations and critiques. Recounting the proliferation of farms and community gardening initiatives in the Lower Ninth Ward, Roseline (from the Village) stressed how nonprofits directed resources away from people who were trying to rebuild their homes and had their own gardens: "So rather than giving the people the money that could have been used to rebuild their own personal farms and their own personal gardens and their homes, you have all these people come with the charity farm, and the charity this, and the charity that." A leader of a museum dedicated to Southern foodways said that although chefs are a focus of their work, chefs don't often support the museum financially or otherwise because they are prioritizing their own foundations and programs: "It's my own frustration, no one supports us. . . . More and more we [even] have people refusing to give us product, like if we have a party. . . . I think they've been over-asked, not just by us but by everything that goes down." In chapter 6, I further consider why chefs start their own initiatives rather than find ways to support organizations such as Mandy's.

Jane reflected at length about reasons to *not* align her business expertise with her charitable engagement. When I asked her if she brings her skills as a restaurateur into her philanthropic work, she told me that she wants to do other things, to learn about other social issues: "I want to broaden my horizon. I want to have other things to talk to people about. Once you've done something for forty years, wouldn't you like to learn something new?" Jane is nearing retirement and is trying to decide how to continue her work on social issues beyond being a member of the board of directors of several organizations: "As I get older, I really like to be in the trenches a little bit more, maybe do some volunteering. But I don't know if I want to be a 'chef teacher.'

Because I'm afraid that I'd be too mean, that I'd treat the kids like my little employees, and that's kind of—you know!" Here Jane acknowledges that the skills required to teach cooking are different from the skills she uses to manage a professional kitchen setting, and that her experience might not transfer well into different contexts.

Conclusion: Acceptable Care and Raising Money

This chapter began with Grow Dat's Dinners on the Farm, showing how an NGO navigates working with celebrity humanitarians. Small nonprofits such as Grow Dat are under constant pressure to raise funds to keep their doors open, and market-based/earned-revenue opportunities such as Dinners on the Farm featuring guest chefs are an attempt to meet this need. However, a significant amount of conflict surrounded the dinners: What does it mean to host an "exclusive" demographic at the "inclusive" farm? Was it antithetical to Grow Dat's mission to be involved with gourmet chef culture? One program leader told me that he finds the practice of calling Farm Dinner attendees "guests" strange because "we [adults] are all guests. It's a *youth* farm. I see myself as a guest in their space; that's who this belongs to." The answer to the question, Who belongs at the farm? remains open, but workshops at the dinners—including the History of the Land—now provide a venue for elite guests to be on the land not only as donors or givers but also as *learners*. As the dinners themselves are expensive to produce and have not raised significant funds, the question remains whether the dinners will result in new donors in the long-term. Overall, I stress that fundraising happens within historical and current power dynamics, both spatial and social (the History of the Land).

Philanthropy is part of marketing and branding strategies for chefs and the restaurant industry in contemporary New Orleans. In the context of hypermasculinized restaurant environments, chefs are expected to act "macho" and are discouraged from being "too emotional," a charge often leveled at women working in kitchens (Harris and Giuffre 2015). I believe that chef philanthropy also serves as a form of acceptable care for male chefs. I imagine that elite chefs desire meaningful connection and want opportunities to show care for others. As the space of the restaurant is largely unsupportive in nourishing these kinds of connections, philanthropy becomes an outlet in which male chefs can express care and find meaning. Philanthropic engagement of the kind that I observed in New Orleans allows chefs an outlet for care that is accepted within the gender confines of their industry, as it largely occurs outside the restaurant environment—for example, when chefs and restaurant workers were disappointed that they had to dig an irrigation ditch at Grow Dat rather than interact with teenagers who work at the farm. While this reflects a specific imaginary of what charitable work is and who it is for, it also shows that chefs seek to meaningfully engage with others and want to feel a sense of connection. As critiques of philanthropy highlight, this form of caring is nonthreatening for chefs, as it keeps hierarchies in place, maintaining racialized and gendered dynamics in the construction of givers and receivers. Philanthropy, as disembedded corporate social responsibility (CSR) (which I explain in chapter 6), allows chefs to maintain their dominant positions in the culinary world without having to challenge the root sources of inequality or oppression that make most food businesses successful.

Non-elite chefs and chefs who do not want to run their own foundation have different systems of knowledge that inform their engagement and understanding of justice or humanitarianism. Chef Luis asserted, "There's no school for this," and I heard this sentiment frequently throughout my research—that chefs had to "make it up" or "figure it out on the fly." Similarly, Brad Pitt shared how "naive" he was and how little he knew about housing when he started Make It Right (see discussion in chapter 1). However, many scholarly disciplines and pedagogical approaches are focused on finding the best ways to address social problems and to enact social change; personally, this has been the most significant thread of my own academic education. Chefs lack formal education, training, and expertise in these arenas, though. Training programs such as the Chef Bootcamp for Policy and Change try to address these gaps. Chef Jane, quoted in the preceding section, doubted that her skills as a kitchen manager with adults would translate into skills as a volunteer culinary teacher with young people.

As I discussed in chapter 4, there is an imperative in CSR to align business and philanthropy, meaning that a business's philanthropic work should be in the same sector or industry as the business. When this alignment occurs, business leaders are assumed to be experts: if they are successful in their industry, they are qualified to intervene on social issues related to their industry. Although many would not agree that these are the necessary credentials, I found it to be a common thread in my research.

As I discuss in chapter 6, the dominant philanthropic focus of chef foundations in New Orleans is preparing youth for the restaurant workforce, either through changing the workforce's demographics (developing more chefs who are white women and POC) or by making sure they have adequate training and credentials for the job. In the example of the JBF, who better to solve the problems of the restaurant industry (the lack of white women and POC) than the wealthy and powerful leaders of the restaurant industry (white men)? However, my findings show that the prevalence of racism and sexism operating within the restaurant industry underpins philanthropic efforts as well. A lack of historical analysis and understanding of oppression limits the ability of these foodscape projects to imagine just social transformations and seriously redress inequality.

CHAPTER SIX

The Next Top Chef

Rebranding Gourmet Foodscapes

This chapter considers the relationships between chef humanitarianism and business. There are strengths that come from philanthropy's positioning within the restaurant industry, most notably the ability to raise money, such as the flawless crawfish boil fundraiser discussed in chapter 4. However, this positioning also risks reproducing the inequalities and exploitations of the restaurant industry. I find that among chefs who engage in business-aligned and business-informed philanthropy, overlap between their corporate and philanthropic worlds can result in the infusion of sexism and racism (common in gourmet foodscapes) into their charitable work as well. Given the backdrop of deeply entrenched inequalities regarding race, gender, and class, is chef philanthropy addressing and redressing such inequalities within their own operations or in their external philanthropic efforts?

In the first part of the chapter, I argue that chef philanthropy serves as a form of aid to the restaurant industry, working to brand and rebrand gourmet foodscapes as ethical. Food service workers earn low wages, white men occupy the majority of well-paid positions as managers (Liu and Apollon 2011, 11), and sexual harassment is pervasive in restaurant workplace culture (Sinclair 2006). A recruitment flyer for Jamie Oliver's Fifteen Apprentice Programme features a determined-looking young woman of color next to the question, "Are YOU the next Top Chef?" (figure 6.1). I argue that chef philanthropic programs targeting the next generation of restaurant workers utilize celebrity imaginaries such as this to justify their interventions, which simultaneously works to rebrand the inequitable industry as a place of glamour and success for women, women of color, and people of color.

I next consider chefs who run restaurants that are focused on ethical practices and who care about building community. Many of these chefs and restaurateurs are small scale and non-elite, but several are celebrities who own celebrated restaurants. In interviews, this group focused on the themes of labor, workplace policies, and justice. I compare how these chefs understand the notion of "doing good in foodscapes" with the priorities and perspectives of chef foundations.[1] I share narratives that highlight the racism and sexism that several beneficiaries and staff experienced within Chefs Move! and the

FIGURE 6.1 A recruitment postcard for Jamie Oliver's apprenticeship program at his restaurant Fifteen in London asks potential beneficiaries, "Are YOU the next Top Chef?" Photo by Jamie Oliver's Fifteen Apprentice Programme.

John Besh Foundation (JBF). These narratives show troubling cultures and practices within the corporate culinary world and give evidence to the importance of embedded corporate social responsibility (CSR) reforms.

In the next section, I propose a conceptualization of embedded and disembedded CSR that builds on Richey and Ponte's (2011) foundational work on engaged and disengaged CSR (see chapter 2, table 2.1). I argue that studying embeddedness is a useful analytical tool. In embedded CSR in restaurants, workplace conditions and politics, environmental impacts, and the purpose of the space (beyond food service) are the focus of reforms. In disembedded CSR, interventions are proximate (made outside the restaurant) and concern social issues that are either related or unrelated to food and foodscapes. I emphasize the spatial dimensions of both the physical location of the intervention or reform and the social problem being addressed. As I assert in chapter 5, chef foundations engage in foodscape projects that occur largely outside the spaces of their restaurants, which allows them an outlet for acceptable care—philanthropic work that allows chefs to remain within the confined gender roles and hierarchies of their industry and that is nonthreatening to power structures.

The chapter concludes with a discussion about causumerism in the restaurant industry and the role that ethical consumption plays in funding chef projects. Looking closely at the JBF's first charitable project, Milk Money, I show how causumer products have been mobilized as branding tools. I also explore how beneficiary farmers (primarily white) were constructed differently than Chefs Move! scholarship winners.

Restaurant Labor and Branding

> Prior to the levee breach—that's blamed on Katrina—New Orleans residents, specifically the Black residents, we had developed a series of survival techniques that were allowing us to actually make a living, despite the fact that most of us were working in the service industry and the pay in the service industry has never afforded middle class liberty. So post-Katrina, the philanthropy that happened, it came as a result of businesspeople and restaurateurs realizing, "Oh my goodness! If we don't do something to get this city back on its feet, our cash cow is done!"
> —Interview with SYLVESTER, community activist at the Village

In the quote that opens this section, Sylvester directly connects the post-levee-breach economy to the rise of chef philanthropy. His comment highlights both the city's economic dependence on the service sector, which is composed of Black low-wage workers, and the idea that restaurant-led philanthropy is somehow connected with these workers and their labor. Sylvester's understanding of the restaurant industry's dependence on racialized low-wage workers follows theorizing by geographers such as Woods, who have argued that containment and enclosure of Black people and workers of color is a key component of wealth creation to benefit the white elite.

The service industry has been a cornerstone of the New Orleans economy, but restaurant jobs are low quality. Even when the industry as a whole is thriving, the majority of workers remain in poverty or near poverty. Of the more than 20 million people working in food systems in the United States, 60 percent (12 million) are employed in the service sector (Liu and Apollon 2011, 2). Drawing on research by the Restaurant Opportunities Centers United (ROC United), the Applied Research Center (now Race Forward) found the following:

> Restaurants pay their employees low wages, offer few benefits in a field with dangerous working conditions, and seldom advance or increase pay or advance workers in their careers. . . . Our findings based on national data also reveal that retail and service workers of color made less than their white colleagues. Half of white workers made $10.63 or less, whereas the median hourly wage for workers of color was $1.32 less per hour. That's $2,418 less in annual median wage. Workers of color were also concentrated in low-wage service jobs, such as food preparation workers or fast food, at 53 percent and 39 percent, respectively. (Liu and Apollon 2011, 218)

On the whole, food service workers earn low wages, and people of color make even less than white people. White food service workers hold most management positions, and white men constitute the majority of managers (Liu and Apollon 2011).

A 2010 study by ROC United, ROC-NOLA, and the New Orleans Restaurant Industry Coalition found that the restaurant industry in the New Orleans metro area employed 8.6 percent of the city's workers, more than 44,000 people. Their findings assert that while there are a few "good" restaurant jobs, the majority are "bad jobs" with very low wages, few benefits, and slim opportunities for advancement. The field is a "predominantly low-wage industry in which violations of employment and health and safety laws are commonplace" (ROC United, ROC-NOLA, and the New Orleans Restaurant Industry Coalition 2010, i). The average national median wage is $7.76 an hour for restaurant workers, and average annual earnings were $16,870.79 in

2008 (i). Workers of color are clustered in the majority of low wage and precarious jobs, while white workers, a small segment of the workforce, hold "the few good jobs." Workers of color report discrimination in hiring, promotion, and discipline, and experience verbal abuse based on race, national origin, and English language facility (ii).

Sexual harassment is also rampant in the industry (Sinclair 2006). Some women chefs in Harris and Giuffre's (2015) study drew a distinction between sexualized behavior and sexual harassment. Sexualized behavior was restricted to "talking about sex or making sexual jokes, . . . considered just part of working in a kitchen," normal "guy talk" (Harris and Giuffre 2015, 110–11). Sexual jokes and teasing served to "determine if women were tough enough for the kitchen. If women were sensitive and got offended by what went on in professional kitchens, this served as proof that they did not belong" (Harris and Giuffre 2015, 114). In contrast, respondents identified sexual harassment as incidents when "there was touching and a definite power differential between coworkers" (Harris and Giuffre 2015, 112). Sexual harassment is underreported in male-dominated jobs overall, as "there is a strong emphasis on being tough and not complaining about the circumstances at work" (Harris and Giuffre 2015, 118). There is pressure for women to conform or accept harassment in order to succeed in the culinary field.

In Sylvester's framing, chefs and restaurants engaged in philanthropy to help rebuild their businesses and to make money post-Katrina. This reflects a concern and debate I heard throughout my research regarding a popular arena of chef-led interventions: restaurant workforce readiness targeted at teenagers. The topic was brought up in interviews, and I was personally part of such conversations as a youth employer at Grow Dat, as teenagers are paid to work at the farm. There is a proliferation of programming in the city that targets young people of color for work in the hospitality industry or service sector, primarily restaurants and hotels. For example, there are at least three local nonprofit organizations that run restaurants and train young people in service-industry skills. Chefs have been financial contributors to or champions of the organizations, and some have won awards from the organizations for their support. The programs vary in their pedagogies and approaches, with, as I understand it, a great deal of nuance. However, the macrolevel concern is that there is too much focus on preparing—or channeling—young people of color into careers in low-wage work. Woods (2017b, 241) has argued that an economy based on tourism and low-wage work can be understood as requiring the preparation of a "trapped labor force."

The first project the Shaya Barnett Foundation (Chef Alon Shaya's foundation) launched was a culinary arts program at a local high school. The project uses the National Restaurant Association's (NRA) ProStart curriculum. The NRA is the country's largest employer resource and has over 500,000 restaurant members, including major corporate chains; in addition, there are nine chapters of the affiliated Louisiana Restaurant Association (LRA) in the state, with more than 7,500 members. In line with its mission "to roll back burdensome regulatory requirements and press Congress for change that helps your business" (NRA 2019), the organization is known for opposing increases to the minimum wage, paid sick leave, and other benefits (Graves and Jilani 2018; ROC United 2014). One of the NRA's celebrated accomplishments is keeping the federal minimum wage for tipped employees at the rate established in 1991: $2.13 an hour.

The Shaya Barnett Foundation's culinary program won an award from the charter management organization that runs the school where the project is based, and local and national press coverage has been limited but positive. Shaya's narrative about his focus on vocational training is personal, as he largely attributes his success to his high school home economics teacher in Philadelphia, and she is now Shaya's partner at the foundation. As a James Beard award winner who owns several restaurants, Shaya's personal biography does not map onto the concern that this kind of training funnels people into low-wage labor.

I contend that celebrity chefs mobilize a form of culinary capital that mitigates concerns or objections to their involvement in this kind of workforce development. Shaya and others do not herald the realities of "bad jobs" in the culinary world; instead, they represent the slim opportunity for wild success. Chefs Move!, the project examined in chapter 4, relies on culinary capital in a similar way, both through its (previous) association with chef John Besh and in its mission and rhetoric about developing the next generation of culinary "leaders," not workers. The JBF program is direct about the fact that people of color are not at the top of the industry's hierarchy and argues that they should be.

In interviews, scholarship winners expressed their dreams and desires to "make it"—to become celebrity chefs themselves or to own culinary businesses. Simultaneously, other winners worried that they were letting the foundation down when they took jobs that were stable but not high profile or prestigious. One winner said that, ironically, her experience fulfilling the required internship made her not want to work in restaurants. She was, for one, disappointed by the low wages at Besh Restaurant Group [BRG] restaurants. Instead, she has been catering for a corporation and loves the lifestyle—high wages and regular working hours—even though she worries that "the foundation won't like it."

I argue that Sylvester's understanding is reflective of how celebrity humanitarianism can provide "aid to brands" (Richey and Ponte 2011). Richey and Ponte describe how "Brand Aid" works to "improve a brand's ethical profile and value."[2] Brands have massive monetary value to corporations—the most successful brands represent more than 40 percent of the owning company's total market value (2011, 10–11). Maintaining the ethical profile of the brand is a key concern, as a brand can lose value and become less profitable when it receives negative media attention. The form of chef philanthropy discussed here aids or assists the restaurant industry. In a sector marked by sexual harassment, racism, and low wages, chefs' philanthropic projects—particularly in the way their rhetoric claims they are developing future celebrity chefs and diverse culinary leaders—help rebrand the restaurant industry as equitable and ethical.

Branding is one of the reasons why chefs launch foundations. In my findings, one of the reasons they run their own programming—rather than following a more traditional grant-making model—is because they and their boards desire their projects to bear their names. The Emeril Lagasse Foundation has been a grant-making private foundation since 2002, but it more recently became a 501(c)(3) nonprofit organization. The foundation fundraises through various methods and has hosted high-profile annual events both nationally and in New Orleans, including the Boudin, Bourbon and Beer festival and Carnivale du Vin. The foundation's director said that the board wanted to move more into programming: "A couple of years ago the board says, 'Well, wait a minute, we just keep raising money and we just give it away. And yes, our name is on a lot of things and that's lovely: Cafe Reconcile, Liberty's Kitchen, St. Michael's, Edible Schoolyard New Orleans, NOCCA [New Orleans Center for Creative Arts high school].' But the board's like, 'Well, wait a minute, we don't run anything, we don't *own* anything. We need something.'" After years of exploring different ideas, in 2018 the foundation announced its branded "signature program"—Emeril's Culinary Garden and Teaching Kitchen. With the goal of being implemented in at least ten elementary schools by 2023, the Lagasse Foundation provides curriculum, builds the gardens and kitchens, and assists in hiring staff, but it does not oversee programming "on the ground." The director outlined that the giving structure will have four components going forward: the signature program; larger community grants, which are made predominantly in places where Lagasse has restaurants; a small grants program; and sponsorships.

This expressed need to "own" something can push philanthropists into launching interventions where they likely lack experience and expertise. In my research, community food organizations and philanthropic advisers said that grants were the best way chefs could support food movements and social change. However, from a business perspective, giving out grants has less branding potential than a signature project, which is owned by the corporation or celebrity brand.

Labor and Human Resources: Accepting/Rejecting Industry Standards

For many of the restaurant owners I interviewed, a concern with ethical operations is built into the structure of their business. Rather than operating primarily as a for-profit venue and then "giving back" later on, the restaurants are concerned with how money is made in the first place. Alexa and Tucker are a couple who own two small bustling restaurants. When I asked them about where they go for information about their charitable work, they stressed a lack of information, primarily in terms of best practices and research regarding human resources (HR) and policies that benefit employees. Alexa lamented that there are "no resources, no restaurant organizations that are actually supportive and helpful." They said they won't use information from the NRA and the LRA because of the NRA's "horrible labor practices" (mentioned previously). Alexa and Tucker's refusal to join and use the resources from these organizations is significant, as they have a large footprint in New Orleans as the industry standard. For example, Richard "Dickie" Brennan Sr. was on the board of the NRA, and Dickie Brennan Jr. (of the Dickie Brennan & Co. restaurants) was the chair of the 2018 NRA Convention.

After expressing distain for the NRA and LRA—the official venues they are supposed to turn to for best practices—Alexa and Tucker continued with the following exchange:

ALEXA: There should be a thing written about that I can steal and take for our organization and apply.

TUCKER: Word!

ALEXA: Instead, I'm trying to make decisions about something that I don't have any background in or know how it's going to work. There's not enough out there for people who are looking. All there is, is the occasional news story that someone will write about: "Oh, this restaurant in California did this and had a really good outcome," but it's very scattered. Nothing comprehensive. They never even know—research wise—what would be the biggest benefit to employees—

TUCKER: Is it more money or health care?

ALEXA: You never know. We have x amount of money that we're just giving back to our employees in cash. But would it be better if we gave everyone five days of paid vacation? I've read articles that paid vacation is so important. But it's the same amount of money regardless. There are so many things that there's just no digestible research on best practices.

The study discussed earlier (ROC United, ROC-NOLA, and the New Orleans Restaurant Industry Coalition 2010) stresses that the industry, as such a significant employer, could become a driver of social progress in the city, a possibility that Alexa and Tucker are aware of. However, they stress that a lack of research and ethical resources on best practices in restaurants leaves them guessing as to what is best for their employees.

Like those discussed in chapter 5, Alexa and Tucker look to what peers in their industry are doing for guidance. They also cited news coverage and said they are inspired by Zingerman's Delicatessen in Michigan, cofounded by Ari Weinzweig (2010). Following many of Weinzweig's practices but with questions still remaining, Alexa and Tucker have pieced together HR policies that they hope align with their ethics and values. They shared with me a nine-page working document for their older restaurant, outlining their mission and vision. The vision statement establishes how community is understood both internally and externally to neighborhood, city, and region: "We believe you cannot do your best work if you aren't happy in your workplace. . . . One of the main ways that we engage with and support our New Orleans and Gulf South communities is through our relationships with local farms and businesses. . . . Another way we contribute to our community is by modeling responsible and sustainable business practices in the service industry." Their mission ends: "By bringing people together around food, we use our business to foster a strong community while we constantly learn and grow." Alexa and Tucker developed the document on their own, piecemeal. Throughout the interview, they stressed that they wish there were more research and information to guide their practices and policies.

Chef Ray is related to esteemed Chef Leah Chase and is involved with the Edgar "Dooky" Jr. and Leah Chase Family Foundation. Like Roseline from the Village, Ray was a beloved guest chef at one of Grow Dat's Community Lunches. An interview with Chef Ray was largely about how he ties equity, labor, and community together. Ray has read Danny Meyer's book *Setting the Table: The Transforming Power of Hospitality in Business* (2006) three times and said that one of the key lessons he takes from Meyer is that the right people to hire are "the people who understand where their restaurant fits in the community. They understand their restaurant is bigger than just a restaurant and making money off of food. I have to sustain this community because this is why my location, my restaurant, is working."

Ray's timescale is longer than most of the other chefs I interviewed, the majority of whom launched restaurants and became famous within the last decade. Ray explained, "When you talk about the ones that have been here for long periods of time, seventy-five years—Commander's getting ready to celebrate a hundred twenty-five years, Antoine's, Galatoire's—they understand where they fit in this community, they understand that they need to reach out and give back and sustain the community that sustains them. The first thing is the community. Without that, nothing will happen." Initially, I thought Ray was defining community in terms of the patrons eating at his restaurants, so I asked, "What is the dynamic of being a restaurant that welcomes the tourist economy but is also fundamentally concerned with sustaining community?" As he responded to this question, it became clear to me that while diners might be a part of the equation, he was primarily speaking about restaurant workers. Ray said he believes that the low wages earned by most workers in the restaurant industry are unjust, especially when compared to the wealth being created by restaurants— wealth that goes to only a few people. He stressed his belief in a living wage and is campaigning in the city for all restaurants to adopt one (it's unclear if his restaurants have or have not adopted it).

Sarah, one of the chefs who left professional cooking and is now a chef teacher, cited the *Equity Toolkit for Restaurant Employers* (ROC United, Race Forward, and the Center for Social Inclusion 2017) as essential to addressing labor justice in the restaurant industry. After working as a chef teacher for years, often involved with nonprofits that train and prepare young people for culinary work, Sarah has been moving into organizing work that aims to raise wages and increase labor standards within restaurants.

"Yes, Chef": Gender, Race, and Sexual Harassment

René, a Chefs Move! scholarship winner, asked if we could talk over coffee. We met at a small café located under a parking garage near the Convention Center before René went to work for an evening shift at a nearby restaurant. Normally abuzz with positivity and enthusiasm, René looked haggard and worn out. It had been a difficult time: Brett Anderson's (2017) investigation about the culture of sexual harassment at the BRG had run in the local newspaper and made the national news six weeks before. René's trauma had resurfaced since the story became public, with nightmares making for restless sleep and memories coming back during the day. René was going to therapy and was on antidepressants, trying to practice self-care and negotiate the challenging time.

As winners began to find out about the allegations against Besh and the BRG, René texted staff from the foundation directly to ask what was happening. Staff responded by denying any abuse and claimed that all Besh's personal actions were "consensual." Despite the foundation's denials, René believed the women's stories because personal efforts to report sexual harassment had been discouraged, downplayed, and ignored by both BRG and the foundation. René had won Chefs Move! several years before and attended the International Culinary Center in New York. After culinary school, winners work an internship at a BRG restaurant back in New Orleans. René, who is Latinx, experienced ongoing harassment from a supervising chef during the required internship at Willa Jean. The chef referred to René as a "dirty pervert," a "maniac," and a "predator"; made pronouncements to other staff such as, "Well, someone must be on their period"; and René was chastised for minimal mistakes and sometimes not mistakes at all—for instance, for "over-prepping" a workstation.

It took a long time for René to share what was happening. René told family members that work was stressful but was afraid to "complain" to leaders at BRG: "I don't want to look bad on my part, I want to be professional." René's parents pushed back, saying that no, these incidents were not a normal part of professional life—that it was harassment. But René saw what was happening to others who spoke up: a coworker went to the restaurant's manager to report that she had been shown pornography in the cold storage, and when she got upset, the chef joked, "She's in a bad mood because she needs dick." The restaurant's manager discouraged her from filing a formal grievance, warning her that she would likely lose her job. Thus, neither René nor the coworker filed complaints. As the BRG lacked an HR department, it's unclear what, if any, formal reporting system would have even been available to them.

The chef harassing René was eventually suspended for other infractions. But when he came back to the restaurant after his period of suspension was lifted, René felt pushed to the limit and decided to finally share what was happening with the JBF. Rene's official mentor, another chef within the BRG, advised René to "wait it out," since the internship period was almost over. JBF staff told René they would look into it, but it was never brought up again.

Marisol, the foundation's former director, also experienced sexual harassment and racism at the BRG, though she worked in the foundation offices rather than in one of its restaurants. To Marisol, however, she "felt like she worked at BRG" instead of a nonprofit organization. She described the BRG and the JBF as having "kind of the same culture." Located above one of the BRG restaurants in the central business district (CBD), the foundation and its staff shared the same floor of office space with BRG corporate employees, including Octavio Mantilla, John Besh, and Emery Whalen. At a Tulane event honoring Besh as an Outstanding Social Entrepreneur, JBF staff attended the awards ceremony alongside BRG executives and restaurant employees. Although there were different legal structures for the corporate BRG and the philanthropic JBF, in practice there was little separation between the entities.

At that time, Whalen was serving as the JBF's first director. She had a mug in her office that said "Oui, Chef," and Marisol thinks "Yes, Chef" captures a large part of the culture of not only the BRG but the foundation as well. The imperative to "keep Chef happy" was pervasive: the women working at the foundation were told to "dress up pretty" for Besh when he was in the office, that they should not dress casually by wearing jeans, and that their nails needed to look "decent." Marisol was the only person of color on the foundation's team, and there was only one other person of color within the larger BRG offices at the time she was hired. As an attractive young woman fresh out of undergraduate school, Marisol described feeling that she was on display as the foundation's "pretty little gem"—a visual marketing tool for the foundation if nothing else.

To recruit applicants for Chefs Move!, Marisol and John Besh walked through the French Quarter to distribute flyers and to speak with restaurateurs about the scholarship, requesting that they encourage promising employees to apply. As they walked, Besh grabbed her hand, stared directly into her eyes, and repeatedly pressured her to join him at one of the many hotel bars they walked past. When she finally relented and they sat down at a bar, she texted friends who worked in the BRG office to join them so she and Besh would not be alone. Besh was disappointed when the other women arrived, questioning Marisol as to why she did not want it to be just the two of them. Marisol described the experience as shameful and disgusting.

Another time, Marisol was attending the culinary school graduation of a scholarship recipient out of state. The night before the ceremony, she developed a migraine and went to bed early at her hotel. When Besh flew into the city after 11 P.M., he called Marisol and asked her to meet him for a nightcap at his hotel across town. He was disappointed when she said no—that she was not feeling well and was already in bed. Emery somehow found out that Marisol had said no—"she couldn't believe it"—and told her that she *had* to go meet Besh, that it was part of her job. Marisol reluctantly went to the bar, where she intentionally sat across from Besh, not next to him. She sipped one glass of wine while he had several drinks, biding her time until she felt like she could excuse herself. Besh seemed disappointed that "it wasn't the night that he had expected." Marisol complained to Emery after the trip that she should not be required to do something like that as part of her job. Both of these incidents are in line with reports in which other employees felt pressured to enter into sexual relationships with Besh, particularly during trips away from New Orleans (Anderson 2017).

Marisol told me that after she quit, it finally became clear and undeniable to her that "when it came to me, race was an issue." Marisol gave notice that she was leaving the foundation shortly after the out-of-town trip. It was the end of a work week, and she was surprised that on the following Monday she was introduced to a white woman who was already set to replace her. Emery had met the new hire through sales, a marketing executive for a beverage company the BRG bought from. She lived elsewhere but wanted to move to New Orleans. Emery described the new hire as the perfect match for the foundation, and Marisol got the sense that everyone already knew and loved her. While Marisol was training her, the new hire complained to Marisol about the starting salary. Marisol was making less than $30,000 a year after promotions with few benefits, and she had to negotiate to have the BRG pay even a portion of her individual Affordable Care Act health-care plan. However, the new director was offered a starting salary close to two and a half times what Marisol was earning. Marisol was shocked, as she believed the new hire was underqualified for the job both experience-wise and academically. Marisol regretted that she "wasn't strong in those moments" and didn't push back, saying that it has taken her some time to be able to articulate the full impact of the discrimination she experienced: "It's been a few years of recovery. I talk about it, I choke up. You're scared. It's not about the money; it's just about dignity. There was none when I was there. It was horrible."

In the months after the publication of Anderson's report, some corporate changes took place at BRG and the foundation: the restaurant group adjusted its legal name to BRG Hospitality, dropping the reference to Besh; Besh stepped down from his public role, although he remained a co-owner; Whalen left BRG with several BRG hotel ventures and launched QED Hospitality with chef Brian Landry (also formerly with BRG); and a BRG employee, Shannon White, became the new CEO. A legal dispute between BRG chef Alon Shaya became public immediately before Anderson's story broke, which resulted in Shaya launching his own restaurant group, Pomegranate Hospitality. The Shaya Barnett Foundation transferred its affiliation to Pomegranate. Several months later, the Link Stryjewski Foundation also had to cancel a high-end fundraising event that featured Mario Batali, another chef accused of sexual harassment in the ongoing #MeToo investigations in the gastronomic world (Plagianos and Greenwald 2017).

The JBF went largely quiet for over a year, removing images of Besh from its website and social media platforms, and canceling planned fundraising events. In a phone interview from Los Angeles about nine months later, Aarón Sánchez said he was separating his scholarship fund from Chefs Move! with the intention of finding another fiscal sponsor. Just shy of a year later in September 2018, the JBF relaunched under the name Made in New Orleans (MiNO) with a new director. As the foundation regroups and MiNO emerges, Chefs Move! winners are navigating if and how they will continue their relationship with the foundation. Some are hopeful, and some are ambivalent; some have increased their involvement with the foundation's Alumni Council, while others have disengaged or completely distanced themselves. Some feel tenuously excited about the new director, a woman of color from New Orleans. The new CEO at BRG is a woman, and Besh is no longer a part of daily operations. However, MiNO launched out of the same foundation office inside the BRG, with Octavio Mantilla still at the helm of the corporation. The personal assistant to MiNO's director worked for the BRG for years. What does it take for entrenched racism and sexism—pervasive throughout the corporate structure—to change?

At the time of our coffee, René had decided to end involvement with the foundation: "It was sort of evil. I'm pretty sure they knew about it [the harassment] and did nothing." René said it was painful to see others remain involved with the foundation who "might not have had the harassment, but I lived it." When we had met six months before, René had expressed nuanced feelings about the foundation but had not mentioned sexual harassment. I asked René how it felt to speak with me that first time: "Emery trained me early on in interviews to say, 'The foundation did great things for me,' so I just stuck to that." It was only after working in kitchens outside BRG that René began questioning this allegiance, asking, "Why am I still trying to protect them? They're not protecting me." René explained how complex the negotiation of determining what to share about the foundation is: "What can I say? What can I not say? They did a good thing for me. They did wrong by me. It's not all good; it's not all bad. It's in-between."

René's and Marisol's experiences of sexual harassment and racism illustrate the hazards of businesses engaging in philanthropy and closely aligning their for-profit and charitable engagements.

Locating CSR: Spatiotemporal Configurations of Chef Philanthropy

In their CSR activity matrix first introduced in chapter 2 (table 2.1), Richey and Ponte (2011, 129) develop engaged CSR (also known as proper CSR) and disengaged CSR. Engaged CSR entails activities that directly affect a business's operations, while disengaged CSR activities are disconnected from or only partially linked to the company's functioning. CSR beneficiaries can be either proximate or distant. In engaged CSR, proximate beneficiaries are located within the corporation or its factories, and in disengaged CSR, beneficiaries are in communities where the corporation operates. In engaged CSR, distant beneficiaries are commodity chain suppliers conscientious of working conditions and environmental issues. "Brand Aid" is in the bottom right corner of the matrix—disengaged CSR with distant beneficiaries. Brand Aid signifies activities that are far from the corporation's headquarters or factories and are distant from the social settings or communities in which the corporation operates.

Building on Richey and Ponte's matrix but reflecting my own ethnographic context, I develop the terms "embedded CSR" and "disembedded CSR." Table 6.1 helps position and chart the spatiotemporal configurations of chef philanthropy in New Orleans. My development of embedded/disembedded

TABLE 6.1 Embedded and disembedded CSR matrix (distance from restaurant, its operations, and its workers, near to far)

I. Embedded CSR: within restaurants and corporate structure	II. Proximate CSR: restaurant industry	III. Proximate CSR: food and foodscapes	IV. Disembedded CSR
Description: Workplace conditions and politics at own restaurants (informed by interviews with chefs and non-elite cooks)	*Description: Corporate philanthropy with beneficiaries in the restaurant industry*	*Description: Corporate philanthropy with beneficiaries more broadly related to food or foodscapes*	*Description: Corporate philanthropy unrelated to restaurant industry or food/foodscapes*
Reforms target:	Foodscape interventions target:	Foodscape interventions target:	
• Wages, benefits, hours: living wage, fair wage, health care, paid time off (PTO)	*Labor/employment*	*Health*	
• Preventing and addressing sexual harassment	• Industry: food education	• Food aid/emergency food aid	
• Challenging segregation in roles and spaces along race, class, and gender lines (leadership; front of house/back of house; hot line and cold line)	• Industry: equity and equality	• Food access	
		• Food education	
• Hiring a diverse workforce and employees who are traditionally less respected (candidates lacking formal education; the formerly incarcerated; the elderly; women with caregiving responsibilities)		*Labor/employment*	
		• Agriculture	
		Multi	
• Addressing environmental impacts: transparency of supply chain, supporting local and organic food systems, serving seasonal products		• Food policy	
• Reduction of foods of animal origin and responsible sourcing of meat and fish			
• Reduction of waste, energy usage			
• Purpose of space beyond food service (political organizing, community space)			

CSR is tailored to smaller corporations and foodscape interventions, and it emphasizes the spatial dimensions of both the physical location of the intervention or reform and the social problem being addressed. Table 6.1 details CSR types according to distance from corporate headquarters and restaurants. Moving from left to right across the chart (from I to IV), reforms or interventions are a step further from the restaurant and foodscapes.

In embedded CSR, workplace conditions and politics, environmental impacts, and the purpose of the space beyond food service are the focus of reforms. The next category (II) is proximate CSR, in which philanthropic efforts are directed toward the restaurant industry specifically. Category III, proximate CSR, broadly targets food and foodscapes. Disembedded CSR, the final category (IV), is disembedded both in its location (interventions occurring outside the restaurant) and in its interventions in social issues that are unrelated to food.

Embedded CSR (category I) focuses on a variety of reforms in workplace conditions. The list of conditions was developed from interview data with chefs and non-elite cooks.[3] Participants emphasized different aspects of the list. For example, Alexa and Tucker focused on HR policies like employee benefits. Tyrione, a Black woman who owns a small restaurant that grew out of a food truck, sees it as her privilege and responsibility to hire previously incarcerated individuals and grandmothers, people "who can't get jobs anywhere else." She stressed how thankful she is that she is able to employ people who need work. Tyrione says that she learned over time that running a restaurant is "bigger than money . . . it isn't about money. It's about being a community leader and giving." Like many small and non-elite restaurateurs, Tyrione *also* engages in proximate and disembedded CSR, sometimes feeding homeless or hungry people who come into her restaurant but cannot afford to pay (category III) and sometimes contributing financially to safe homes and shelters for women and children (category IV). When asked why she does not exclusively focus on foodscape issues, she explained that her life experiences, particularly growing up in the Lower Ninth Ward, make her "look at the bigger picture all around, what the whole situation is." Tyrione tries to find where there is the most need for her help; sometimes it involves food, and sometimes it does not.

Chefs like Nikki from the Cajun restaurant aim to address the environmental impact of their restaurants.[4] Restaurants are contributors to climate change and environmental degradation, as they use large amounts of energy, and most source food products from industrial food systems that require energy-intensive agriculture and petrochemical fertilizers (Nesheim, Oria, and Yih 2015). Industrial food systems have negative environmental impacts, such as increases in carbon emissions, increases in greenhouse gases, and deterioration of water quality (Nesheim, Oria, and Yih 2015, 127). Scholars studying environmental sustainability in restaurants have proposed that researchers should fundamentally be concerned with the question: "How effectively and to what extent are sustainable restaurants contributing to the quality of life of the local community in which they reside?" (Barneby and Mills 2015, 302). This holistic approach, focused on the broader impacts of restaurants—how a restaurant serves its community—reflects my findings about the values and priorities of restaurants that are not elite or do not have a celebrity chef at the helm.

The final component of embedded CSR regards the purpose of the space beyond food service. Dooky Chase's Restaurant is an excellent example of this aspect because the history that unfolded (and continues to unfold) within the restaurant's walls is about the creation of a space that challenged legal segregation, fostered relationships, and supported organizing efforts for the civil rights movement (Bell 2018; Edge 2017, 80–81; Loyola University n.d.). As just one example, in an upstairs dining room at the restaurant, chef Leah Chase served gumbo to Dr. Martin Luther King Jr. and visiting Freedom Riders as they met with organizers of the bus boycotts in Baton Rouge to strategize and plan their next effort. It was thus upstairs at Dooky Chase's where much of Rosa Parks's refusal to give up her seat at the front of a public bus in Montgomery, Alabama (a turning point of the movement) was planned.

Unlike the global reach of the corporations studied by Richey and Ponte, the restaurant groups and associated foundations in my research are smaller scale and have a primary footprint in New Orleans. However, philanthropic expansion beyond New Orleans is likely as restaurant corporations grow. Emeril Lagasse opened his first restaurant in New Orleans in the early 1990s, and the Emeril Lagasse Foundation was founded in 2002. The Lagasse Foundation is now one of the more established chef foundations in New Orleans, and Emeril's Culinary Garden and Teaching Kitchen is a project being implemented in various locations across the United States. An example beyond the New Orleans context is World Central Kitchen, the popular food-aid project of Spanish-born chef José Andrés. World Central Kitchen has worked in New Orleans (Firth 2022) but also extensively nationally and internationally, with current projects supporting Ukrainians both within the country and in Romania, Moldova, Hungary, Slovakia, Spain, and Germany. Andrés's first restaurant opened in 1993, and the José Andrés Group (formerly Think-FoodGroup, LLC, co-founded with Rob Wilder) now has at least eighteen international restaurants. According to the group's website, the company's "singular" mission is to "Change the World Through the Power of Food."[5] With the scale of restaurants and philanthropy built into its corporate mission, national and international CSR by similarly sized restaurant corporations and chefs is likely to continue to grow.

Causumerism and Ethical Consumption

> [Food is] what we're about and it's what we like and it goes to a good cause. So when you think about that—it's perfect. So you think, "Okay, I'm spending this much money on this ticket" but then if it's going to such a great cause you feel so much better about it. You know? Because it's going to do something else, other than just line their pockets.
>
> —RHONDA, John Besh Foundation donor

In reflecting on her decision to buy a ticket to attend the JBF fundraiser Fêtes Fest, Rhonda said she enjoys fine dining and that when she knows there is a fundraising element tied to the food event, she feels "so much better about it." At a Dinner on the Farm featuring the executive chef of Shaya (a JBF restaurant), I sat near a young white woman in her early thirties who had given her boyfriend tickets to the dinner as a present: "When I'm giving gifts, I try to do gifts that are doing good," and she said that she had previously gifted a "stove to a woman in a developing country."

The primary emergent engagement strategy for those who want to support chefs' charitable work is causumerism. Causumerist practices, or ethical consumption, contend that consumer spending can be directed toward humanitarian concerns and can be used to solve social problems (see Lewis and Potter 2011). Mainstream US food movement trends—such as calls to "vote with your fork" through buying sustainable, organic, or local food—align with causumerism. Food is often positioned as a commodity or consumer good in advanced capitalist societies and, accordingly, is available for causumer mobilization. It is significant that the chefs engaging in this philanthropy are well-known and have some degree of celebrity status. As discussed in chapter 2, celebrities are considered especially effective conduits of market-based and causumer-based approaches to humanitarian aid.

For most chef projects, the majority of financial support does not come from an individual's private wealth but must be fundraised. Causumerism is a key fundraising strategy they employ, and it takes two primary forms: consumer goods/commodities and experiences. Research on causumerism has primarily studied material commodities, but my research shows the need to expand our understanding of causumerism to include experience. In this form, the causumer good is an event in which donors buy a charitable experience, such as the crawfish boil at Besh's home (chapter 4) or any number of the special events that chefs (or organizations, such as Grow Dat Youth Farm) use to fundraise. Rhonda, a white woman who grew up in New Orleans and claims that for her family, "everything we do is about food," found out about the Besh Foundation when her daughter brought her to a cooking demonstration and meal with Aarón Sánchez at BRG restaurant Johnny Sánchez. Rhonda insisted that culinary-themed events are the perfect fundraiser for the local context: "In this city, what do you do for fun? You go out. So a venue [event] like that is going to be a good winner."

Ofra Koffman, Shani Orgad, and Rosalind Gill (2015, 158) propose that the focus of the humanitarian gaze is changing with an emergent "'selfie humanitarianism' in which helping others is intimately connected to entrepreneurial projects of the self." Drawing on theorizing by Lilie Chouliaraki, Koffman, Orgad, and Gill argue that the solidarity offered in selfie humanitarianism is not animated by solidarity and calls for redistribution or social justice but offers "makeovers of subjectivity" for the humanitarian donor. In tracking how humanitarian communication has changed over time, Chouliaraki (2013, 3) notes "the emergence of a self-oriented morality, where doing good to others is about 'how I feel' and must, therefore, be rewarded by minor gratifications to the self." My ethnography complicates the notion of who counts as a beneficiary. Is the person who attends a chef's private fundraising party or purchases a causumer product a *beneficiary* of an intervention? This feels aligned with the change noted by Ponte and Richey (2011, 2060) in celebrity-led causumerism from "conscious consumption" based on product-related information to "compassionate consumption," which regards managing consumer affect.

At Willa Jean, a BRG-owned bakery in the CBD, customers can purchase a $6.00 Milk Money latte (figure 6.2). The latte is advertised as a way to "support local farmers," as a portion of sales from each latte will go toward the foundation's microlending efforts. One such customer was René, the former Chefs Move! winner, who ordered a steaming Milk Money latte in a tall white cup at the Willa Jean to-go counter before sitting down for our first interview. I asked about it: "The milk that they use for this latte, they actually get from one of the farms that got a microloan from Besh, and part of the proceeds that they get from selling it, they give it back to them. So, they're getting something from me buying it which is why I always get it.

FIGURE 6.2 A sign advertising the Milk Money latte at Willa Jean restaurant in the CBD. The text reads: "Support local farmers with the Milk Money Latte: A portion of the proceeds from every Milk Money Latte goes towards The John Besh Foundation's Milk Money Microloan Initiative." Photo by the author.

And it tastes delicious." René misunderstood how the financing works, believing that the money, at least in part, goes directly to the dairy farmer who supplied the milk. As shown in the section that follows, René's misunderstanding illustrates concerns by one of the farmers about how the loans are represented.

Milk Money and Donor Imaginaries

Milk Money was the first project the Besh Foundation launched in 2011, with the stated mission of helping the "many farmers in Louisiana who have a marketable, delicious product" increase their production and sell their goods in local food systems, including farmers markets, grocery stores, and restaurants, by giving them access to microloans (JBF website 2015, site discontinued). Leo is a young white farmer who has a small diversified family farm on the Northshore of Lake Pontchartrain. His mother oversees a cut flower business on the same property, and I saw them selling a wide array of vegetables and beautiful bouquets several times at the bustling Covington Farmers Market on Saturday mornings.

In the early 2010s, Leo needed to buy a tractor to expand his heritage chicken operation. Leo had sold chickens to a BRG restaurant and heard about Milk Money through one of John Besh's friends, who was a mutual acquaintance. Leo applied through the foundation for a $10,000 loan, which was then financed through Hope Credit Union. He was told that the foundation had a partnership with the Tulane University MBA program and that loan recipients would also receive additional marketing and business strategy support, but at least for Leo, nothing materialized in this regard (which he cited as a disappointment).

Leo thought the loan itself was great and unique because a traditional bank loan would not finance what he wanted: a used 1980s Kubota tractor. To Leo, the essential benefit of Milk Money was that the JBF "legitimized" the loan for the credit union to approve it—that the Besh endorsement made the credit union feel comfortable about cutting the check. Leo stressed that everything else was the same as a regular loan. He was concerned about the loan being misrepresented as an award or a grant:

> I know my check goes to the Hope Federal Credit Union, not to the Besh Foundation, when I pay back the loan that I got. There was something in the paper about how we got this "award" or something. And we had a couple of customers congratulate us and refer to it as a grant. I remember in one instance I was like, "Well, we got a loan," and they were surprised that it wasn't free money. I went to a bank and got a loan and I pay it back on a timeframe with interest. . . . Besh didn't just give me the money. It's a loan. "Yeah, you made it easier and I appreciate that, but it wasn't free." . . . I don't think they should be painted as like, "We're giving away seed money." No, they should be saying, "We facilitate regular ass bank loans between farmers and the bank."

Here Leo acknowledges the presence of a small gift—the use of the Besh name as an intermediary to legitimize the loan—but to Leo, it is only a gift in this limited sense.

The last time someone from BRG or the foundation visited his farm was several years before our interview, and Leo thought that the majority of the foundation's attention was directed toward the Chefs Move! program. Leo said that the loan almost didn't happen due to delays and a lack of communication from the foundation for almost a year:

LEO: Every time I would send her [Emery] an email I would get an auto response that she was dealing with Chefs Whatever—the other program we were talking about—?
ME: Chefs Move?
LEO: Yeah. "I'm in New York, I'll be back Monday"—this after this after this and like never [hearing from her].

Ruth, one of JBF's staff members, reiterated Leo's assertion about the foundation's priorities in a different way, saying that Milk Money is "a really cool part of our foundation that it is not really focused on. It's not quite as flashy, it's not a $65,000 scholarship."

The dynamics of Milk Money are significantly different from what was described by Chefs Move! beneficiaries, as discussed earlier. The gift is less, or as in Leo's understanding, there is not much of a gift at all. Milk Money beneficiaries subsequently feel less of a need to engage in reciprocity. Milk Money beneficiaries are white rural farmers, while Chefs Move! winners are young urban people of color; in a sociohistorical context, they are positioned drastically differently as receivers. There is significantly less visual representation of Milk Money winners: I never saw a farmer standing onstage next to Besh at a public event, and there is little media coverage about the program. On the Milk Money section of the JBF website, instead of portraits of farmers there is a close-up photograph of a fuzzy cow with big eyes (figure 6.3).

As the foundation is focused on fundraising, the lack of representation of farmer beneficiaries serves a strategic purpose, even if it is not conscious. What makes the scholarship more flashy? Who looks deserving of a (white) donor's charity? Who do donors "want to see"? The construction of the "deserving beneficiary" is not uncomplicated: indeed, donors could view beneficiaries of color as evidence of racial justice, and that aim is a purported goal of the foundation. Based on interviews, donors may hold racial equity as a goal, but the way they spoke of winners reflected a more simplistic and enduring imaginary, one in which hardworking young people of color are marked as both deserving and needy—in need of their white charity.

FIGURE 6.3 The web page promoting the Milk Money program, November 2015. Image from John Besh Foundation website.

Conclusion: Brand Signaling and "Ethical" Restaurants

This chapter analyzes chef humanitarianism and business regarding branding, CSR, and ethical consumption. I find that for chefs and restaurants that engage in business-aligned and business-informed philanthropy, overlap between their corporate and philanthropic structures and practices can infuse the culinary world's problems of sexism and racism into chefs' charitable work. I introduced an analytical tool that charts the spatiotemporal configurations of chef philanthropy in New Orleans. In table 6.1, I highlighted differences between embedded, proximate, and disembedded CSR in relation to foodscape interventions. I see this analysis as vitally important due to a push in CSR to align standard operations and corporate philanthropy. In this movement, businesses target areas of external need that are closely aligned with their work (table 6.1, Proximate CSR, categories II & III) — a goal or best practice promoted in CSR efforts (Brandt, personal communication, 2017). Following a logic that businesses should "do what they know best" in all their areas of engagement, CSR initiatives are being pushed toward continuity between a business's for-profit work and its philanthropic work. My research studies such alignment closely and attempts to illuminate the potentials, complexities, and pitfalls of this trend.

In chapter 4, I showed that chef foundations align for-profit work and daily operations, mobilizing a form of philanthropy that is based on corporate practices, procedures, and knowledge. In my findings about the restaurant industry in New Orleans, celebrity chefs often skip over embedded CSR (for example, the BRG not having an HR department, paying low wages, and not addressing endemic sexual harassment) and focus heavily on category II, proximate CSR in the restaurant industry (such as starting service industry training programs and giving away scholarships to culinary school). As I discussed earlier, proximate CSR in the restaurant industry in New Orleans has been unable to address root causes of racism and sexism in the industry and risks channeling young people of color into low-wage work through the kinds of programming and interventions they support.

To close this chapter, I end with a reflection about branding and causumerism. Meeting for the first time in the fall of 2018, the new director of MiNO (the rebranded JBF) shared that the foundation had decided to focus on Chefs Move! and had closed the Milk Money program, with the possibility of relaunching it in the future. I was not surprised to hear this, as Milk Money had appeared to be winding down for years. Biking past Willa Jean bakery on my way back to my apartment immediately after our meeting, a curiosity overtook me and I pulled up onto the sidewalk and peered inside. Behind the long bakery counter loaded with breads, cakes, and cookies, a sign advertising the $6.00 Milk Money latte still hung above the espresso machine.

Nine months later, I returned to Willa Jean again, and the Milk Money latte was still listed on the menu. There has been no public announcement, but perhaps MiNO has decided to start the project back up again. Regardless, I always found the latte to be somewhat of an enigma and this further increased my sense of the oddness of it: Why would JBF fundraise for a loan that was financed by a credit union? When I asked about it, the explanation was kept simple: that the latte funded Milk Money. Promotional materials about the project are vague, such as the sign in figure 6.2 that reads "A portion of the proceeds from every Milk Money Latte goes towards The John Besh Foundation's Milk Money Microloan Initiative." Funds raised could be used for administrative costs, or perhaps JBF created an emergency savings account that could be used if farmers defaulted on their loans and the bank called on JBF to pay up. These are just hypotheses, however, and I think most customers assume that buying a Milk Money latte means you are somehow giving a gift to a local farmer. Given that that is not the case, I argue that the latte serves purposes beyond fundraising.

Having the latte on the menu is a form of brand signaling, telling customers that they can feel good about spending their money at the expensive restaurant in the gentrifying CBD. The latte signals to customers "we're good people." In an industry where sexual harassment, racism, and low wages are endemic, the sweetness of the Milk Money latte helps the restaurant project itself as an ethical space, aiding the restaurant's brand (Richey and Ponte 2011, 10–11). In this instance, aid to the restaurants might be the only form of aid happening at all.

CHAPTER SEVEN

Conclusion

Uneven Geographies of Giving

> As globalization drives a move toward homogenization, cultural
> distinction becomes an important competitive advantage. . . . By any
> economic measure, Louisiana has a competitive advantage in its culture.
>
> —MT. AUBURN ASSOCIATES, *Louisiana: Where Culture Means Business*

In the State of Louisiana's 2005 report on cultural economic development
(see figure 7.1; discussed in chapter 3), this quote reflects what the report
refers to as the "competitive advantage of authenticity." The commodifica-
tion and instrumentalist use of culture for economic growth was key to rebranding the city post-disaster for outside investment and tourism promotion.
New Orleans's distinctive foodways have been mobilized in branding strategies that emphasize multicultural harmony (gumbo), sustainability (local
produce featured in local dishes), and the continuing resilience of the city
(Tom Fitzmorris's restaurant tracker). As "authentic" cultural icons imbued
with culinary capital, chefs became leaders of the city's recovery and rebuilding efforts after Katrina. Some chefs, propelled by the economic boom
of the city's "restaurant renaissance," have formalized and institutionalized
their philanthropic efforts into the form of foundations, which continue to
emerge in New Orleans. Restaurants, heralded as forces of recovery, are also
part of the uneven redevelopment of the city (chapter 3). Such uneven redevelopment has, at least in part, contributed to chefs' success, allowing them
to move into philanthropic spaces and become humanitarian leaders.

Charting the rapid proliferation of foundations being launched by chefs,
we can examine the implications of the "new" New Orleans and the future
being imagined by philanthropists in the city. As discussed in chapter 3,
Woods (2017b, 3) writes: "Through the eye of Katrina, we see the old dry
bones of both the Freedom Movement and the plantation oligarchy walking
again in daylight." After the levees failed, New Orleans was not a tabula
rasa that erased the city's social geographies shaped by enslavement, segregation, and unequal economic investment; the inequalities shaping the
city's rebuilding are related to unfinished Black freedom struggles. In trac-

FIGURE 7.1 Cover of July 2005's report *Louisiana: Where Culture Means Business*. Published a month before Katrina by the Department of Culture, Tourism and Recreation, the report recommends strategies that would rebrand the state as a "cultural hub." Image by Mt. Auburn Associates, 2005.

ing the geographies of the gift, philanthropy occurs within, and continues to further shape, the city's unequal social geographies.

The proliferation of chef-led foodscape interventions in New Orleans is reflective of international trends in which celebrities are leaders in humanitarian efforts and agendas. Geographic engagement with giving has been limited, and literature in other disciplines has largely neglected to consider how giving in the context of the United States is situated spatially and constructed historically. Geographies of giving are shaped by the history of the land; practices of giving are cultivated within a landscape of social inequality and social relations, which shape what forms of philanthropy become possible and legible. Gift geographies must consider giving's uneven spatiality and historicity.

Geographies of corporate giving in foodscapes can be analyzed through a framework of embedded and disembedded CSR (table 6.1). This tool uses a spatial lens to reveal the nuanced formulations and implications of the politics, potentials, and limitations of business-based involvement in foodscapes and social change. Using this framework while attending to the geographies of giving—giving's spatial, historical, and intersectional construction—allows elite and corporate philanthropy to be studied more robustly, with greater potential insight and impact in research findings. Although developed in the context of New Orleans and foodscapes, these lenses or tools can be useful in other interdisciplinary research on giving.

This project attempts to write an intimate feminist ethnography that "studies up." Themes of land, history, and narration animate my personal biography and have informed my methodological approach, studying places and institutions where I am personally enmeshed. Place, history, and power must be carefully considered in order to understand the gift and its manifestations in foodscapes. I join calls from feminist, antiracist, and Indigenous scholars and activists (among others) to radically rethink philanthropy. Although I hold no sweeping answers, we must engage with questions that challenge business as usual and historical patterns of inclusion and exclusion.

In this final chapter, I highlight core themes of the gift, fundraising/financing, and the history of the land. I review my core arguments and findings; highlight limitations of the research and areas for future research; and discuss implications of my research for theory, policy, and practice.

Implications for Practice: Knowledge Exchange with Chef Foundations

Although I feel diffident to suggest best practices, there are practical findings pertinent to share with practitioners of chef philanthropy.[1] These findings could also be useful for chefs who do not have foundations, helping them make more informed choices about their charitable engagement. Chefs start nonprofit organizations and foundations for different reasons, as noted primarily in chapter 5. Chefs and restaurants are frequently approached for donations and can become overwhelmed by requests when they lack an administrative structure to process and evaluate inquiries. Thus, one reason chefs start foundations is to create or formalize a structure that is dedicated to their philanthropic efforts. Chefs also start foundations to have more control over their philanthropy, wanting to set their own humanitarian agenda rather than respond to requests by others. They worry about the fallout of supporting a "bad" organization; thus, I observed a pattern of replication, in which chefs follow avenues established by peers and undertake the same forms of philanthropic engagement with the same or similar organizations. Chefs can overextend their capacity when they start a foundation or engage in philanthropic projects: they are often unaware of the labor required to run a nonprofit organization, particularly one that is not endowed and requires constant fundraising.

Starting a foundation is not necessarily a reflection of wealth or generosity; indeed, chefs run foundations as part of their branding strategies and often fundraise from individual donors to be able to run their organization. The increasingly common use of the inaccurate term "foundation" (chapter 4) has been strategically useful for chef foundations as it suggests that chefs hold significant wealth even if they do not, and it signals the idea that chefs are generous, sharing wealth from their business's success, even when the money is actually being fundraised from external sources.

Ethical consumption and causumerism are mobilized to help fund chef projects. I argue that fundraising events are a form of causumerism and that "the fundraiser" is a prominent spatiotemporal configuration of chef philanthropy that is essential to how this philanthropy operates. Fundraisers are sites of financial gain for foundations; branding and meaningful engagement for chefs; pleasure and ethical consumption for donors; and opportunities, intense racialized histories, and contested representations for beneficiaries. In food movements in the United States, a widespread belief that food systems can be reformed by "voting with your fork" has limited our collective imagination and curtails potential for more systemic change.

I contend that another reason chefs engage in philanthropy and humanitarian work is because it provides an outlet for "acceptable care." In hypermasculinized restaurant environments, philanthropy provides a meaningful way for male chefs to show care for others. As chef philanthropy is largely disembedded and happens outside the spaces of corporate offices and restaurants, it does not threaten white men's dominant positioning within culinary spaces, and boundaries of traditional and heteronormative gender roles can be maintained or managed. Philanthropy can also be a way for chefs to firm up those boundaries or to reinforce relationships of power and privilege. For example, the Lagasse Foundation's Boudin, Bourbon and Beer Festival capitalizes on "macho" food and drink, and the four chef co-chairs of 2019's event were men, three of which were white. In both proximate and disembedded philanthropy (table 6.1), chefs enact relationships of giving that are imbued with power differentials, such as the racialized and gendered dynamics observed at the crawfish boil at John Besh's home.

Chef foundations engage in disembedded forms of CSR and draw on business-based knowledge and solutions that inform their areas of engagement and enable their fundraising efforts. Although experience in producing events makes them effective at fundraising, chefs lack knowledge, expertise, and experience in the social problems their foodscape interventions target. Chefs often hire from their professional restaurant networks to staff their nonprofit organizations, but this practice puts into power leaders who do not have appropriate skills and experience to facilitate social programming. In particular, I find that chefs lack skills in power analysis and understanding their own positionality.

The Shaya Barnett Foundation uses curriculum from the controversial National Restaurant Association to train teenagers as future culinary workers. The John Besh Foundation attempted to tackle widespread racism within the restaurant industry through culinary education for individual young people of color. Speaking about the Chefs Move! initiative, Besh has said: "We can't allow education to become the stumbling point that keeps somebody with huge potential from realizing that potential" (Sivewright 2017). However, as Jabari Brown countered (chapter 4), "What if lacking credentials isn't the problem?" These decidedly individualistic approaches to social change tend to disregard—and are unlikely to dismantle—pervasive structures of racial and other forms of inequality within the restaurant industry. Due to the celebrity status of the benefactors leading these projects,

I find that chef philanthropy provides a form of "Brand Aid" (Richey and Ponte 2011) to the restaurant industry, working to brand and rebrand the gourmet culinary world as ethical. A lack of robust analysis around race, class, and gender in these initiatives suggests that the transformative power of these projects is limited at best and even risks reifying systems of oppression within foodscapes. The lack of an anti-oppression orientation and intersectional perspective can have consequences for beneficiaries, as I found with regard to sexual harassment in chef philanthropy.

Beneficiaries have diverse and complex understandings of the gifts that they have received, with variations in their experience as unique individuals and due to differences in race, class, and gender. Beneficiaries often stress that any criticism they hold is not directed toward an individual chef. They think deeply about reciprocity—what is "owed" to the chefs and foundations that supported them. Evaluating the effectiveness of chefs' programs was not a research goal, but I found that ignoring gender, class, and other axes of power and historical exclusion affects beneficiaries and inhibits a foundation's ability to meet its purported social mission. Overall, chef foundations lack analysis about power, and would benefit greatly from learning anti-oppression modalities. As mentioned in chapter 5, Grow Dat has used the VISIONS model since 2012, and for several years I have been training and facilitating VISIONS work with other institutions as well. Working in this framework, I have seen individuals and organizations come to understand their role in systemic oppression and how good intentions often cause harm.

As discussed in chapter 1, Holt-Giménez and Shattuck (2011) and Levkoe (2011) draw distinctions between issue-based and system-based initiatives. New Orleans's foodscape initiatives are primarily issue-based and limited in their scope. Chef interventions, as part of traditional philanthropic structures and nonprofit institutions, seldom align with system-based food movements and are thus most commonly engaged in neoliberal and reformist interventions (Holt-Giménez and Shattuck 2011) rather than more transformative food politics (Levkoe 2011).

Future Research: Afterlives of Aid and Connections across the Gulf

There is need to study private interventions that failed or shut down, such as Wendell Pierce's Sterling Farms and Frank Stronach's Magnaville/ Canadavillle. I conceptualize this as the "afterlife of aid," a consideration of the worlds created by philanthropic projects beyond their official end. Following what are often splashy media-intensive launches, many celebrity aid initiatives seem to vanish almost overnight. As interventions are part of branding strategies for celebrities or corporations, when projects falter or fail, they often fade quickly from the public sphere so as not to damage a celebrity's brand. Why do projects fail, and after they shut their doors or end their formal operations, what remains? Studying failed projects will open up another avenue of vital information about geographies of giving.

My ethnography is limited to New Orleans, but there is a need to conduct more research across North–South divides (J. Robinson 2011), and I propose that the Gulf of Mexico is a particularly salient arena for such thinking, collaborations, and scholarship. Although I focused this research on chef philanthropy in New Orleans, philanthropic foodscape projects in Mexico, Cuba, and the US states that border the Gulf are proliferating and are worthy of comparative study. Cross-cutting environmental issues such as climate change, which are not bounded by geopolitical borders, require this sort of thinking and action. Feminist scholarship calls on us to make "connections among diverse geographical locations and related socio-economic processes within colonial and neo-colonial contexts that influence gendered livelihoods, social movements and control over resources" (Oberhauser and Johnston-Anumonwo 2014, 2). Transnational perspectives and analysis that crosses borders acknowledges the global nature of inequality, food systems, and environmental degradation, and demonstrates that only global responses will adequately address the challenges we face. I hope this research helps spur other inquiries that will invest in making these connections across diverse locations.

Giftlessness and the Rightful Share

If gifts are inherently ambivalent in Berking's sense or even impossible in Derrida's formulation, as discussed in chapter 2, why do we continue to think in terms of giving? I see a practical need to engage other practices that are not based on the gift. Wealth is commonly dispersed in six primary ways: taxation, paid labor, investments (including trust funds or other methods of intergenerational wealth transfer), charity or philanthropy, individual contributions (which are often tied to paid labor, such as pensions or unemployment funds in the United States), and distribution or cash transfers (either conditional or unconditional). Here it is expedient to consider ways (other than gift exchange) in which people access resources. How is a country's wealth distributed or shared? Who should distribute it, and who should be the recipient?

I want to consider the notion of giftlessness. In James Ferguson's (2015, 178) writing on the politics of distribution, such as basic income grants or unconditional cash transfers, "no one is giving anyone anything." In development and aid practices, poor people access money primarily through labor market participation or charitable interventions. Charitable interventions often target labor. The popular saying from which Ferguson takes the book's title — "Give a man a fish and you feed him for a day; teach a man to fish and you feed him for a lifetime" — suggests not only a masculine self-sufficiency but also entrepreneurialism. I have seen this sentiment in other formulations, such as the phrase "a hand up, not a hand out," which was frequently invoked in interviews with founders and staff of Frank Stronach's Canadaville project.

In the "politics of distribution," Ferguson (2015, 51) claims that "some of the most potent and radical political demands in the region today turn less on abstract rights than on very specific claims to a share of material goods." Here, Ferguson begins developing the idea that social payments are ownership shares. "Transfer" and "social payment" are the terms used most frequently in southern Africa, and this reflects an important terminological distinction, as they mean something different from aid or grants. It is my contention that the key difference is that aid and grants imply giving and gifts, and that these transfers are importantly *not* gifts. Ferguson draws on both corporate capitalism's use of shares and anthropological studies on sharing to develop the concept of "the share" instead of "the gift." He asks, "What if a poor person should receive a distributive payment neither as reciprocal exchange for labor (wages) or good conduct (the premise of conditional cash transfers) nor as an unreciprocated gift (assistance, charity, a helping hand) but instead as a share, a rightful allocation due to a rightful owner?" (Ferguson 2015, 178).

Thinking about Mauss, Derrida, Diprose, and now Ferguson inspires me to ask: Does a gift require inequality or unequal power relations? As a gift is given by one entity to another (be it collective or individual) and hierarchies mediate human interactions, is inequality inherent among the exchangers? Even if we affirm that equality can exist between the entities to begin with, does the functioning of the cycle of reciprocity create inequity? Or, as Hattori (2001, 641) believes about foreign aid, is it possible that inequities apparent in the reciprocal cycle "signal and euphemize" hierarchies but no not "actively reinforce, mitigate, or worsen" hierarchies? The redistribution of wealth that occurs through elite philanthropy risks overlooking or even accepting the vast inequality that created such a context to begin with. Through giftlessness, such politics of distribution do away with the messy gift completely, suggesting that there are other ways to redistribute wealth.

Closing Reflections

In "The Gift of Good Land," Wendell Berry posits that Judeo-Christian teachings focus too much on heroism and heroes, emphasizing the unique and exceptional actions of individualistic "great men" (1981, 276). Berry argues that secular US culture embraced the idea of the hero postindustrialization, and that people are encouraged to embrace "the ambition to be a 'pioneer' of science or technology, to make a 'breakthrough' that will 'save the world' from some 'crisis' (which now is usually the result of some previous 'breakthrough')" (1981, 277–78). In Berry's critique of heroism, I see parallels to the savior mentality (Flaherty 2016) and white savior industrial complex (Cole 2012), defined as a "confluence of practices, processes, and institutions that reify historical inequities to ultimately validate white privilege" (A. Anderson 2013, 39). Philanthropic reformer Edgar Villanueva (2018, 5) calls philanthropy "the savior mentality in institutional form." Who gets to be a hero? How often do our heroes become heroic due to systems of power and privilege that undergird their accomplishments? As Tajee asked in chapter 4, "Why did it come to this? Why did this person"—a hero—"need to create this opportunity for me to take?"

Charitable celebrity chefs are indicative of cultural norms in which "the extraordinary actions of 'great men'" are desired and celebrated (Berry 1981, 276). Berry (1981, 280) argues that what is necessary to do good work is "not to invent new technologies or methods, not to achieve 'breakthroughs,' but to determine what tools and methods are appropriate to specific people, places, and needs, and to apply them correctly. Application (which the heroic approach ignores) is the crux." Berry thinks that application is the most important aspect of doing good work. However, this is a slow, modest, complex, and often collective process, which is antithetical to individualistic heroism.

In my research, chef foundations struggle with application. As Teju Cole (2012) writes, "There is much more to doing good work than 'making a difference.'" Many chef foundations aim to train the next generation of chefs, some with the explicit goal of making young chefs of color the new leaders of the culinary world. These are laudable goals, but attention to the *processes* through which these missions are realized—how these missions are applied and who applies them—is crucial. An employee at a chef foundation reflected: "All these things, they look great on paper, but once you really start to get into [the] details of it—this is not realistic or sustainable." Chef foundations focus on formal culinary training, but education and credentials are inadequate to dismantle the multifaceted racism and sexism of the restaurant industry. In that light, we must take seriously the fact that chef philanthropy reflects the industry that created it. Chef engagement in humanitarianism holds potential to offer more just futures, but the path to liberatory outcomes is not an easy one given the background of inequality that has largely enabled the success of elite chefs.

Over the course of my research, I sensed a growing belief that chefs *should* be charitable, that they are *expected* to become humanitarian leaders. Starting a foundation is good for business and is a status symbol—a "chic way of saying 'I've made it'" (as described in chapter 4). Starting a foundation is also a significant responsibility. Restaurants large and small reported being inundated with requests for help. Chefs are asked to cook on-site at "dine around" fundraising events, to donate gift cards and food, to become board members at NGOs, to champion causes, to sponsor events. Despite the glossy sheen that celebrity chef culture promotes, most restaurant jobs pay low wages, and even well-known chefs report struggling to keep their restaurants open due to tight profit margins. Why is a woman who owns two restaurants approached more than 500 times each year to donate food to charity? Why is there so much focus on chefs "giving back" to the larger community, while little attention is paid to how chefs control working conditions and environmental impacts in their own kitchens? These are signs of fractured financial systems and inequalities that fail to make our collective social fabric robust and secure.

I'll close with a question I keep returning to: What happens when we turn our collective humanitarian gaze not to gifts (charity), heroes (celebrity chefs), and selfies (our causumer selves) but to the history of the land, the rightful share, social movements, and collective efforts? What new futures become possible?

Notes

Chapter One

1. Gaines is a pseudonym, as are all names other than celebrities and public figures.

2. "Minority" is the term used by the John Besh Foundation.

3. The mission of Grow Dat Youth Farm is to nurture a diverse group of young leaders through the meaningful work of growing food. Grow Dat launched its first leadership program in 2011 and is a nonprofit 501(c)(3) organization. For more information, visit www.growdatyouthfarm.org.

4. "Causumerism" refers to consumerism with a cause — that is, shopping for a charitable purpose.

5. Food apartheid is a critical alternative to thinking and scholarship on food deserts (see Reese [2019, 5–7] on anti-Blackness and food apartheid). Leah Penniman (2018, 4) explains that food apartheid "makes clear that we have a human-created system of segregation that relegates certain groups to food opulence and prevents others from accessing life-giving nourishment."

6. Chef Alon Shaya left the Besh Restaurant Group shortly before sexual harassment allegations against the company became public and founded his own enterprise, Pomegranate Hospitality. (For more background, see Burton [2018].)

7. For further discussion of chefs' COVID-19 pandemic responses, see Firth (2022).

8. The term "foodscape" was coined by geographers to "identify and analyze the socio-spatial manifestation of human–food activities, foodstuffs and subsequent social or health implications" (Panelli and Tipa 2009, 456). The term has been widely used in urban studies, public health, and sociology. Norah MacKendrick (2014, 16) stresses that "the foodscape is never fixed; its boundaries shift depending on how the food environment expands and contracts."

9. Publication of the World Bank's *World Development Report* in 1990 ushered in a widespread approach to global poverty reduction, defined at the time as the New Poverty Agenda (Lipton and Maxwell, 1992) or New Policy Agenda (M. Robinson 1993).

10. For an overview of key definitions and debates about food systems, see Feagan 2007 on local and community food systems and Roberts 2008 on world food and "modernist" systems.

11. Azra Sayeed and Norma Maldonado (2013, 21) continue in their description of food sovereignty:

> It drives an anti-colonialist agenda in food production and consumption, upholding the right of small producers to have access and control over their productive resources including land, forests, water sources, and seeds. It emphatically acknowledges the central role of women as producers across

various sectors including agriculture and fisheries. These conditions are critical to ensuring access to affordable, safe and nutritious food for all, including urban marginalized communities. In particular, food sovereignty emphasizes domestic production based on traditional agro-ecological methods of food production, ensuring household and community food security first, and then distribution to wider domestic markets. It also emphasizes cooperation—rather than competition—in food and agriculture trade, rejecting and resisting trade liberalization as a means of controlling the production and livelihoods of small farmers producing for local markets. It also advocates a spirit of cooperation with respect to food aid, especially in the face of natural and climate disasters, and rejects the use of food aid as a means of controlling food and agriculture commodities markets.

12. "Community" is a contested term, and for the purposes of my research, it primarily designates third-sector activity and engagement in social issues. In my ethnography, I try to illuminate the contested meanings of community throughout the text by continually reflecting on inclusion, exclusion, and power.

13. A 2010 study by the USDA Economic Research Service (Ralston et al. 2010) found no consensus on a definition for "local food system"; I follow Watts (1983, 521) in defining food systems as "complexes of human activity and interaction that affect the production, consumption, appropriation, trading and circulation of food."

14. Gotham and Greenberg (2014) argue that New Orleans is a "crisis city," marked not just by the disaster of Katrina itself but by a large-scale and long-term breakdown after the hurricane. They claim that a disaster triggers a crisis (the large-scale and long-term breakdown) if the conditions are right in the underlying "landscape of risk and resilience": "where risk and inequality are intense and widespread protections are weak, crises will likely ensue" (6).

15. See Sam Karlin (2019) on Louisiana's Motion Picture Production Tax Credit.

Chapter Two

1. For more on philanthropic history, see Olivier Zunz (2012) and INCITE! Women of Color Against Violence (2007) for critical debates. For broader perspectives on contemporary philanthropy and social justice not limited to the context of the United States, see Morvaridi (2015).

2. As an example, the photograph on the cover of the INCITE! volume (2007) is from a fundraiser taking place in front of the offshore oil rig "habitat" exhibit at Audubon Aquarium in New Orleans. The exhibit, in which visitors can "explore an underwater oil rig in the Aquarium's Gulf of Mexico exhibit and meet the aquatic animals that thrive around its barnacled pilings" (https://audubonnatureinstitute .org/gulf-of-mexico), was sponsored by Shell, BP, Exxon Mobile, and other oil corporations.

3. Philanthropic leader Courtney Harvey predicts that this will change in the coming years: a massive transfer of global wealth is anticipated in the next twenty years, and

women will be the main inheritors "simply due to the fact that they live longer" (Harvey, personal communication).

4. Questions about care work and what counts as a gift and who counts as a giver arise here. Care work is important to consider, as simplistic notions of reciprocity in giving are inadequate to explain the complex, relational nature of caregiving. Gift giving, if it does not include giving of one's time and one's labor, risks ignoring significant aspects of women's giving specifically. Nurturing relationships are stressed in Genevieve Vaughan's (2007) work on gift economies.

5. LaFleur and Brainard (2009, 9–13) identify these five new leaders: venture philanthropists, corporations, the poor, the public, and celebrities.

6. I take a pluralist view on development, which "covers a multitude of theoretical and political stances and a wide diversity of practices" (Cornwall, Harrison, and Whitehead 2007, 1), and draw on Woods (2017a) as he engages with development thought specifically in the context of the US South.

7. For a sociological history and overview of the discipline of celebrity studies, see Ferris 2007.

8. See also Turner's (2014, 3–30) introduction to his *Understanding Celebrity* for further discussion on defining celebrity.

9. "Brand Aid" is a phenomenon "based on three pillars: a brand, one or more aid celebrities, and a cause" (Richey and Ponte 2011, 10–15). See discussion in chapter 7.

10. The term "causumerist" is attributed to Ben Davis, cofounder of buylesscrap .org (Ponte and Richey 2011, 2066).

11. See also King (2006) on breast cancer philanthropy and the corporate "market for generosity."

Chapter Three

1. Post-9/11, Homeland Security absorbed FEMA (the Federal Emergency Management Agency).

2. The growth coalition was operating under a contract with the International Regional Development Council set up by the City of New Orleans and Greater New Orleans, Inc. (Gotham and Greenberg 2014).

3. CAN describes itself as "a non-profit organization that gives back to the chefs who cook from their souls, donate their time and talent, and help us better understand the many complex issues related to food." Visit the CAN website at https:// chefaction.squarespace.com/who-we-are.

4. Galatoire's is one of the city's oldest restaurants, and Fitzmorris (1996, 143) refers to it as the "cornerstone of fine Creole dining."

5. Willie Mae's was rebuilt through celebrity chef efforts, which I detail in the forthcoming section, "Humanitarian of the Year."

6. The website for the Shrimp and Petroleum Festival is accessible at www .shrimpandpetroleum.org/.

7. The John Besh Foundation was recast as the Made in New Orleans Foundation (MiNO) in 2018 after sexual harassment accusations against the Besh Restaurant Group became public in 2017. See chapter 6.

8. The renovation of the historic St. Roch Market (originally built in 1875) was at the center of gentrification debates in New Orleans (see White 2015).

9. Research on the gendered impacts of PPPs in women's health is from Gideon and Porter (2015).

Chapter Four

1. Sociologists Josée Johnston and Shyon Baumann (2015, x) study the boundaries of gourmet foodscapes by documenting how "foodies"—"a person who devotes considerable time and energy to eating and learning about good food, however 'good food' is defined"—distinguish themselves through "high-brow and low-brow" eating practices.

2. See Zunz (2012) for a history of the legal battles about the creation of foundations and government regulation of foundations.

3. *Garden & Gun* is a monthly culture and lifestyle magazine focused on the US American South.

4. At the restaurants, young and slim women were also hired into roles that had greater levels of public visibility, such as hostesses (Anderson 2017).

5. See Patricia Turner (2008) on the history of the term "Uncle Tom." Contemporarily, it is often used as a slur, meaning an African American man who is subservient or obsequious, "who will sell out any black man if it will curry the favor of a white employer."

6. "Large scale plantations" were defined as having a "big house" and more than a hundred enslaved persons living and working on the property (Vlach 1993, 8).

7. "Cajun" refers to an ethnic group descended from French ancestors expelled from Acadia (Nova Scotia) in the mid-1700s who settled in Louisiana (see Gutierrez 1992, 3–33).

8. The television show ran from 2013 to 2017; it was canceled after the sexual harassment allegations became public.

Chapter Five

1. See Dylan Rodríguez (2007) on the nonprofit industrial complex.

2. The legal drinking age is twenty-one in the United States, and most program participants are between fifteen and nineteen years old.

3. As I discuss in chapter 3, "community" primarily designates third-sector activity and engagement in social issues.

4. Houston, Texas, experienced intense flooding in late August 2017 after Hurricane Harvey.

5. The term "downtown" usually refers to areas of the city east of Canal Street; west of Canal is "uptown." However, the CBD is often part of descriptions of downtown, grouped with the Convention Center and the French Quarter (see Campanella 2006).

6. Media venues such as ProPublica (Elliott and Umansky 2016) have been investigating the Red Cross, reporting failures in its response to several disasters, including Superstorm Sandy in 2012, the Haiti earthquake in 2010, and flooding in Mississippi in 2016.

7. Red beans and rice is a traditional New Orleans dish (see Beriss 2012).

Chapter Six

1. See Firth (2022) for further discussion of caring in times of crisis and on the professionalization of chef philanthropy.

2. Richey and Ponte's (2011, 10–15) formulation of "Brand Aid" is composed of three pillars: brands, aid celebrities, and causes, or Brand + Aid Celebrity + Cause = Brand Aid.

3. Alexandra Ketchum (2018) outlines how restaurants can utilize and enact feminist principles to further expand these aspects of workplace conditions.

4. See Sloan, Legrand, and Hindley (2015) on sustainability in restaurants (further expanding these aspects of environmental impact).

5. José Andrés Group's website, https://joseandres.com/mission/.

Chapter Seven

1. The term "chefs" is used as a shorthand throughout this section to refer not only to individual chefs but also to institutions (chef foundations and their staff teams) more generally.

Bibliography

Adams, Jessica. 2007. *Wounds of Returning: Race, Memory, and Property on the Postslavery Plantation.* Chapel Hill: University of North Carolina Press.

Adams, Vincanne. 2013. *Markets of Sorrow, Labors of Faith: New Orleans in the Wake of Katrina.* Durham, N.C.: Duke University Press.

Ahn, Christine E. 2007. "Democratizing American Philanthropy." In *The Revolution Will Not Be Funded: Beyond the Non-profit Industrial Complex,* edited by INCITE! Women of Color Against Violence, 64–76. Cambridge, Mass.: South End Press.

Alderman, Derek, David Butler, and Stephen Hanna. 2015. "Memory, Slavery, and Plantation Museums: The River Road Project." *Journal of Heritage Tourism* 11 (3): 209–18.

Allen, Greg. 2015. "Some Moved On, Some Moved In and Made a New New Orleans." *All Things Considered.* NPR, August 26, 2015. www.npr.org/2015/08/26 /434288564/some-moved-on-some-moved-in-and-made-a-new-new-orleans.

Anderson, Ashlee. 2013. "Teach for America and the Dangers of Deficit Thinking." *Critical Education* 4 (11): 28–47.

Anderson, Brett. 2017. "John Besh Restaurants Fostered Culture of Sexual Harassment, 25 Women Say." *Times-Picayune.* October 21, 2017.

Ashlee, Aeriel A., Bianca Zamora, and Shamika N. Karikari. 2017. "We Are Woke: A Collaborative Critical Autoethnography of Three 'Womxn' of Color Graduate Students in Higher Education." *International Journal of Multicultural Education* 19, no. 1 (2017): 89–104. https://doi.org/10.18251/ijme.v19i1.1259.

Associated Press. 2010. "Louisiana to Spend $5 Million in BP Money on Tourism Every 3 Months." *NOLA.Com Times-Picayune,* November 20, 2010. https://www .nola.com/news/gulf-oil-spill/index.ssf/2010/11/louisiana_to_spend_5_million_i .html.

———. 2010. "State to Spend $5M in BP Money Every 3 Months." New Orleans CityBusiness. November 22, 2010. https://neworleanscitybusiness.com/blog/2010 /11/22/state-to-spend-5m-in-bp-money-every-3-months/.

Barneby, Charles, and Juline E. Mills. 2015. "The Sustainable Restaurant: Does It Exist?" In *The Routledge Handbook of Sustainable Food and Gastronomy,* edited by Philip Sloan, Willy Legrand, and Clare Hindley, 297–304. Oxford: Routledge.

Barnes, Christine. 2014. "Mediating Good Food and Moments of Possibility with Jamie Oliver: Problematising Celebrity Chefs as Talking Labels." *Geoforum* 74:169–78.

Barnett, Michael, and Thomas Weiss. 2008. "Humanitarianism: A Brief History of the Present." In *Humanitarianism in Question: Politics, Power, Ethics,* edited by Michael Barnett and Thomas Weiss, 1–48. Ithaca, N.Y.: Cornell University Press.

Bell, Janet Dewart. 2018. *Lighting the Fires of Freedom: African American Women in the Civil Rights Movement.* New York: New Press.

Beriss, David. 2007. "Authentic Creole: Tourism, Style and Calamity in New Orleans." In *The Restaurants Book: Ethnographies of Where We Eat*, edited by David Beriss and David Sutton, 151–66. Oxford: Berg.

——. 2012. "Red Beans and Rebuilding: An Iconic Dish, Memory and Culture in New Orleans." In *Rice and Beans: A Unique Dish in a Hundred Places*, edited by Richard Wilk and Livia Barbosa, 241–63. London: Berg.

Beriss, David, and David Sutton. 2007. "Restaurants, Ideal Postmodern Institutions." In *The Restaurants Book: Ethnographies of Where We Eat*, edited by David Beriss and David Sutton, 1–13. Oxford: Berg.

Berking, Helmuth. 1999. *Sociology of Giving*. London: SAGE.

Berry, Wendell. 1969. "A Native Hill." *Hudson Review* 21 (4): 601–34.

——. 1981. "The Gift of Good Land." In *The Gift of Good Land: Further Essays Cultural and Agricultural*, 267–81. New York: North Point Press.

Besh, John. 2011. *My Family Table: A Passionate Plea for Home Cooking*. Kansas City: Andrews McMeel.

Bishop, Matthew, and Michael Green. 2008. *Philanthrocapitalism: How the Rich Can Save the World*. New York: Bloomsbury.

Bohannon, John, and Martin Enserink. 2005. "Scientists Weigh Options for Rebuilding New Orleans." *Science* 309 (5742): 1808–9.

Boltanski, Luc, and Laurent Thévenot. 2006. *On Justification: Economies of Worth*. Translated by Catherine Porter. Princeton, N.J.: Princeton University Press.

Boorstin, Daniel J. 1971. *The Image: A Guide to Pseudo-Events in America*. New York: Atheneum.

Bornstein, Erica. 2012. *Disquieting Gifts: Humanitarianism in New Delhi*. Stanford, Calif.: Stanford University Press.

Boykoff, Maxwell T., and Michael K. Goodman. 2009. "Conspicuous Redemption? Reflections on the Promises and Perils of the 'Celebritization' of Climate Change." *Geoforum* 40 (3): 395–406.

Bradshaw, Sarah. 2013. *Gender, Development and Disasters*. Cheltenham: Edward Elgar.

Brockington, Dan. 2009. *Celebrity and the Environment: Fame, Wealth and Power in Conservation*. London: Zed Books.

——. 2014. *Celebrity Advocacy and International Development*. Oxford: Routledge.

Brown, Jabari, Kevin Connell, Jeanne Firth, and Theo Hilton. 2020. "The History of the Land: A Relational and Place-Based Approach for Teaching (More) Radical Food Geographies." *Human Geography* 13 (3): 242–52.

Brown, Jabari, Leo Gorman, and Kevin Connell. 2016. "The History of the Land." In *Cultivating Tomorrow's Leaders: Foundations for Lasting Change*, edited by Jeanne Firth, 124–29. New Orleans: Grow Dat Youth Farm.

Browne, Katherine E. 2015. *Standing in the Need: Culture, Comfort, and Coming Home after Katrina*. Austin: University of Texas Press.

Budabin, Alexandra Cosima, and Lisa Ann Richey. 2021. *Batman Saves the Congo: How Celebrities Disrupt the Politics of Development*. Minneapolis: University of Minnesota Press.

Burns, Robert, and Matthew Thomas. 2015. *Reforming New Orleans: The Contentious Politics of Change in the Big Easy*. Ithaca, N.Y.: Cornell University Press.

Burton, Monica. 2018. "Alon Shaya and John Besh End Legal Fight over the Shaya Name." *EATER.* April 12, 2018. www.eater.com/2018/4/12/17228666/john-besh -alon-shaya-lawsuit-settlement.

Bush, Leigh Chavez. 2019. "The New Mediascape and Contemporary American Food Culture." *Gastronomica: The Journal of Critical Food Studies* 19 (2): 16–28.

Byrd, Kaitland M. 2015. "Modern Southern Food: An Examination of the Intersection of Place, Race, Class, and Gender in the Quest for Authenticity." In *A Place-Based Perspective of Food in Society*, edited by Kevin Fitzpatrick and Don Willis, 103–19. New York: Palgrave Macmillan.

Cairns, Kate, and Josée Johnston. 2015. *Food and Femininity.* London: Bloomsbury.

Calkin, Sydney. 2015a. "Feminism, Interrupted? Gender and Development in the Era of 'Smart Economics.'" *Progress in Development Studies* 15 (4): 295–307.

———. 2015b. "Post-Feminist Spectatorship and the Girl Effect: 'Go Ahead, Really Imagine Her.'" *Third World Quarterly* 36 (4): 654–69.

Callahan, David. 2017. *The Givers: Wealth, Power and Philanthropy in a New Gilded Age.* New York: Alfred A. Knopf.

Camp, Jordan T., and Laura Pulido. 2017a. "The Cornerstone of a Third Reconstruction." In *Development Drowned and Reborn: The Blues and Bourbon Restorations in Post-Katrina New Orleans* by Clyde Woods, edited by Laura Pulido and Jordan T. Camp, 291–97. Athens: University of Georgia Press.

———. 2017b. "The Dialectics of Bourbonism and the Blues." In *Development Drowned and Reborn: The Blues and Bourbon Restorations in Post-Katrina New Orleans,* by Clyde Woods, edited by Laura Pulido and Jordan T. Camp, xxi–xxix. Athens: University of Georgia Press.

Campanella, Richard. 2006. "Uptown/Downtown: Shifting Perceptions, Shifting Lines." In *Geographies of New Orleans: Urban Fabrics Before the Storm*, 157–67. Lafayette: Center for Louisiana Studies, University of Louisiana.

Carney, Judith. 2009. *Black Rice: The African Origins of Rice Cultivation in the Americas.* Cambridge, Mass.: Harvard University Press.

Carney, Judith, and Richard Nicholas Rosomoff. 2009. *In the Shadow of Slavery: Africa's Botanical Legacy in the Atlantic World.* Berkeley: University of California Press.

Chant, Sylvia. 2016. "Addressing World Poverty through Women and Girls: A Feminised Solution?" *Sight and Life* 30 (2): 58–62.

Chouliaraki, Lilie. 2006. *The Spectatorship of Suffering.* London: SAGE.

———. 2010. "Post-Humanitarianism: Humanitarian Communication beyond a Politics of Pity." *International Journal of Cultural Studies* 13 (2): 107–26.

———. 2013. *The Ironic Spectator: Solidarity in the Age of Post-Humanitarianism.* Cambridge: Polity Press.

Cole, Teju. 2012. "The White-Savior Industrial Complex." *Atlantic*, March 21, 2012.

Cooper, Andrew Fenton. 2008. *Celebrity Diplomacy.* Boulder: Paradigm.

Cooper, Christopher, and Robert Block. 2006. *Disaster: Hurricane Katrina and the Failure of Homeland Security.* New York: Henry Holt.

Cornwall, Andrea, Elizabeth Harrison, and Ann Whitehead, eds. 2007. "Introduction: Feminisms in Development: Contradictions, Contestations and Challenges." In

Feminisms in Development: Contradictions, Contestations and Challenges, 2–18. London: Zed Books.

Crouch, Colin. 2004. *Post-Democracy*. Cambridge: Polity Press.

David, Emmanuel, and Elaine Enarson. 2012. *The Women of Katrina: How Gender, Race, and Class Matter in an American Disaster*. Nashville: Vanderbilt University Press.

Davis, Dàna-Ain, and Christa Craven. 2016. *Feminist Ethnography: Thinking through Methodologies, Challenges, and Possibilities*. Lanham, Md.: Rowman & Littlefield.

Dempsey, Sarah E., and Kristina E. Gibson. 2015. "Make Good Choices, Kid: Biopolitics of Children's Bodies and School Lunch Reform in Jamie Oliver's Food Revolution." *Children's Geographies* 13 (1): 44–58.

Derickson, Kate. 2014. "The Racial Politics of Neoliberal Regulation in Post-Katrina Mississippi." *Annals of the Association of American Geographers* 104 (4): 889–902.

Derrida, Jacques. 1992. *Given Time: I. Counterfeit Money*. Chicago: University of Chicago Press.

———. 2002. *Negotiations: Interventions and Interviews, 1971–2001*. Edited by Elizabeth Rottenberg. Stanford, Calif.: Stanford University Press.

———. 2007. *Psyche: Inventions of the Other*. Vol. 1. Edited by Peggy Kamuf and Elizabeth Rottenberg. Stanford, Calif.: Stanford University Press.

DeVault, Marjorie L. 1991. *Feeding the Family: The Social Organization of Caring as Gendered Work*. Chicago: University of Chicago Press.

Dieter, Heribert, and Rajiv Kumar. 2008. "The Downside of Celebrity Diplomacy: The Neglected Complexity of Development." *Global Governance: A Review of Multilateralism and International Organizations* 14 (3): 259–64.

Diouf, Sylviane A. 2014. *Slavery's Exiles: The Story of the American Maroons*. New York: New York University Press.

Diprose, Rosalyn. 2002. *Corporeal Generosity: On Giving with Nietzsche, Merleau-Ponty, and Levinas*. Albany: State University of New York Press.

Doherty, Bob, Iain A. Davies, and Sophi Tranchell. 2013. "Where Now for Fair Trade?" *Business History* 55 (2): 161–89.

Dorell, Oren. 2005. "Louisianans Get Few Post-Katrina Contracts." *USA Today*, December 10, 2005. http://usatoday30.usatoday.com/news/washington/2005-10-12-katrina-contracts_x.htm.

Douglas, Mary. 2002. "Forward: No Free Gifts." In *The Gift*, edited by Marcel Mauss, ix–xxiii. London: Routledge.

DuBois, W. E. B. 1899. *The Philadelphia Negro: A Social Study*. Philadelphia: University of Pennsylvania Press.

Eckstein, Justin, and Anna Young. 2015. "Cooking, Celebrity Chefs, and Public Chef Intellectuals." *Communication and Critical/Cultural Studies* 12 (2): 205–8.

Edge, John T. 2017. *The Potlikker Papers: A Food History of the Modern South*. New York: Penguin Press.

Edwards, Michael. 2014. *Civil Society*. 3rd ed. Cambridge: Polity Press.

Egerton, John. 1993. *Southern Food: At Home, on the Road, in History*. Chapel Hill: University of North Carolina Press.

Elliott, Justin, and Eric Umansky. 2016. "We Want You to Help Report on the Red Cross: Introducing the Red Cross Reporting Network." ProPublica, June 21, 2016. www.propublica.org/article/introducing-the-red-cross-reporting-network.

Farah, Nuruddin. 1999. *Gifts*. London: Penguin Books.

Fassin, Didier. 2012. *Humanitarian Reason: A Moral History of the Present*. Berkeley: University of California Press.

Fausset, Richard. 2016. "Baton Rouge Is Passionate, and Peaceful, After Shooting of Alton Sterling." *New York Times*, July 7, 2016.

Feagan, Robert. 2007. "The Place of Food: Mapping Out the 'Local' in Local Food Systems." *Progress in Human Geography* 31 (1): 23–42.

Federici, Silvia. 2012. "Feminism and the Politics of the Commons." In *The Wealth of the Commons: A World Beyond Market & State*, edited by David Bollier and Silke Helfrich. Amherst, Mass.: Levellers Press.

Feldman, Brian. 2016. "Brutal Sign Shames Airbnb-Using NOLA Tourists: 'Enjoy Our Former Homes Y'all!!!'" *New York Magazine: Intelligencer*, April 27, 2016. http://nymag.com/intelligencer/2016/04/new-orleans-residents-are-not-fond-of-jazz-fest-airbnb-guests.html.

Felton, Emmanuel. 2016. "New Orleans' Uphill Battle for More Black and Homegrown Teachers." The Hechinger Report. https://hechingerreport.org/new-orleans-uphill-battle-black-homegrown-teachers/.

Ferguson, James. 2015. *Give a Man a Fish: Reflections on the New Politics of Distribution*. Durham, N.C.: Duke University Press.

Fernando, Jude L., ed. 2004. *Microfinance: Perils and Prospects*. Oxford: Routledge.

Ferris, Marcie Cohen. 2014. *The Edible South: The Power of Food and the Making of an American Region*. Reprint. Chapel Hill: University of North Carolina Press.

Firth, Jeanne. 2012. "Healthy Choices and Heavy Burdens: Race, Citizenship and Gender in the 'Obesity Epidemic.'" *Journal of International Women's Studies* 13 (2): 33–50.

———. 2022. "Crisis Caring: Chef Foundations, Branding, and Responsibility in Foodscapes." *Food, Culture & Society*, October 2022.

Firth, Jeanne, and Catarina Passidomo. 2022. "New Orleans' 'Restaurant Renaissance,' Chef Humanitarians, and the New Southern Food." *Food, Culture & Society* 25 (2): 183–200.

Fisher, Carolyn. 2007. "Selling Coffee, or Selling Out? Evaluating Different Ways to Analyze the Fair-Trade System." *Culture & Agriculture* 29 (2): 78–88.

Fitzmorris, Tom. 2010. *Tom Fitzmorris's Hungry Town: A Culinary History of New Orleans, the City Where Food Is Almost Everything*. New York: Abrams.

Flaherty, Jordan. 2016. *No More Heroes: Grassroots Challenges to the Savior Mentality*. Chico, Calif.: AK Press.

Fouts, Sarah. Forthcoming. *Right to Remain: Street Vendors and Day Laborers in Post-Katrina New Orleans*. Chapel Hill: University of North Carolina Press.

Fuqua, Joy V. 2011. "Brand Pitt: Celebrity Activism and the Make It Right Foundation in Post-Katrina New Orleans." *Celebrity Studies* 2 (2): 192–208.

Fussell, Elizabeth, Narayan Sastry, and Mark VanLandingham. 2010. "Race, Socioeconomic Status, and Return Migration to New Orleans after Hurricane Katrina." *Population and Environment* 31: 20–42.

Gautier, Arthur, and Anne-Claire Pache. 2015. "Research on Corporate Philanthropy: A Review and Assessment." *Journal of Business Ethics* 126 (3): 343–69.

Gideon, Jasmine, and Fenella Porter. 2015. "Unpacking "Women's Health" in the Context of PPPs: A Return to Instrumentalism in Development Policy and Practice?" *Global Social Policy* 16 (1): 68–85.

Giridharadas, Anand. 2018. *Winners Take All: The Elite Charade of Changing the World.* New York: Alfred A. Knopf.

González de la Rocha, Mercedes. 2001. "From the Resources of Poverty to the Poverty of Resources? The Erosion of a Survival Model." *Latin American Perspectives* 28 (4): 72–100.

Goodman, Michael K. 2013. "ICare Capitalism? The Biopolitics of Choice in a Neo-Liberal Economy of Hope." *International Political Sociology* 7 (1): 103–5.

Gotham, Kevin Fox, and Miriam Greenberg. 2014. *Crisis Cities: Disaster and Redevelopment in New York and New Orleans.* New York: Oxford University Press.

Graves, Lisa, and Zaid Jilani. 2018. "The Restaurant Industry Ran a Private Poll on the Minimum Wage. It Did Not Go Well for Them." *The Intercept,* April 17, 2018. https://theintercept.com/2018/04/17/the-restaurant-industry-ran-a-private-poll -on-the-minimum-wage-it-did-not-go-well-for-them/.

Gutierrez, C. Paige. 1992. *Cajun Foodways.* Jackson: University Press of Mississippi.

Guzman-Lopez, Adolfo. 2019. "Group Brings a Mexican Flavor to New Orleans's Mardi Gras." *Washington Post,* February 25, 2019.

Hackler, M. B. 2010. "'Louisiana's New Oil': Planning for Culture on the New Gulf Coast." In *Culture After the Hurricanes: Rhetoric and Reinvention on the Gulf Coast,* edited by M. B. Hackler, 3–16. Jackson: University Press of Mississippi.

Hale, Grace Elizabeth. 1998. *Making Whiteness: The Culture of Segregation in the South, 1890–1940.* New York: Pantheon.

Hall, Gwendolyn Midlo, and Pippin Frisbie-Calder. 2018. "San Malo Maroons." Paper Monuments. New Orleans Historical. Last updated October 19, 2018. https://neworleanshistorical.org/items/show/1403.

Haraway, Donna. 1989. *Primate Visions: Gender, Race, and Nature in the World of Modern Science.* New York: Routledge.

———. 1998. *How Like a Leaf: An Interview with Thyrza Nichols Goodeve.* New York: Routledge.

Harris, Deborah, and Patti Giuffre. 2015. *Taking the Heat: Women Chefs and Gender Inequality in the Professional Kitchen.* New Brunswick, N.J.: Rutgers University Press.

Harris, Jessica. 1989. *Iron Pots and Wooden Spoons: Africa's Gifts to New World Cooking.* New York: Atheneum.

———. 1995. *The Welcome Table: African-American Heritage Cooking.* New York: Fireside.

———. 2011. *High on the Hog: A Culinary Journey from Africa to America.* New York: Bloomsbury.

Hattori, Tomohisa. 2001. "Reconceptualizing Foreign Aid." *Review of International Political Economy* 8 (4): 633–60.

Hay, Iain, ed. 2013. *Geographies of the Super Rich.* Cheltenham: Edward Elgar.

Hay, Iain, and Samanatha Muller. 2014. "Questioning Generosity in the Golden Age of Philanthropy: Towards Critical Geographies of Super-Philanthropy." *Progress in Human Geography* 38 (5): 635–53.

Heldke, Lisa M. 2003. *Exotic Appetites: Ruminations of a Food Adventurer*. New York: Routledge.

Hiltner, Stephen. 2018. "Vietnamese Forged a Community in New Orleans. Now It May Be Fading." *New York Times*, May 5, 2018.

Hobson, Marian. 1998. *Jacques Derrida: Opening Lines*. London: Routledge.

Holmes, Su, and Sean Redmond. 2010. "A Journal in Celebrity Studies." *Celebrity Studies* 1 (1): 1–10.

Holt-Giménez, Eric. 2010. "Food Security, Food Justice, or Food Sovereignty?" *Food First Backgrounder* 16 (4): 1–4.

Holt-Giménez, Eric, and Annie Shattuck. 2011. "Food Crises, Food Regimes and Food Movements: Rumblings of Reform or Tides of Transformation?" *Journal of Peasant Studies* 38 (1): 109–44.

Horowitz, Andy. 2020. *Katrina: A History, 1915–2015*. Cambridge, Mass: Harvard University Press.

Hozić, Aida A., and Jacqui True. 2016. "Making Feminist Sense of the Global Financial Crisis." In *Scandalous Economics: Gender and the Politics of Financial Crises*, 3–20. New York: Oxford University Press.

Huliaras, Asteris, and Nikolaos Tzifakis. 2010. "Celebrity Activism in International Relations: In Search of a Framework for Analysis." *Global Society* 24 (2): 255–74.

INCITE! Women of Color Against Violence. 2007. *The Revolution Will Not Be Funded: Beyond the Non-profit Industrial Complex*. Cambridge, Mass.: South End Press.

IRS (Internal Revenue Service). 2018. "Public Charities." 2018. www.irs.gov/charities -non-profits/charitable-organizations/public-charities.

Ishiwata, Eric. 2011. "'We Are Seeing People We Didn't Know Exist': Katrina and the Neoliberal Erasure of Race." In *The Neoliberal Deluge: Hurricane Katrina, Late Capitalism, and the Remaking of New Orleans*, edited by Cedric Johnson, 32–59. Minneapolis: University of Minnesota Press.

Jaffe, Rivke, Eveline Dürr, Gareth A. Jones, Alessandro Angelini, Alana Osbourne, and Barbara Vodopivec. 2019. "What Does Poverty Feel Like? Urban Inequality and the Politics of Sensation." *Urban Studies* 57 (5): 1–17.

Jaffee, Daniel. 2012. "Weak Coffee: Certification and Co-optation in the Fair Trade Movement." *Social Problems* 59 (1): 94–116.

Jaffee, Daniel, and Philip H. Howard. 2010. "Corporate Cooptation of Organic and Fair Trade Standards." *Agriculture and Human Values* 27 (4): 387–99.

Jochum, Kimberly, Amanda Knight, and University of New Orleans History Department. 2019. "City Park." New Orleans Historical. 2019. https://neworleans historical.org/tours/show/9.

Jochum, Kimberly, and Michael Mizell-Nelson. 2019. "Segregation in City Park." New Orleans Historical. Last modified August 19, 2019. https://neworleanshistorical.org /items/show/203?tour=9&index=6.

Johnson, Cedric. 2011a. "Charming Accommodations: Progressive Urbanism Meets Privatization in Brad Pitt's Make It Right Foundation." In *The Neoliberal Deluge:*

Hurricane Katrina, Late Capitalism, and the Remaking of New Orleans, edited by Cedric Johnson, 187–224. Minneapolis: University of Minnesota Press.

———. 2011b. "Introduction: The Neoliberal Deluge." In *The Neoliberal Deluge: Hurricane Katrina, Late Capitalism, and the Remaking of New Orleans*, edited by Cedric Johnson, xvii–l. Minneapolis: University of Minnesota Press.

———. 2011c. *The Neoliberal Deluge: Hurricane Katrina, Late Capitalism, and the Remaking of New Orleans*. Minneapolis: University of Minnesota Press.

———. 2015. "Gentrifying New Orleans: Thoughts on Race and the Movement of Capital." *Souls: A Critical Journal of Black Politics, Culture, and Society* 17 (3–4): 175–200.

Johnston, Josée, and Shyon Baumann. 2015. *Foodies: Democracy and Distinction in the Gourmet Foodscape*. 2nd ed. New York: Routledge.

Kabeer, Naila. 2005. "Is Microfinance a 'Magic Bullet' for Women's Empowerment? Analysis of Findings from South Asia." *Economic and Political Weekly*, 4709–18.

Kapoor, Ilan. 2012. *Celebrity Humanitarianism: The Ideology of Global Charity*. Oxford: Routledge.

Karim, Lamia. 2011. *Microfinance and Its Discontents: Women in Debt in Bangladesh*. Minneapolis: University of Minnesota Press.

Karlin, Sam. 2019. "Film Tax Break Costs Louisiana Millions, New Study Shows; Supporters Rally at Entertainment Summit." *Advocate*, March 28, 2019.

Kelting, Lily. 2016. "The Entanglement of Nostalgia and Utopia in Contemporary Southern Food Cookbooks." *Food, Culture & Society* 19 (2): 361–87.

Kendall, Diana. 2002. *The Power of Good Deeds: Privileged Women and the Social Reproduction of the Upper Class*. Lanham, Md.: Rowman & Littlefield.

Ketchum, Alexandra. 2018. *How to Start a Feminist Restaurant*. Portland, Ore.: Microcosm.

Kimmerer, Robin Wall. 2013. *Braiding Sweetgrass: Indigenous Wisdom, Scientific Knowledge, and the Teachings of Plants*. Canada: Milkweed.

King, Samantha. *Pink Ribbons, Inc.: Breast Cancer and the Politics of Philanthropy*. Minneapolis: University of Minnesota Press, 2006.

Koffman, Ofra, Shani Orgad, and Rosalind Gill. 2015. "Girl Power and 'Selfie Humanitarianism.'" *Continuum: Journal of Media and Cultural Studies* 29 (2): 157–68.

Kummer, Corby. 2006. "Open for Business." *Atlantic*, March 2006.

LaFleur, Vinca, and Lael Brainard. 2009. "Making Poverty History? How Activists, Philanthropists, and the Public Are Changing Global Development." In *Global Development 2.0: Can Philanthropists, the Public, and the Poor Make Poverty History?*, edited by Lael Brainard and Derek Chollet, 9–41. Washington, D.C.: Brookings Institution Press.

Laidlaw, James. 2002. "A Free Gift Makes No Friends." In *The Question of the Gift: Essays Across Disciplines*, edited by Mark Osteen, 45–66. Oxford: Routledge.

Lax, Jacob, and Angela Mertig. 2020. "The Perceived Masculinity of Meat: Development and Testing of a Measure across Social Class and Gender." *Food, Culture & Society* 23 (3): 416–26.

LEDC (Louisiana Economic Development Council). 1999. "Louisiana: VISION 2020, State of Louisiana Master Plan for Economic Development."

Levkoe, Charles Zalman. 2011. "Towards a Transformative Food Politics." *Local Environment: The International Journal of Justice and Sustainability* 16 (7): 687–705.

Lewis, David. 2014. *Non-governmental Organizations, Management and Development.* 3rd ed. Oxford: Routledge.

Lewis, Tania, and Emily Potter, eds. 2011. *Ethical Consumption: A Critical Introduction.* London: Routledge.

Lipton, Michael, and Simon Maxwell. 1992. "The New Poverty Agenda: An Overview." IDS Discussion Paper No. 306. Brighton: Institute of Development Studies at the University of Sussex.

Little, Amanda. 2010. "Rebuilding New Orleans—the Green Way." *O, The Oprah Magazine*, September 2010. www.oprah.com/world/brad-pitts-make-it-right -foundation-in-new-orleans-katrina/all.

Littler, Jo. 2015. "The New Victorians? Celebrity Charity and the Demise of the Welfare State." *Celebrity Studies* 6 (4): 471–85.

Liu, Yvonne Yen, and Dominique Apollon. 2011. *The Color of Food.* Applied Research Center. February 2011. www.raceforward.org/sites/default/files/downloads/food _justice_021611_F.pdf.

Lorde, Audre. 2007. "The Master's Tools Will Never Dismantle the Master's House." In *Sister Outsider: Essays and Speeches*, 110–14. Berkeley, Calif.: Crossing Press.

Löwenthal, Leo. 1961. *Literature, Popular Culture, and Society.* New Jersey: Prentice-Hall.

Loyola University. n.d. "'A Haven for All of Us:' Documenting the World of Dooky Chase Restaurant in the Era Before Desegregation." Loyola University New Orleans, Department of History, Documentary and Oral History Studio. Accessed May 17, 2023. http://cas.loyno.edu/history/haven-all-us-documenting -world-dooky-chase-restaurant-era-desegregation.

MacCash, Doug. 2015. "Brad Pitt: 'I Feel Fantastic" about Make It Right.' *Times-Picayune*, August 15, 2015. www.nola.com/news/article_c28e8b3e-62ed-5e01-8f74 -d8980ce92269.html.

MacKendrick, Norah. 2014. "Foodscape." *Contexts* 13 (2): 16–18.

Mackenzie, Catriona, and Natalie Stoljar, eds. 2000. *Relational Autonomy: Feminist Perspectives on Autonomy, Agency, and the Social Self.* Oxford: Oxford University Press.

Mansky, Jackie. 2017. "Food Historian Reckons with the Black Roots of Southern Food." *Smithsonian*, January 8, 2017. www.smithsonianmag.com/arts-culture /food-historian-reckons-black-roots-southern-food-180964285/.

Marshall, David. 1984. "Adam Smith and the Theatricality of Moral Sentiments." *Critical Inquiry* 10 (4): 592–613.

Marshall, Neill, Stuart Dawley, Andy Pike, and Jane Pollard. 2018. "Geographies of Corporate Philanthropy: The Northern Rock Foundation." *Environment and Planning A* 50 (2): 266–87.

Martin, Brett. 2019. "The Provocations of Chef Tunde Wey." *GQ*, June 3, 2019.

Maurer, Bill. 2016. Foreword to *The Gift*, by Marcel Mauss, rev. ed., ix–xvii. Translated by Jane I. Guyer. Chicago: Hau Books.

Mauss, Marcel. 2002. *The Gift.* Translated by W. D. Halls. Oxford: Routledge. Originally published as "Essai sur le don" in *L'Année sociologique.*

———. 2016. *The Gift.* Rev. ed. Translated by Jane I. Guyer. Chicago: Hau Books.

Mawdsley, Emma. 2011. "The Changing Geographies of Foreign Aid and Development Cooperation: Contributions from Gift Theory." *Transactions of the Institute of British Geographers* 37 (2): 256–72.

Mayoux, Linda. 1999. "Questioning Virtuous Spirals: Micro-Finance and Women's Empowerment in Africa." *Journal of International Development* 11 (7): 957.

McCline, Richard L., M. von Nkosi, Adrine Harrell-Carter, and Emily Boness. 2015. "Expanding Opportunity for Minority-Owned Businesses in Metro New Orleans." The Data Center. July 2015. www.datacenterresearch.org/reports_analysis /minority-businesses/.

McGoey, Linsey. 2015. *No Such Thing as a Free Gift: The Gates Foundation and the Price of Philanthropy.* London: Verso.

McKinsey. 2010. "The Business of Empowering Women." London: McKinsey.

McKittrick, Katherine. 2006. *Demonic Grounds: Black Women and the Cartographies of Struggle.* Minneapolis: University of Minnesota Press.

McMichael, Philip. 2009. "A Food Regime Genealogy." *Journal of Peasant Studies* 36 (1): 139–69.

McNulty, Ian. 2019. "As New Orleans Mourns Two Legends, What Does It Take to Make More?" *New Orleans Advocate,* July 6, 2019. www.theadvocate.com/new _orleans/entertainment_life/food_restaurants/article_bd06067c-896d-11e9-8ab1 -3fe43839925a.html.

Meyer, Danny. 2006. *Setting the Table: The Transforming Power of Hospitality in Business.* New York: HarperCollins.

Moeller, Kathryn. 2018. *The Gender Effect: Capitalism, Feminism, and the Corporate Politics of Development.* Oakland: University of California Press.

Mohan, John, and Beth Breeze. 2016. *The Logic of Charity: Great Expectations in Hard Times.* Houndmills: Palgrave Macmillan.

Molyneux, Maxine. 2006. "Mothers at the Service of the New Poverty Agenda: Progresa/Oportunidades, Mexico's Conditional Transfer Programme." *Social Policy & Administration* 40 (4): 425–49.

Morago, Greg. 2015. "How New Orleans' Drinking and Dining Scene Helped Rebuild and Reinvent the City." *Houston Chronicle,* August 28, 2015. www .houstonchronicle.com/life/travel/destinations/article/How-New-Orleans-bar -and-restaurants-helped-6442627.php.

Morris, Benjamin. 2010. "Soul Food: Katrina and the Culinary Arts." In *Culture after the Hurricanes: Rhetoric and Reinvention on the Gulf Coast,* edited by M. B. Hackler, 91–106. Jackson: University Press of Mississippi.

Morvaridi, Behrooz, ed. 2015. *New Philanthropy and Social Justice: Debating the Conceptual and Policy Discourse.* Bristol: Policy Press.

Moser, Caroline. 1996. "Confronting Crisis: A Comparative Study of Household Responses to Poverty and Vulnerability in Four Poor Urban Communities." Environmentally Sustainable Development Studies and Monographs Series No. 8. Washington, D.C.: World Bank.

Mostafanezhad, Mary. 2013. "'Getting in Touch with Your Inner Angelina': Celebrity Humanitarianism and the Cultural Politics of Gendered Generosity in Volunteer Tourism." *Third World Quarterly* 34 (3): 485–99.

Mt. Auburn Associates. 2005. *Louisiana: Where Culture Means Business.* Baton Rouge: State of Louisiana, Office of the Lt. Governor, Department of Culture, Recreation and Tourism.

Naccarato, Peter, and Kathleen Lebesco. 2012. *Culinary Capital.* London: Berg.

Nader, Laura. 1972. "'Up the Anthropologist: Perspectives Gained From Studying Up.'" *Institute of Education Sciences (Ed.Gov)*, 1–28. https://eric.ed.gov/?id =ED065375.

———. 1974. "Up the Anthropologist—Perspectives Gained from Studying Up." In *Reinventing Anthropology*, edited by Dell Hymes, 284–311. Ann Arbor: University of Michigan Press.

Nath, Jemál. 2011. "Gendered Fare? A Qualitative Investigation of Alternative Food and Masculinities." *Journal of Sociology* 47 (3): 261–78.

Nesheim, Malden C., Maria Oria, and Peggy Tsai Yih, eds. 2015. *A Framework for Assessing Effects of the Food System.* Washington, D.C.: Institute of Medicine and National Research Council, National Academies Press.

New Orleans CityBusiness. 2006. "Besh, N.O. Chefs Honored by James Beard Foundation." May 9, 2006. https://neworleanscitybusiness.com/blog/2006/05/09 /besh-no-chefs-honored-by-james-beard-foundation/.

New Orleans Preservation Timeline Project. 2019. "The Historic Faubourg St. Mary Corporation Is Established, September 23, 1978." New Orleans: Tulane School of Architecture. http://architecture.tulane.edu/preservation-project/timeline-entry /1433.

NRA (National Restaurant Association). 2019. "Our Mission." 2019. https://www .restaurant.org/About/Mission.

Oberhauser, Ann M., and Ibipo Johnston-Anumonwo. 2014. *Global Perspectives on Gender and Space: Engaging Feminism and Development.* Oxford: Routledge.

OECD (Organisation for Economic Co-operation and Development). 2015. "The Role of Philanthropy in Financing for Development." Third Annual Conference on Financing for Development, Addis Ababa, July 2015. www.oecd.org/dac/financing -sustainable-development/Addis%20flyer%20-%20PHILANTHROPY.pdf.

Okun, Tema. 2010. *The Emperor Has No Clothes: Teaching about Race and Racism to People Who Don't Want to Know.* Charlotte, N.C.: Information Age.

Opie, Frederick Douglass. 2008. *Hog and Hominy: Soul Food from Africa to America.* New York: Columbia University Press.

Osteen, Mark, ed. 2002. Introduction to *The Question of the Gift: Essays across Disciplines*, 1–41. Oxford: Routledge.

Panelli, Ruth, and Gail Tipa. 2009. "Beyond Foodscapes: Considering Geographies of Indigenous Well-Being." *Health & Place* 15 (2): 455–65.

Parry, Jonathan. 1986. "Money and the Morality of Exchange." *Man (N.S.)* 21: 453–73.

Passidomo, Catarina. 2017. "'Our' Culinary Heritage: Obscuring Inequality by Celebrating Diversity in Peru and the U.S. South." *Humanity & Society* 41 (4): 427–45.

Payton, Robert. 1988. *Philanthropy: Voluntary Action for the Public Good.* New York: Macmillan.

Pelot-Hobbs, Lydia. 2023. *Prison Capital: Mass Incarceration and Struggles for Abolition Democracy in Louisiana.* Durham, N.C.: University of North Carolina Press.

Penniman, Leah. 2018. *Farming While Black: Soul Fire Farm's Practical Guide to Liberation on the Land.* White River Junction, Vt.: Chelsea Green.

Pinchin, Karen. 2014. "How Slaves Shaped American Cooking." *National Geographic.* https://www.nationalgeographic.com/culture/article/140301-african-american-food-history-slavery-south-cuisine-chefs.

Piper, Nick. 2013. "Audiencing Jamie Oliver: Embarrassment, Voyeurism and Reflexive Positioning." *Geoforum* 45:346–55.

Plagianos, Irene, and Kitty Greenwald. 2017. "Mario Batali Steps Away from Restaurant Empire Following Sexual Misconduct Allegations." *EATER,* December 11, 2017. https://ny.eater.com/2017/12/11/16759540/mario-batali-sexual-misconduct-allegations.

Plaisance, Stacey. 2009. "Pitt Laughs over New Orleans Mayor T-Shirt Push." *Houma Today,* August 13, 2009. www.houmatoday.com/news/20090813/pitt-laughs-over-new-orleans-mayor-t-shirt-push.

Ponte, Stefano, and Lisa Ann Richey. 2011. "(PRODUCT)REDTM: How Celebrities Push the Boundaries of 'Causumerism.'" *Environment and Planning A* 43 (9): 2060–75.

Price, Todd. 2016. "Chef John Besh Wins First T.G. Solomon Excellence in Innovation Award." *NOLA.Com Times-Picayune,* July 20, 2016. www.nola.com/dining/index.ssf/2016/07/john_besh_wins_first_tg_solomo.html.

Prügl, Elisabeth. 2010. "Gendered Knowledge in the Postmodern State: The Case of Agricultural Trade Liberalization in Europe." In *Gender Knowledge and Knowledge Networks in International Political Economy,* edited by Brigitte Young and Christoph Scherrer, 115–29. Germany: Nomos Verlagsgesellschaft, Baden-Baden.

Prügl, Elisabeth, and Jacqui True. 2014. "Equality Means Business? Governing Gender through Transnational Public-Private Partnerships." *Review of International Political Economy* 21 (6): 1137–69.

Ralston, Katherine, Travis Smith, Stephen Vogel, Shellye Clark, Luanne Lohr, Sarah Low, and Constance Newman. 2010. "Local Food Systems: Concepts, Impacts, and Issues." ERR 97. Washington, D.C.: USDA Economic Research Service.

Reese, Ashanté M. 2019. *Black Food Geographies: Race, Self-Reliance, and Food Access in Washington, D.C.* Durham, N.C.: University of North Carolina Press.

———. 2020. "'D.C. Is Mambo Sauce': Black Cultural Production in a Gentrifying City." *Human Geography* 13 (3): 253–62.

Reich, Rob. 2018. *Just Giving: Why Philanthropy Is Failing Democracy and How It Can Do Better.* Princeton, N.J.: Princeton University Press.

Repo, Jemima, and Riina Yrjölä. 2011. "The Gender Politics of Celebrity Humanitarianism in Africa." *International Feminist Journal of Politics* 13 (1): 44–62.

Richey, Lisa Ann, ed. 2016. *Celebrity Humanitarianism and North-South Relations: Politics, Place and Power.* Oxford: Routledge.

Richey, Lisa Ann, and Stefano Ponte. 2011. *Brand Aid: Shopping Well to Save the World.* Minneapolis: University of Minnesota Press.

Roberts, Adrienne. 2012. "Financial Crisis, Financial Firms . . . and Financial Feminism? The Rise of 'Transnational Business Feminism' and the Necessity of Marxist-Feminist IPE." *Socialist Studies/Études Socialistes* 8 (2).

———. 2015. "The Political Economy of 'Transnational Business Feminism.'" *International Feminist Journal of Politics* 17 (2): 209–31.

Roberts, Adrienne, and Susanne Soederberg. 2012. "Gender Equality as "Smart Economics"? A Critique of the 2012 *World Development Report*." *Third World Quarterly* 33 (5): 949–68.

Roberts, Wayne. 2008. *The No-Nonsense Guide to World Food*. Oxford: New Internationalist Publications Ltd.

Robinson, Jennifer. 2011. "Cities in a World of Cities: The Comparative Gesture." *International Journal of Urban and Regional Research* 35 (1): 1–23.

Robinson, Mark. 1993. "Governance, Democracy and Conditionality: NGOs and the New Policy Agenda." In *Governance, Democracy and Conditionality: What Role for NGOs?*, edited by Andrew Clayton. Oxford: INTRAC.

ROC United (Restaurant Opportunities Centers United). 2014. *The Other NRA: Unmasking the Agenda of the National Restaurant Association*. New York: Restaurant Opportunities Centers United.

ROC United, Race Forward, and the Center for Social Inclusion. 2017. *Adding Racial Equity to the Menu: An Equity Toolkit for Restaurant Employers*. New York: Restaurant Opportunities Centers United.

ROC United, ROC-NOLA, and the New Orleans Restaurant Industry Coalition. 2010. *Behind the Kitchen Door: Inequality, Instability, and Opportunity in the Greater New Orleans Restaurant Industry*. New York: Restaurant Opportunities Centers United.

Rodríguez, Dylan. 2007. "The Political Logic of the Non-Profit Industrial Complex." In *The Revolution Will Not Be Funded: Beyond the Non-Profit Industrial Complex*, edited by INCITE! Women of Color Against Violence, 21–40. Cambridge, Mass.: South End Press.

Rosamond, Annika Bergman. 2016. "Humanitarian Relief Worker Sean Penn: A Contextual Story." In *Celebrity Humanitarianism and North-South Relations: Politics, Place and Power*, edited by Lisa Ann Richey, 149–69. Oxford: Routledge.

Rousseau, Signe. 2012. *Food Media: Celebrity Chefs and the Politics of Everyday Interference*. London: Berg.

Roy, Ananya. 2012. "Ethnographic Circulations: Space-Time Relations in the Worlds of Poverty Management." *Environment and Planning A* 44:31–41.

Rubin, Gayle. 1975. "The Traffic in Women: Notes on the 'Political Economy' of Sex." In *Toward an Anthropology of Women*, edited by Rayna R. Reiter, 157–210. New York: Monthly Review Press.

Sanborn, Cynthia, and Felipe S. Portocarrero, eds. 2005. Introduction to *Philanthropy and Social Change in Latin America*, xi–xx. Cambridge, Mass.: Harvard University David Rockefeller Center for Latin American Studies.

Sayeed, Azra, and Norma Maldonado. 2013. "Food Sovereignty and Women's Rights." In *Gender Equality, Women's Rights and Women's Priorities: Recommendations for the Proposed Sustainable Development Goals (SDGs) and the Post-2015 Development Agenda*, by Women's Major Group (WMG), 16–22.

Sbicca, Joshua. 2018. *Food Justice Now! Deepening the Roots of Social Struggle.* Minneapolis: University of Minnesota Press.

Severson, Kim. 2007. "From Disaster, a Chef Forges an Empire." *New York Times,* October 31, 2007.

———. 2015. "The New Orleans Restaurant Bounce, after Katrina." *New York Times,* August 4, 2015.

Sharpless, Rebecca. 2010. *Cooking in Other Women's Kitchens: Domestic Workers in the South, 1865–1960.* Chapel Hill: University of North Carolina Press.

Shreck, Aimee. 2005. "Resistance, Redistribution, and Power in the Fair Trade Banana Initiative." *Agriculture and Human Values* 22 (1): 17–29.

Silk, John. 2004. "Caring at a Distance: Gift Theory, Aid Chains and Social Movements." *Social & Cultural Geography* 5 (2): 229–51.

Sinclair, Alicia. 2006. "'On the Line': Identifying Workplace Stressors in the Restaurant Kitchen." New York: Columbia University.

Sivewright, Dacey Orr. 2017. "One-Night-Only Dinners in New Orleans—for a Cause." *Garden & Gun,* March 9, 2017. https://gardenandgun.com/articles/one -night-dinners-new-orleans-cause/.

Skågeby, Jörgen. 2013. "The Performative Gift: A Feminist Materialist Conceptual Model." *Communication +1* 2 (7): 1–22.

Sloan, Philip, Willy Legrand, and Clare Hindley, eds. 2015. "Part 6: A Sustainable Restaurant System." In *The Routledge Handbook of Sustainable Food and Gastronomy,* 243–304. Oxford: Routledge.

Slocum, Rachel. 2013. "Race in the Study of Food." In *Geographies of Race and Food: Fields, Bodies, Markets,* edited by Rachel Slocum and Arun Saldanha, 25–60. Oxford: Routledge.

Slocum, Rachel, and Arun Saldanha. 2013. "Geographies of Race and Food: An Introduction." In *Geographies of Race and Food: Fields, Bodies, Markets,* edited by Rachel Slocum and Arun Saldanha, 1–24. Oxford: Routledge.

Smirl, Lisa. 2015. *Spaces of Aid: How Cars, Compounds and Hotels Shape Humanitarianism.* London: Zed Books.

Smith, Andrea. 2007. Introduction to *The Revolution Will Not Be Funded: Beyond the Non-profit Industrial Complex,* edited by INCITE! Women of Color Against Violence, 1–18. Cambridge, Mass.: South End Press.

Smith, Bobby J. 2019. "Building Emancipatory Food Power: Freedom Farms, Rocky Acres, and the Struggle for Food Justice." *Journal of Agriculture, Food Systems, and Community Development* 8 (4): 33–43.

Sobal, Jeffery. 2005. "Men, Meat, and Marriage: Models of Masculinity." *Food and Foodways* 13 (1): 135–58.

Somerville, Annie. 2012. "Why Chefs Matter to Farmers." *CUESA: Cultivating a Healthy Food System* (blog). August 6, 2012. https://cuesa.org/article/why-chefs -matter-farmers.

Southern Poverty Law Center. 2007. "U.S. Labor Department Ignored Rampant Worker Abuses in Post-Katrina New Orleans." June 25, 2007.

Spivak, Gayatri. 1993. *Outside in the Teaching Machine.* New York: Routledge.

Stirrat, R. L., and Heiko Henkel. 1997. "The Development Gift: The Problem of Reciprocity in the NGO World." *Annals of the American Academy of Political and Social Science* 554: 66–80.

Stokes, Ashli Quesinberry, and Wendy Atkins-Sayre. 2016. *Consuming Identity: The Role of Food in Redefining the South.* Jackson: University of Mississippi Press.

Strathern, Marilyn. 1988. *The Gender of the Gift.* Berkeley: University of California Press.

Szczesiul, Anthony. 2017. *The Southern Hospitality Myth: Ethics, Politics, Race and American Memory.* Athens: University of Georgia Press.

Tabbush, Constanza. 2010. "Latin American Women's Protection after Adjustment: A Feminist Critique of Conditional Cash Transfers in Chile and Argentina." *Oxford Development Studies* 38 (4): 437–59.

Thomas, Lynnell L. 2014. *Desire and Disaster in New Orleans: Tourism, Race, and Historical Memory.* Durham, N.C.: Duke University Press.

Thomas, Mary. 2011. *Multicultural Girlhood: Racism, Sexism, and the Conflicted Spaces of American Education.* Philadelphia: Temple University Press.

Thomas, Robert J. 1993. "Interviewing Important People in Big Companies." *Journal of Contemporary Ethnography* 22 (1): 80–96.

Tipton-Martin, Toni. 2015. *The Jemima Code: Two Centuries of African American Cookbooks.* Austin: University of Texas Press.

Toledano, Ben. 2007. "New Orleans—an Autopsy." *Commentary,* September 2007, 27–32.

Toohey, Grace. 2018. "Charges Ruled Out against Protesters, Journalists Arrested after Alton Sterling Was Killed." *Advocate,* July 13, 2018. www.theadvocate.com /baton_rouge/news/article_85003d24-86d0-11e8-9592-6306d1de58f5.html.

Touré. 2011. *Who's Afraid of Post-Blackness? What It Means to Be Black Now.* New York: Free Press.

Truong, Thanh. 2020. "The Future of New Orleans Restaurants Is in the Hands of Locals." *4WWL Eyewitness News,* November 2, 2020. www.wwltv.com/article /entertainment/dining/new-orleans-restaurants-post-pandemic-covid-19-future /289-6e03384b-8ca0-4d10-be91-5a1a568c6bfc.

Tsaliki, Liza, Christos A. Frangonikolopoulos, and Asteris Huliaras, eds. 2011. *Transnational Celebrity Activism in Global Politics: Changing the World?* Bristol: Intellect Books.

Tsing, Anna Lowenhaupt. 2005. *Friction: An Ethnography of Global Connection.* New Jersey: Princeton University Press.

Turner, Graeme. 2014. *Understanding Celebrity.* 2nd ed. Los Angeles: SAGE.

Turner, Patricia. 2008. "Why African-Americans Loathe 'Uncle Tom.'" Interview by Michel Martin. *Tell Me More,* NPR, July 30, 2008. www.npr.org/templates/story /story.php?storyId=93059468.

Twitty, Michael W. 2017. *The Cooking Gene: A Journey through African American Culinary History in the Old South.* New York: HarperCollins.

United Nations. 2015. "Transforming Our World: The 2030 Agenda for Sustainable Development." New York: UN General Assembly.

US Bureau of Labor Statistics. 2017a. "Chefs and Head Cooks." Occupational Outlook Handbook. https://www.bls.gov/ooh/food-preparation-and-serving /chefs-and-head-cooks.htm#tab-1.

———. 2017b. "35–1011 Chefs and Head Cooks." Occupational Employment and Wages. https://www.bls.gov/oes/current/oes351011.htm#st.

US Census Bureau. 2016. "Orleans Parish, Louisiana, QuickFacts." http://quickfacts.census.gov/qfd/states/22/22071.html.

———. n.d. "Quick Facts: New Orleans City, Louisiana." Accessed February 26, 2019. www.census.gov/quickfacts/fact/table/neworleanscitylouisiana#.

Vaughan, Genevieve. 2007. "Introduction: A Radically Different Worldview Is Possible." In *Women and the Gift Economy: A Radically Different Worldview Is Possible*, edited by Genevieve Vaughan, 1–40. Toronto: Inanna.

Villanueva, Edgar. 2018. *Decolonizing Wealth: Indigenous Wisdom to Heal Divides and Restore Balance*. Oakland, Calif.: Berrett-Koehler.

Vlach, John Michael. 1993. *Back of the Big House: The Architecture of Plantation Slavery*. Chapel Hill: University of North Carolina Press.

Warin, Megan. 2011. "Foucault's Progeny: Jamie Oliver and the Art of Governing Obesity." *Social Theory & Health* 9 (1): 24–40.

Watts, Michael. 1983. *Silent Violence: Food, Famine, and Peasantry in Northern Nigeria*. Berkeley: University of California Press.

Wedge, Roberta. 2019. "Whoever Wields the Pen Stirs the Pot: Wikipedia's Power to Shape Reality." Lecture presented at the Oxford Food Symposium, July 12–14, 2019, St. Catherine's College, Oxford, England.

Weinzweig, Ari. 2010. *A Lapsed Anarchist's Approach to Building a Great Business: Zingerman's Guide to Good Leading*. Ann Arbor: Zingerman's Press.

Werman, Marco. 2013. "The Language of New Orleans in One Word: Gumbo." *The World*. Public Radio International, July 18, 2013. www.pri.org/stories/2013-07-18/language-new-orleans-one-word-gumbo.

West, Darrell. 2008. "Angelina, Mia, and Bono: Celebrities and International Development." In *Global Development 2.0: Can Philanthropists, the Public and the Poor Make Poverty History?*, edited by Lael Brainard and Derek Chollet, 74–84. Washington, D.C.: Brookings Institution Press.

Wheeler, Mark. 2013. *Celebrity Politics*. Cambridge: Polity Press.

White, Jaquetta. 2015. "Vandalization of New St. Roch Market Reflects Community's Dissatisfaction, Disappointment in Finished Product, Residents Say." *New Orleans Advocate*, February 5, 2015. www.theadvocate.com/new_orleans/news/article_7510c345-484a-5637-a93b-ff696712b6a6.html.

White, Monica M. 2018. *Freedom Farmers: Agricultural Resistance and the Black Freedom Movement*. Chapel Hill: University of North Carolina Press.

Whitehall, Geoffrey, and Cedric Johnson. 2011. "Making Citizens in Magnaville: Katrina Refugees and Neoliberal Self-Governance." In *The Neoliberal Deluge: Hurricane Katrina, Late Capitalism, and the Remaking of New Orleans*, edited by Cedric Johnson, 60–84. Minneapolis: University of Minnesota Press.

Widmer, William. 2016. "After Louisiana Floods, Help Needed." *AARP (Online)*, August 2016. www.aarp.org/politics-society/advocacy/info-2016/louisiana-floods-photo.html#slide2.

Wilkinson-Maposa, Susan, Alan Fowler, Ceri Oliver-Evans, and Chao F. N. Mulenga. 2005. "The Poor Philanthropist: How and Why the Poor Help Each

Other." Cape Town: Southern African-United States Centre for Leadership and Public Values, Graduate School of Business, University of Cape Town.

Williams, Cocoa M. 2017. "Suppers in St. Bernard: An Ethnographic Look into the Supper-Giving Tradition." Paper presented at the 2017 Graduate Student Conference, Foodways & Social Justice, University of Mississippi, September 11–12, 2017.

Williams, Jessica. 2020. "New Orleans Airport and Coronavirus: Passenger Traffic Down, but 'Improving Steadily.'" *New Orleans Advocate*, June 28, 2020. www.nola .com/news/politics/article_3e154fdc-b566-11ea-88db-2fd33f8420e3.html.

Wilson, Kalpana. 2011. "'Race,' Gender and Neoliberalism: Changing Visual Representations in Development." *Third World Quarterly* 32 (2): 315–31.

Wilson, Samuel, Jr. 1998. "Early History of Faubourg St Mary." In *New Orleans Architecture, Volume II: The American Sector*, edited by Mary Louise Christovich, Roulhac Toledano, Betsy Swanson, and Pat Holden, 3–48. Gretna, La.: Pelican.

Woods, Clyde. 2002. "Life after Death." *Professional Geographer* 54 (1): 62–66.

———. 2017a. *Development Arrested: The Blues and Plantation Power in the Mississippi Delta*. London: Verso.

———. 2017b. *Development Drowned and Reborn: The Blues and Bourbon Restorations in Post-Katrina New Orleans*. Edited by Jordan T. Camp and Laura Pulido. Athens: University of Georgia Press.

Yrjölä, Riina. 2009. "The Invisible Violence of Celebrity Humanitarianism: Soft Images and Hard Words in the Making and Unmaking of Africa." *World Political Science* 5 (1).

Zadrozny, Brandy. 2018. "Brad Pitt Sued by New Orleans Residents Who Say Make It Right Sold Them 'Defective' Homes." *NBC News*, July 9, 2018. www.nbcnews .com/news/us-news/brad-pitt-sued-new-orleans-residents-who-say-make-it -n907656.

Ziv, Stav. 2015. "U.N. Hopes Campaign Will Make Its 'Global Goals' as Famous as Beyoncé." *Newsweek*, April 9, 2015.

Zunz, Olivier. 2012. *Philanthropy in America: A History*. Princeton, N.J.: Princeton University Press.

Zuras, Matthew. 2016. "Why New Orleans Needs to Protect Its Culinary Culture." *Munchies VICE*, April 21, 2016. https://munchies.vice.com/en_us/article/kbky33 /why-new-orleans-needs-to-protect-its-culinary-culture.

Index

care work, and giving practices, 175n4

Carney, Judith, 112

Carnivale du Vin, 72

causumerism: and branding, 160–61; causumer experiences as form of giving, 4, 154–55; and corporate engagement in social issues, 40, 154; and ethical consumption, 21, 22, 24, 37, 38, 40, 138, 154–56, 159, 165; and Grow Dat Youth Farm's Dinner at the Farm, 105, 108, 154; products as branding tools, 138; research on, 28, 154–55; in restaurant industry, 138; as shopping for charitable purposes, 110, 173n4; and T-shirt sales, 98

celebrities: as ambassadors for nongovernmental organizations, 36, 103; and consumer-based solutions in development, 8, 17; and defining of celebrity, 35–36, 106; as development actors, 36; "Draft Brad for Mayor" campaign, 24–26; "gifts" offered to New Orleans, 4–5; as objects of consumption, 37; and sustainable development goals, 8

celebrity chefs: authenticity of, 27, 38; and Baton Rouge flooding, 20; culinary capital held by, 21, 22, 39, 44, 50–51, 70, 103, 119, 141, 162, 166–67; culture of, 120, 170, 171; and decisions based on bodies of business knowledge, 40; and food policy issues, 51; and foodscape philanthropy, 9, 37; and Grow Dat Youth Farm's Dinners on the Farm, 19, 22, 103, 105, 106, 110; interviews with, 12; organizations supported by, 125; people of color as, 106; proliferation of projects led by, 4; prominence of, 44; and relief efforts, 46; and tabula rasa discourse, 49

celebrity humanitarianism: and branding, 142, 168; changing nature of, 3, 51; and consumer-based models of development, 37, 154; and defining

celebrity, 35–36; and development, 35, 175n6; and flooding from Hurricane Katrina, 4–5, 28; and foodscapes, 9, 37, 63; interdisciplinary literature on, 36; international trends in, 164; and Make It Right Foundation, 24–27; and new development era, 21, 35; and nongovernmental organizations, 22, 103, 133; and nontraditional development actors, 35, 175n5; positive perspectives on, 38; and post-democracy, 36–37; and post-Katrina redevelopment, 21, 36, 38–39, 44, 62; and regulatory vacuums at post-disaster sites, 62–63; and relief efforts, 46; skeptical perspectives on, 38

celebrity studies, 35

Cell, John C., 85

Central Business District (CBD), New Orleans, 66, 68–69, 70, 77, 123, 176n5

ceremonial humanitarianism, fundraising events as sites of, 4, 22, 72–73

Chant, Sylvia, 7–8

charity: beneficiaries of charitable causes, 12, 74; debates on definition of, 28–29, 122; models of philanthropy compared to, 28; vetting of organizations, 125

Charity Navigator, 125

Chase, Dooky, 59, 153

Chase, Leah, 55, 59, 64, 65, 145, 153

Chavez, Cesar, 126

Chawasha people, 112

Chef Action Network (CAN), 51, 175n3

Chef Bootcamp for Policy and Change, 51, 130, 131, 134

chef foundations: affiliation with Besh Restaurant Group, 6, 72, 77, 97; and application, 170–71; and branding strategies, 142–43, 159, 165, 166, 168, 171; and causumerism, 38; characteristics of, 12, 23, 27, 72–73, 119, 138, 165; competition among, 93, 131–32; as components of disaster infrastructure, 20, 63; and friendly public

class and classism: and chef philanthropy, 10, 27, 80, 166; entrenchment of, 80; and ethnographic fieldwork, 17; and foodscape interventions, 7, 8; and fundraising events, 22, 74, 87–90, 92–93, 100; and impact of Katrina, 48; and inequalities, 13; and policing practices, 70; and positionality, 16; and staff attire, 116. *See also* middle class; poor people; white elites

climate change and instability: 27, 168

Cole, Teju, 170–71

colonialism: and cultures of food, 52; humanitarian work in wealthy countries with history of, 9; settler-colonial expansion, 102, 112, 114; violences of, 7

Colquitt, Martha, 85

Commander's Palace restaurant, 145

common goods, 29, 169

community: Black chefs' recognition for community work, 64; chefs' building of, 136; and restaurant industry, 144–45, 152–53; as third-sector activity, 174n12, 176n3; and uniform narrative, 48; "village style of living" in, 121

community cooks: chef philanthropists compared to, 119; and food as axis for social engagement, 12; and giving practices, 34; women's community food work, 129–30

community food activists, 119, 120–23, 143

Connell, Kevin, 110–11

consumer-based solutions in development, 8, 17, 37

consumption: and ethical consumption, 21, 22, 24, 37, 38, 40, 138, 154–56, 159, 165; and humanitarianism, 3, 8; and T-shirt sales, 98

Cooper, Christopher, 45–46

corporate capitalism, 37, 169

corporate food regime, 11

corporate social responsibility (CSR): and alignment between standard operations and philanthropy, 101, 134, 159, 160; and chef philanthropy, 41, 150, 152–54, 158, 159–60, 166; disembedded and embedded forms of, 9, 23, 41, 134, 138, 150, 152–54, 159, 160, 164, 166; engaged and disengaged activities, 41, 150, 152; and environmental responsibility, 40, 138, 152–53; and internal business reforms, 9, 23, 41; and labor exploitation, 40; national and international growth of, 154; proximate forms of, 159, 160, 166; scholarship on, 21, 28; and spatial dimensions of interventions, 23, 41, 150, 152, 159, 164; and wealth accumulation, 40, 41–42; and workplace conditions and politics, 138, 152

corporations: branding strategies of, 51; building of corporate patriotism, 35; and consumer-based solutions in development, 8, 17; and "doing well by doing good," 39; geographies of corporate giving, 8–9; multinational corporations, 39–40; production of development knowledge, 40; spatial dimensions of corporate engagement, 9

cosmopolitanism, 55

COVID-19 pandemic, 5, 6–7, 20

Covington Farmers Market, 157

Crouch, Colin, 36

Cuba, and foodscape projects, 168

culinary capital: and "authentic" cultural icons, 162; of celebrity chefs, 21, 22, 39, 44, 50–51, 70, 103, 119, 141, 162, 166–67; and informal and non-elite interventions, 119

culinary culture: and Black service workers, 3, 138–39; and consumers as media makers, 104; culinary capital held by celebrity chefs, 21, 22, 39, 44, 50–51, 70, 103, 119, 141, 162, 166–67; and Grow Dat Youth Farm's Dinners on the Farm, 103; rebranding as

102; as nonprofit organization, 142; practices of, 124–25

Emeril's Culinary Garden and Teaching Kitchen, 142–43, 153

enslaved people: devaluing of work of, 10; and Indigenous people, 112, 114; and large scale plantations, 85, 176n6; maroon communities of, 114

enslavement: and cultures of food, 52, 80, 112, 114; and land histories, 102; and Southern hospitality myth, 94; spatial and social legacies of, 74, 87, 112, 114, 162; spatial politics of, 49; violences of, 7

entrepreneurialism, 169

environmental responsibility, and corporate social responsibility, 40, 138, 152–53

Ernest N. Morial Convention Center, 46

fair trade, 40

"Fall in Love with New Orleans All Over Again" campaign, 49

Faubourg Marigny, New Orleans, 70

Federal Emergency Management Agency (FEMA), 46, 68

Federal Writers' Project, 85

Federici, Silvia, 29

feminist scholarship: consideration of "the gift," 10; and geographies of giving, 9, 164; and nontraditional development leaders, 35; and relational autonomy, 33; and transnational perspectives, 168

Ferguson, James, 169

Ferris, Marcie Cohen, 52

Fertel, Randy, 4

Fields, Kelly, 6, 63, 77

Fifteen: Apprentice Programme, 136–37; restaurant, 99

Fitzmorris, Tom, 48, 64–65, 162, 175n4

flooding: of African American neighborhoods, 45; in Baton Rouge, 20–21, 126; and celebrity humanitari-anism, 4–5, 28; daily life in New Orleans shaped by, 20; levee system failure in New Orleans, 4, 44, 45, 47, 48, 64, 70, 122, 138; in Mississippi, 176n6; social and physical landscape shaped by Hurricane Katrina, 1, 20–21, 28

Folse, John, 56

food apartheid, 5, 44, 173n5

Food as Medicine, 131–32

food deserts, 173n5

food geographies, 7, 52

"foodie", 72, 120, 176n1

food justice, 11

food movements: and causumerism, 38, 154; chefs as leaders in, 10–11, 103; and consumerism, 11, 17; and food systems, 11, 167; funding of, 17; as progressive or radical, 11; and urban agriculture, 56, 58, 63

Food Network, 50–51

foodscapes: and celebrity chefs, 9, 37; and chef philanthropy, 7, 10–13, 27, 44, 63–64, 102, 128, 136, 152, 159; elite foodscape philanthropy, 10; and fundraising events, 103; and geographies of corporate giving, 9; and giving practices, 23, 164; gourmet foodscapes, 136, 176n1; and interventions, 7, 8, 62, 119, 164, 166, 167; and issue-based initiatives, 11, 167; and land histories, 19; of New Orleans, 52–53, 56, 64–66, 155, 162, 167; oppressive structure within, 14, 167; philanthropy in, 9, 22; and power dynamics of post-Katrina reconstruction, 7, 49, 52; racial justice movements in, 130; shifting boundaries of, 173n8; and socio-spatial manifestation of human-food activities, 173n8; and system-based initiatives, 11, 167

food sovereignty movement, 11, 173–74n11

food studies, 9

food systems: consumer-spending based reform of, 10, 17, 165–66; defining of, 174n13; and food movements, 11, 167; and gender, 7–8; global nature of, 168

foodways: African foodways, 7, 52, 79, 80. *See also* Southern food

foreign aid, 31

"Forever New Orleans" campaign, 49, 54

foundations: legal definition of, 73, 165; as "public good" institutions, 73; use of term in chef philanthropy, 96–97. *See also* chef foundations

Fouts, Sarah, 69

Freedom Farm Cooperative, 16

Freedom Riders, 153

free people of color, 61

Free Southern Theater, 16

French Quarter, New Orleans, 66, 70, 123, 176n5

friction, concept of, 29

fundraising events: and boundaries of political communities, 73; and causumerism, 155, 165; and chef philanthropy, 22, 42, 43, 72, 74, 101–2, 123, 166; and class, 22, 74, 87–90, 92–93, 100; "dine around" fundraising, 125–26, 130, 171; and donor experiences, 98–100; effectiveness of, 74; and foodscapes, 103; gala model for, 125; as informal/casual events, 87; and land histories, 23, 76, 85–87, 94, 103, 176n6; live and silent auctions at, 87–88; market-based fundraising, 18, 104, 108–10, 133; marketing of, 72; polyvalent nature of, 22, 74; and power relations, 110; product lines showcased at, 102; and race, 22, 74, 81–85, 90, 92, 100, 166; as sites of ceremonial humanitarianism, 4, 22, 72–73; spatiotemporal configuration of, 72, 74; and tourists, 75, 91, 93, 99; and white elites, 92–93, 103

Galatoire's Restaurant, 54, 145, 175n4

Garcia, Adolfo, 64

Garden & Gun, 75, 81, 93, 99, 176n3

Garden District, New Orleans, 66, 70

Garrison, Kansas, 14

gastrodiplomacy, in cookbooks, 80

gender: and John Besh's connection to domestic space, 93–94, 95; and celebrity humanitarianism, 38; and chef foundations, 27; and chef philanthropy, 10, 166, 167; cook/chef distinction, 94, 95, 119, 120; and culinary boundaries, 95; and culinary spaces, 94, 95, 119; and differentiation in media representation, 129; and foodscape interventions, 7, 8; and forms of acceptable care, 133–35, 138, 166; and fundraising events, 22, 74, 115, 166; and gift cycles, 30–31, 34, 174–75n3; and impact of Katrina, 48; and impact of public-private partnerships (PPP), 68; and inequalities, 13; and masculine self-sufficiency, 169; and policing practices, 70; and prevalence of sexual harassment, 129; and staff attire, 116; and unpaid reproductive labor of "feeding the family," 7

geographies of giving: and chef philanthropy, 9, 27; and corporate giving, 8–9, 164; and corporate social responsibility, 164; and failed projects, 168; land histories shaping, 9, 27, 74, 164; and social relations shaping, 30; and spatiality and historicity of giving, 8–9, 30, 35; and unequal social geographies, 164

German Civil Code, 24, 169, 170, 171

Gill, Rosalind, 155

Gilligan, Johanna, 109

Giuffre, 94, 97, 119, 129, 140

GiveNOLA Day, 6

"giving a supper," 64–65

giving practices: and altruism, 34; and care work, 175n4; complexity of, 30; and foodscapes, 23, 164; and fundraising events, 22, 72; and

philanthropy: arguments against, 29; and basic income grants, 24; bias and inequalities shaping contours of, 28; and corporate self-interest, 35; and disembedded CSR, 9, 23, 41; elite philanthropy, 7, 36, 42–43, 170; and geographies of giving, 9; land histories tied to, 4; models of charity compared to, 28; as new development, 8; poor people's contributions to, 34; rethinking of, 164; venture philanthropy, 29; as voluntary giving, 33. *See also* chef philanthropy

Picayune Place, New Orleans, 68

Pierce, Wendell, 4, 63, 120, 167

Pitt, Brad, 4, 24–27, 38, 62, 100, 134. *See also* Make it Right Foundation

place-based histories, 103. *See also* Grow Dat Youth Farm, History of the Land

plantation logics and legacies: and chef philanthropy, 10, 27; and plantation estates, 76, 85–87, 94, 103, 117, 118, 176n6

political communities, boundaries of, 73

Pollan, Michael, 105

Pomegranate Hospitality, 149, 173n6

Pontchartrain Park, 120–21

Ponte, Stefano: on "Brand Aid," 23–24, 37, 142, 175n9, 177n2; on celebrity humanitarianism, 37; on compassionate consumption, 155; on corporate social responsibility, 23, 40–41, 138, 150, 153; on geographies of corporate giving, 9

poor people: as contributors to the supply side of philanthropy, 34; and distributive payment, 169; intimate ethnography of, 17; and nontraditional development actors, 8, 29, 175n5; and philanthropy as charity, 28; and power dynamics of post-Katrina reconstruction, 63; and scholarship winners, 100; and service workers, 139. *See also* class and classism

Portocarrero, Felipe, 29

positionality, of author, 14–17, 19

post-democratic model, 36–37

power and power relations: awareness of, 3; and celebrity humanitarianism, 38; in charitable work, 23; and donor-recipient relationships, 21, 23, 31, 107, 109–10, 115, 118, 167; and fundraising, 110; and giving practices, 21, 23, 31, 169; and heroism, 170

Preston, Kelly, 4

privatization, trends in, 62

privilege: and access to capital and resources, 128; awareness of, 3; and chef philanthropy, 166; gift-giving as vehicle for preservation of, 35; memorialization of generosity of the privileged, 10, 34; and southern hospitality myth, 94; and white savior industrial complex, 170. *See also* celebrities; white elites

Project Home Again, 62

ProPublica, 176n6

Prudhomme, Paul, 52, 53

Prügl, Elisabeth, 35, 68

public chef intellectual (PCI), 51

public-private divide, and gendered nature of culinary spaces, 94

public-private partnerships (PPP), 8, 50, 62, 68

Puck, Wolfgang, 53

Pulido, Laura, 47

QED Hospitality, 149

race and racism: and chef foundations, 13, 27; and chef philanthropy, 10, 136, 159, 166; and Chefs Move! scholarships, 2–3, 7, 13, 79–85, 87, 90, 106, 136, 138, 166; and donor-recipient relationships, 74, 84, 85–87, 90, 116–18, 134, 158, 167; entrenched racism, 80, 84; and food geographies, 7, 52; and foodscape interventions, 7,

white savior industrial complex, 170
white supremacy: legacies of, 43; and
    New Orleans City Park, 118; and
    removal of monuments, 114; and
    Southern hospitality myth, 94
Widmer, William, 16, 20, 42
Wilder, Rob, 153
Wilkinson-Maposa, Susan, 34
Willa Jean bakery, 77, 93, 127, 146,
    155–56, 160
Willie Mae's Scotch House, 54, 64,
    175n5
Winfrey, Oprah, 5, 62
wokeness, defining of, 2–3
women: attractive white women as
    hostesses, 115, 176n4; Black women's
    evacuation from New Orleans, 45;
    Black women's "giving a supper," 64;
    Black women working in plantation
    kitchens, 7, 52; as culinary instructors,
    129–30, 132–33; as domestic cooks, 94,
    95, 119; as independent chefs, 108; as
    professional chefs, 103, 119, 120, 129,
    133, 134, 140; as restaurant cooks, 119,
120; as servers, 118; as visual market-
    ing tool for foundations, 147
Woods, Clyde: on containment and
    enclosure of Black people, 139; on
    development, 123, 175n6; on disaster
    infrastructure, 20, 44–45; on land-
    holding elite, 53; trapped labor force,
    140; on ruling "Bourbon elite," 70; on
    wealth accumulation of antebellum
    planters, 86, 162
Works Progress Administration, 114
World Bank, *World Development Report*,
    173n9
World Central Kitchen, 51, 153. *See also*
    José Andrés
WWOZ, 59

Yes Ma'am Foundation, 6, 63, 72, 77
Young, Anna, 51

Zamora, Bianca, 2–3
Zingerman's Delicatessen, Michigan, 144
Žižek, Slavoj, 36
Zunz, Olivier, 28

Printed in the USA
CPSIA information can be obtained
at www.ICGtesting.com
LVHW041955171023
761387LV00005B/28